Taste of Home
MEDITERRANEAN
FAVORITES

TASTE OF HOME BOOKS · RDA ENTHUSIAST BRANDS, LLC · MILWAUKEE, WI

International Standard Book Number:
979-8-88977-015-2

Content Director: Mark Hagen
Creative Director: Raeann Thompson
Senior Editors: Christine Rukavena,
Julie Kuczynski
Senior Art Director: Courtney Lovetere
Editors: Hazel Wheaton, Christine Campbell
Assistant Art Director: Carrie Peterson
Senior Designer: Jogesh Antony
Deputy Editor, Copy Desk: Ann Walter
Copy Editor: Suchismita Ukil

Cover Photography:
Photographer: Dan Roberts
Set Stylist: Stacey Genaw
Food Stylist: Shannon Norris

Pictured on front cover:
Greek Ouzo Pork Kabobs, p. 211

Pattern:
Gokcemim/Getty Images

Pictured on title page:
Veggie Frittata, p. 36

Pictured on page 5:
Homemade Meatless Spaghetti Sauce , p. 164

Pictured on back cover:
Spinach Shrimp Fettuccine, p. 72; Bella Basil
Raspberry Tea, p. 43; The Best Eggplant
Parmesan, p. 180; White Chocolate Fruit
Tart, p. 286

Printed in China

*SANTORINI
LAMB SLIDERS,
PAGE 47*

CONTENTS

SMART CHOICES, MADE EASY

The recipes in this book help you eat great the whole day through!

BREAKFAST

SAVORY TOMATO & OLIVE OATMEAL – PAGE 15

Whole-grain oats are lower on the glycemic index than refined grains, so they keep you feeling fueled throughout the morning. Fresh garden produce boosts this dish's fiber and volume, and an optional egg on top adds a satisfying meat-free protein.

LUNCH

CUMIN-SPICED LENTIL BURGERS – PAGE 148

These lentil-and-bulgur patties have an exotic taste from a unique blend of onions, herbs and spices. Cooked in heart-healthy canola oil, piled high with veggies and tucked into flatbreads, these burgers make a wholesome hand-held meal.

DINNER

TILAPIA FLORENTINE – PAGE 104

Work in a serving of fish plus a healthy dose of fresh spinach when you serve this easy, family-pleasing dinner. The dish gets a flavor boost from lemon juice and a modest amount of Italian cheeses.

EMBRACE THE MEDITERRANEAN WAY OF LIFE

*You might not be able to jet off to Greece or Italy tonight, but with **Mediterranean Favorites**, you can savor the flavors of the renowned coast right at home. Incorporate health benefits by following these key ideas.*

FOCUS ON FRESH PRODUCE
Make veggies and fruits the hero of your meals, letting them take up at least half the plate.

EAT MORE FISH & SEAFOOD
A good starting goal is the USDA's recommendation— 8 ounces per week for an average adult's 2,000-calorie-per-day diet.

GO MEATLESS MORE OFTEN
Let the 28 entrees in our Vegetarian Mains chapter help you get started.

CHOOSE HEALTHY FATS
Reach for heart-healthy olive oil more often than butter, coconut oil and other fats that are solid at room temperature.

PREFER WHOLE GRAINS
Brown rice, whole wheat flour, barley, bulgur and oats are all smart choices.

LEAN ON LENTILS & LEGUMES
These high-fiber plants help you feel fuller for longer and are a good, eco-friendly protein source.

TAKE IT SLOW
Eat slowly, without distractions such as work or TV. When possible, eat meals with others. Aim to spend at least 20 minutes eating your meal.

RESTRICT HIGHLY PROCESSED FOODS
Cured meats, convenience products, refined grains and sugars, and foods with long ingredient lists are eaten far less on a Mediterranean diet.

ENJOY IN MODERATION
While no food is off-limits, red meats, high-fat dairy products and alcohol are enjoyed in moderation.

SNACK ON NUTS
Add a serving (¼ cup) at least 3 times per week as an alternative to highly processed chips and crackers.

The recipes in **Mediterranean Favorites** are appropriate for many lifestyles. While some dishes include dairy and red meat, many do so in moderation. Unlock the fresh coastal flavors of the Mediterranean today!

AT-A-GLANCE ICONS
Icons throughout indicate slow-cooker 🍲 and five-ingredient 5i dishes (may also call for water, salt, pepper and cooking oil).

*GREEN SHAKSHUKA,
PAGE 31*

GOOD MORNINGS

Start your mornings right with mini frittatas, homemade yogurt or honey coffee. These feel-good dishes get you ready to take on the day—every day!

51 QUINOA BREAKFAST BOWL

Quinoa has been around for a while, but I'm just now jumping on the quinoa breakfast bowl bandwagon. I've made it several times as a savory side or salad but never as a warm breakfast cereal. I finally did it last weekend and loved it!
—Erica Schmidt, Kansas City, KS

TAKES: 20 MIN. • **MAKES:** 4 SERVINGS

2 cups 2% or coconut milk
1 cup quinoa, rinsed
Optional: Ground cinnamon, vanilla Greek yogurt, sugar substitute blend, honey, brown sugar, raisins, fresh blueberries, chopped apple, chia seeds and fresh mint leaves

In a large saucepan, bring milk to a boil over medium heat, stirring occasionally. Add quinoa. Reduce heat; simmer, covered, until liquid is absorbed, 12-15 minutes. Remove from heat; fluff with a fork. If desired, stir in any combination of optional ingredients.

¾ CUP: 217 cal., 5g fat (2g sat. fat), 10mg chol., 59mg sod., 33g carb. (6g sugars, 3g fiber), 10g pro. **DIABETIC EXCHANGES:** 1½ starch, ½ reduced-fat milk.

PROSCIUTTO-PESTO BREAKFAST STRATA

I'd never tried prosciutto before this recipe, and it instantly made me a big-time fan! The layers of flavor in this dish are brilliant, making it well worth the time and a must for your recipe box.
—Vicki Anderson, Farmington, MN

PREP: 25 MIN. + CHILLING • **BAKE:** 50 MIN. • **MAKES:** 10 SERVINGS

2 cups 2% milk
1 cup white wine or chicken broth
1 loaf (1 lb.) French bread, cut into ½-in. slices
¼ cup minced fresh basil
¼ cup minced fresh parsley
3 Tbsp. olive oil
½ lb. thinly sliced smoked Gouda cheese
½ lb. thinly sliced prosciutto
3 medium tomatoes, thinly sliced
½ cup prepared pesto
4 large eggs
½ cup heavy whipping cream
½ tsp. salt
¼ tsp. pepper

1. In a shallow bowl, combine milk and wine. Dip both sides of bread in milk mixture; squeeze gently to remove excess liquid. Layer bread slices in a greased 13x9-in. baking dish.

2. Sprinkle with basil and parsley; drizzle with oil. Layer with half the cheese, half the prosciutto, and tomatoes; drizzle with half the pesto. Top with remaining cheese, prosciutto and pesto.

3. In a small bowl, whisk eggs, cream, salt and pepper until blended; pour over top. Refrigerate, covered, several hours or overnight.

4. Preheat oven to 350°. Remove strata from refrigerator while oven heats. Bake, uncovered, until top is golden brown and a knife inserted in center comes out clean, 50-60 minutes. Let stand 5-10 minutes before serving.

1 PIECE: 440 cal., 26g fat (10g sat. fat), 138mg chol., 1215mg sod., 30g carb. (7g sugars, 2g fiber), 22g pro.

QUINOA
BREAKFAST
BOWL

MINI ITALIAN FRITTATAS

I created this recipe when my friends and I had a picnic breakfast. I wanted an egg meal that was portable and easy to make. These crowd-pleasing frittatas were the result!
—Jess Apfe, Berkeley, CA

PREP: 20 MIN. • **BAKE:** 20 MIN. • **MAKES:** 1 DOZEN

¼ cup sun-dried tomatoes
    (not packed in oil)
¾ cup shredded part-skim
    mozzarella cheese, divided
½ cup chopped fresh spinach
⅓ cup water-packed artichoke hearts,
    rinsed, drained and chopped
⅓ cup chopped roasted
    sweet red peppers
¼ cup grated Parmesan cheese
¼ cup ricotta cheese
2 Tbsp. minced fresh basil
1 Tbsp. prepared pesto
2 tsp. Italian seasoning
¼ tsp. garlic powder
8 large eggs
½ tsp. pepper
¼ tsp. salt

1. Preheat oven to 350°. Pour ½ cup boiling water over tomatoes in a small bowl; let stand for 5 minutes. Drain and chop tomatoes.

2. In a bowl, combine ½ cup mozzarella cheese, spinach, artichokes hearts, red peppers, Parmesan cheese, ricotta cheese, basil, pesto, Italian seasoning, garlic powder and tomatoes. In a large bowl, whisk eggs, pepper and salt until blended; stir in cheese mixture.

3. Fill 12 greased or foil-lined muffin cups three-fourths full. Sprinkle with remaining mozzarella cheese. Bake until set, 18-22 minutes. Cool 5 minutes before removing from pan. Serve warm, with additional pesto if desired.

1 MINI FRITTATA: 95 cal., 6g fat (3g sat. fat), 149mg chol., 233mg sod., 2g carb. (1g sugars, 0 fiber), 8g pro. **DIABETIC EXCHANGES:** 1 lean meat, 1 fat.

🗗 SALSA SHAKSHUKA WITH AVOCADOS

I was watching a cooking show and the host put several ingredients into a pan for her shakshuka. *I realized those ingredients were essentially the makings for salsa, so that's how I ended up with this fresh morning meal.*
—Patty Crouse, Warren, PA

PREP: 10 MIN. • **GRILL:** 20 MIN. • **MAKES:** 6 SERVINGS

1   jar (24 oz.) salsa
6   large eggs
¼   tsp. salt
⅛   tsp. pepper
6   whole pita breads
1   medium ripe avocado, peeled and sliced
     Optional: Cotija cheese, sliced radishes and fresh cilantro leaves

1. Spread salsa into a large cast-iron or other heavy skillet; place on grill rack. Grill, covered, over medium heat until bubbly, 13-15 minutes, stirring occasionally.

2. With back of spoon, make 6 wells in salsa; break an egg into each well. Sprinkle with salt and pepper. Grill, covered, until egg whites are completely set and yolks begin to thicken but are not hard, 6-8 minutes. Serve with pita bread, avocado and toppings of your choice.

1 SERVING: 312 cal., 9g fat (2g sat. fat), 186mg chol., 946mg sod., 43g carb. (5g sugars, 3g fiber), 12g pro.

◇◇

🗗 HOMEMADE YOGURT

You'll be surprised by how easy it is to make homemade yogurt. Top with granola and your favorite berries.
—*Taste of Home* Test Kitchen

PREP: 5 MIN. + CHILLING • **COOK:** 20 MIN. + STANDING • **MAKES:** ABOUT 2 QT.

2   qt. pasteurized whole milk
2   Tbsp. plain yogurt with live active cultures

1. In a Dutch oven, heat milk over medium heat until a thermometer reads 200°, stirring occasionally to prevent scorching. Remove from heat; let stand until a thermometer reads 112°-115°, stirring occasionally. (If desired, place pan in an ice-water bath for faster cooling.)

2. Whisk 1 cup warm milk into yogurt until smooth; return all to pan, stirring gently. Transfer mixture to warm, clean jars, such as 1-qt. canning jars.

3. Cover jars; place in oven. Turn on oven light to keep mixture warm, about 110°. Let stand, undisturbed, until yogurt is set, 6-24 hours, tilting jars gently to check consistency. (Yogurt will become thicker and more tangy as it stands.)

4. Refrigerate, covered, until cold. Store in refrigerator up to 2 weeks.

1 CUP: 151 cal., 8g fat (5g sat. fat), 25mg chol., 107mg sod., 12g carb. (12g sugars, 0 fiber), 8g pro. **DIABETIC EXCHANGES:** 1 whole milk.

*SALSA SHAKSHUKA
WITH AVOCADOS*

SAVORY OATMEAL TIPS

What else can you put in savory oatmeal? *You can top savory oatmeal with some diced avocado and crumbled feta cheese, and add some fresh or dried herbs like oregano or parsley to the mixture. Feel free to add additional protein, like cooked Italian pork sausage or cooked ground chicken.*

How else can you cook savory oatmeal? *To make savory oatmeal in the microwave, combine all the ingredients besides the olives and basil in a microwaveable bowl and cook for 1½-2 minutes or until oats are cooked. When it's done, add the olives and basil on top.*

Can you use other kinds of oats to make savory oatmeal? *Feel free to use ½ cup old-fashioned oats or ¼ cup steel-cut oats instead of quick oats in this recipe—and adjust the cooking time accordingly. If using steel-cut oats, give them a long head start before adding the tomato and other ingredients.*

SAVORY TOMATO & OLIVE OATMEAL

SAVORY TOMATO & OLIVE OATMEAL

Who says oatmeal has to be sweet? I love this recipe because it starts my day in a healthy, fulfilling way.
The fresh garlic, tomatoes and basil are bright notes in a breakfast that keeps me satisfied until lunch.
The oatmeal gives me protein and fiber, and I add a splash of extra virgin olive oil at the end for heart health.
—Roland McAmis Jr., Greeneville, TN

TAKES: 20 MIN. • **MAKES:** 1 SERVING

1   cup reduced-sodium chicken broth
1   medium tomato, chopped
½   cup quick-cooking oats
1   garlic clove, minced
3   Greek olives, chopped
1   Tbsp. chopped fresh basil
    Optional: Additional chopped
    fresh basil, grated Parmesan
    cheese, sunny-side up large egg
    and extra virgin olive oil

In a small saucepan, bring broth to a boil over medium-high heat. Stir in tomato, oats and garlic; reduce heat and simmer 2 minutes. Remove from heat; stir in olives and basil. Add toppings as desired.

1½ CUPS: 222 cal., 6g fat (1g sat. fat), 0 chol., 761mg sod., 35g carb. (5g sugars, 5g fiber), 10g pro. **DIABETIC EXCHANGES:** 2 starch, 1 vegetable, 1 fat.

MEDITERRANEAN BROCCOLI & CHEESE OMELET

My Italian mother-in-law taught me to make this omelet years ago—she would make it for breakfast,
lunch or dinner and eat it on Italian bread. This is one of my favorite ways to use up leftover broccoli.
—Mary Licata, Pembroke Pines, FL

TAKES: 30 MIN. • **MAKES:** 4 SERVINGS

2½ cups fresh broccoli florets
6   large eggs
¼   cup 2% milk
½   tsp. salt
¼   tsp. pepper
⅓   cup grated Romano cheese
⅓   cup sliced pitted Greek olives
1   Tbsp. olive oil
    Shaved Romano cheese and
    minced fresh parsley

1. Preheat broiler. In a large saucepan, place steamer basket over 1 in. water. Place broccoli in basket. Bring water to a boil. Reduce heat to a simmer; steam, covered, until crisp-tender, 4-6 minutes.

2. In a large bowl, whisk eggs, milk, salt and pepper. Stir in cooked broccoli, grated cheese and olives. In a large cast-iron or other ovenproof skillet, heat oil over medium heat; pour in egg mixture. Cook, uncovered, until eggs are nearly set, 4-6 minutes.

3. Broil 3-4 in. from heat until eggs are completely set, 2-4 minutes. Let stand 5 minutes. Cut into wedges. Sprinkle with shaved cheese and parsley.

1 WEDGE: 229 cal., 17g fat (5g sat. fat), 290mg chol., 775mg sod., 5g carb. (1g sugars, 1g fiber), 15g pro.

⑤ⅰ BRUNCH RISOTTO

This light, flavorful and inexpensive risotto makes a surprising addition to a traditional brunch menu. It's gotten lots of compliments from my friends.
—Jennifer Dines, Brighton, MA

PREP: 10 MIN. • **COOK:** 30 MIN. • **MAKES:** 8 SERVINGS

5¼ to 5¾ cups reduced-sodium chicken broth
¾ lb. Italian turkey sausage links, casings removed
2 cups uncooked arborio rice
1 garlic clove, minced
¼ tsp. pepper
1 Tbsp. olive oil
1 medium tomato, chopped

1. In a large saucepan, heat broth and keep warm. In a large nonstick skillet, cook sausage until no longer pink, breaking it into crumbles, 3-4 minutes; drain and set aside.

2. In the same skillet, saute rice, garlic and pepper in oil for 2-3 minutes. Return sausage to skillet. Carefully stir in 1 cup heated broth. Cook and stir until all the liquid is absorbed.

3. Add remaining broth, ½ cup at a time, stirring constantly. Allow liquid to absorb between additions. Cook just until risotto is creamy and rice is almost tender, about 20 minutes total. Add tomato and heat through. Serve immediately.

⅔ CUP: 279 cal., 6g fat (2g sat. fat), 23mg chol., 653mg sod., 42g carb. (1g sugars, 1g fiber), 12g pro. **DIABETIC EXCHANGES:** 2½ starch, 1 lean meat, ½ fat.

HONEY COFFEE

For a soothing pick-me-up, sip this pleasantly sweet coffee, inspired by the taste of a traditional Spanish latte.
—*Taste of Home* Test Kitchen

TAKES: 10 MIN. • **MAKES:** 4 SERVINGS

2 cups hot strong brewed coffee (French or other dark roast)
½ cup whole milk
¼ cup honey
⅛ tsp. ground cinnamon
   Dash ground nutmeg
¼ tsp. vanilla extract

In a small saucepan, combine coffee, milk, honey, cinnamon and nutmeg. Cook and stir until heated through. (Do not boil.) Remove from heat; stir in vanilla. Pour into cups or mugs; serve immediately.

½ CUP: 86 cal., 1g fat (1g sat. fat), 4mg chol., 18mg sod., 19g carb. (18g sugars, 0 fiber), 1g pro.

POACHED EGGS WITH TARRAGON ASPARAGUS

I adapted this recipe from a dish I had in Napa Valley. I decided to add toasted bread crumbs as a garnish. The result was a breakfast option that everyone loves.
—Jenn Tidwell, Fair Oaks, CA

TAKES: 30 MIN. • **MAKES:** 4 SERVINGS

1   lb. fresh asparagus, trimmed
1   Tbsp. olive oil
1   garlic clove, minced
1   Tbsp. minced fresh tarragon
½   tsp. salt
¼   tsp. pepper
1   Tbsp. butter
¼   cup seasoned bread crumbs
4   large eggs

1. Place 3 in. water in a large skillet with a high side; bring to a boil. Add asparagus; cook, uncovered, 2-4 minutes or until asparagus turns bright green. Remove asparagus and immediately drop into ice water. Drain and pat dry.

2. In a separate large skillet, heat oil over medium heat. Add garlic; cook and stir 1 minute. Add asparagus, tarragon, salt and pepper; cook asparagus 2-3 minutes or until crisp-tender, turning occasionally. Remove from pan; keep warm. In same skillet, melt butter over medium heat. Add bread crumbs; cook and stir 1-2 minutes or until toasted. Remove from heat.

3. Add 2-3 in. fresh water to same skillet used to cook asparagus. Bring to a boil; adjust heat to maintain a gentle simmer. Break cold eggs, 1 at a time, into a small bowl; holding bowl close to surface of water, slip egg into water.

4. Cook eggs, uncovered, 3-4 minutes or until whites are completely set and yolks begin to thicken but are not hard. Using a slotted spoon, lift eggs out of water; serve over asparagus. Sprinkle with toasted bread crumbs.

1 SERVING: 170 cal., 12g fat (4g sat. fat), 194mg chol., 513mg sod., 8g carb. (2g sugars, 1g fiber), 9g pro. **DIABETIC EXCHANGES:** 1½ fat, 1 vegetable, 1 medium-fat meat.

READER REVIEW
"I love poached eggs on asparagus. I changed this up just a little bit by roasting the asparagus with garlic. The tarragon was a nice touch. My husband added a bit of freshly shaved Parmesan cheese and coarsely ground black pepper to his dish. If you're not a fan of tarragon, rosemary works well too. I will definitely make this again."
—EBRAMKAMP, TASTEOFHOME.COM

SHAKSHUKA BREAKFAST PIZZA

I turned traditional shakshuka *into a fun morning pizza. Its sweet, spicy and crunchy ingredients make it perfect for morning, noon or night.*
—Phillipe Sobon, Harwood Heights, IL

PREP: 35 MIN. • **BAKE:** 15 MIN. • **MAKES:** 6 SERVINGS

1   Tbsp. olive oil
1   large onion, thinly sliced
1   Tbsp. ground cinnamon
1   Tbsp. paprika
2   tsp. ground cumin
2   garlic cloves, minced
⅛   tsp. cayenne pepper
1   can (14½ oz.) whole plum tomatoes, undrained
1   tsp. hot pepper sauce
½   tsp. salt
¼   tsp. pepper
1   loaf (1 lb.) frozen pizza dough, thawed
6   large eggs
½   cup crumbled feta cheese

1. Preheat oven to 400°. In a large saucepan, heat oil over medium-high heat. Add onion; cook and stir until tender, 4-5 minutes. Add cinnamon, paprika, cumin, garlic and cayenne; cook 1 minute longer. Stir in tomatoes, hot sauce, salt and pepper; cook and stir over medium heat until thickened, about 10 minutes.

2. Meanwhile, grease a 12-in. pizza pan. Roll dough to fit pan. Pinch edge to form a rim. Bake until edge is lightly browned, 10-12 minutes.

3. Spread crust with tomato mixture. Using a spoon, make 6 indentations in tomato mixture; carefully break an egg into each. Sprinkle with feta. Bake until egg whites are completely set and yolks begin to thicken but are not hard, 12-15 minutes.

1 SERVING: 336 cal., 12g fat (3g sat. fat), 191mg chol., 654mg sod., 41g carb. (4g sugars, 5g fiber), 16g pro.

GREEK TOFU SCRAMBLE

I created this recipe over a decade ago. I was in college, and it was the first time I ever had tofu. I wanted to eat tofu and be earthy like all my cool vegetarian friends. Well, the vegetarian diet may not have stuck with me, but this recipe is still popular with my family!
—Jennifer Garcia, Franklin, MA

TAKES: 25 MIN. • **MAKES:** 2 SERVINGS

1   pkg. (9 oz.) fresh spinach
    (about 10 cups)
1   Tbsp. butter
⅔   lb. firm tofu, drained
    and crumbled
¼   cup coarsely chopped
    kalamata olives
2   Tbsp. fresh lemon juice
2   tsp. minced fresh oregano
    or 1 tsp. dried oregano
¼   tsp. pepper
¼   cup crumbled feta cheese
    Optional: Grated lemon zest
    and diced tomatoes

1. Place spinach and 1 Tbsp. water in a large skillet. Cook over medium-high heat until spinach is wilted, 2-3 minutes. Transfer to a colander; drain, pressing out as much liquid as possible. Coarsely chop spinach.

2. In same skillet, melt butter over medium-high heat. Add tofu, olives, lemon juice, oregano, pepper and spinach. Cook, stirring frequently, until heated through, 3-4 minutes. Add feta; cook until slightly melted. Serve immediately; sprinkle with lemon zest and tomatoes if desired.

1½ CUPS: 240 cal., 17g fat (6g sat. fat), 23mg chol., 481mg sod., 9g carb. (2g sugars, 3g fiber), 17g pro.

FRESH VEGETABLE FRITTATA

This breakfast dish is perfect if you want to incorporate fresh veggies into your meal.
—Pauline Howard, Lago Vista, TX

PREP: 15 MIN. • **BAKE:** 20 MIN. • **MAKES:** 2 SERVINGS

4   large eggs, lightly beaten
1   cup sliced fresh mushrooms
½   cup chopped fresh broccoli
¼   cup shredded reduced-fat
    cheddar cheese
2   Tbsp. finely chopped onion
2   Tbsp. finely chopped green pepper
2   Tbsp. grated Parmesan cheese
⅛   tsp. salt
    Dash pepper

1. In a large bowl, combine all ingredients. Pour into a shallow 2-cup baking dish coated with cooking spray.

2. Bake, uncovered, at 350° until a knife inserted in the center comes out clean, 20-25 minutes. Serve immediately.

½ FRITTATA: 230 cal., 14g fat (6g sat. fat), 386mg chol., 485mg sod., 6g carb. (2g sugars, 1g fiber), 20g pro. **DIABETIC EXCHANGES:** 3 medium-fat meat, 1 vegetable.

KITCHEN TIP

To drain fresh tofu, wrap the block in a clean tea towel or several layers of paper towels. Place on a plate and top with another plate. Place something heavy, like a skillet or cans of food, on top. Let stand, occasionally draining excess water from the plate, until tofu is the desired consistency. This method should only be used with firm and extra-firm tofu.

GREEK TOFU SCRAMBLE

EGGS FLORENTINE

I wanted to impress my family with a holiday brunch, but keep it healthy too. So I lightened up the hollandaise sauce in a classic egg recipe. No one could believe this tasty dish was good for them!
—Bobbi Trautman, Burns, OR

TAKES: 30 MIN. • **MAKES:** 4 SERVINGS

- 2 **Tbsp. reduced-fat stick margarine**
- 1 **Tbsp. all-purpose flour**
- ½ **tsp. salt, divided**
- 1¼ **cups fat-free milk**
- 1 **large egg yolk**
- 2 **tsp. lemon juice**
- ½ **tsp. grated lemon zest**
- ½ **lb. fresh spinach**
- ⅛ **tsp. pepper**
- 4 **large eggs**
- 2 **English muffins, split and toasted**
  Dash paprika

1. In a large saucepan, melt margarine. Stir in flour and ¼ tsp. salt until smooth. Gradually add milk. Bring to a boil; cook and stir until thickened, 1-2 minutes. Remove from heat.

2. Stir a small amount of sauce into egg yolk; return all to pan, stirring constantly. Bring to a gentle boil; cook and stir 2 minutes. Remove from heat; stir in lemon juice and zest. Set aside and keep warm.

3. Place spinach in a steamer basket. Sprinkle with pepper and remaining salt. Place in a saucepan over 1 in. water. Bring to a boil; cover and steam until wilted and tender, 3-4 minutes.

4. Meanwhile, in a skillet or omelet pan with high side, bring 2-3 in. water to a boil. Reduce heat; simmer gently. Break cold eggs, 1 at a time, into a custard cup or saucer. Holding dish close to the surface of simmering water, slip eggs, 1 at a time, into water. Cook, uncovered, until whites are completely set and yolks begin to thicken, 3-5 minutes. Lift out of water with a slotted spoon.

5. Place spinach on each muffin half; top with an egg. Spoon 3 Tbsp. sauce over each egg. Sprinkle with paprika. Serve immediately.

NOTE: This recipe was tested with Parkay Light stick margarine.

1 SERVING: 229 cal., 10g fat (3g sat. fat), 267mg chol., 635mg sod., 21g carb. (0 sugars, 2g fiber), 14g pro. **DIABETIC EXCHANGES:** 1 starch, 1 lean meat, 1 fat, ½ fat-free milk.

🍲 SLOW-COOKER SPANAKOPITA FRITTATA SANDWICHES

Years ago my husband and I took a cruise through the Greek islands for our 10th anniversary. Delicious and nutritious foods like this were served on our ship all day, every day. I enjoyed re-creating the flavors in this brunch sandwich.
—Laura Wilhelm, West Hollywood, CA

PREP: 20 MIN. • **COOK:** 2 HOURS + STANDING • **MAKES:** 8 SERVINGS

12 large eggs
½ cup 2% milk
2 tsp. Greek seasoning
2 cups fresh baby spinach
1½ cups crumbled feta cheese
1 cup sliced fresh mushrooms
½ cup roasted sweet red pepper strips
½ cup shredded Italian cheese blend
¼ tsp. smoked paprika
8 ciabatta rolls, bagels or English muffins, split and toasted

1. In a large bowl, whisk eggs, milk and Greek seasoning until blended. Stir in spinach, feta cheese, mushrooms and pepper strips. Pour into a greased 3.5-qt. slow cooker.

2. Cook, covered, on high 2-3 hours or until eggs are set and a thermometer reads 160°. Remove lid; sprinkle frittata with shredded Italian cheese blend and paprika. Turn off slow cooker; remove insert. Let stand until cheese is melted, about 10 minutes. Cut and serve on bread of your choice.

1 SANDWICH: 481 cal., 14g fat (6g sat. fat), 296mg chol., 1115mg sod., 60g carb. (11g sugars, 3g fiber), 27g pro.

SPINACH BRUNCH PIZZA

Whether you serve it for your morning meal or for supper, this flavorful pie is a good fix for hunger pangs.
—Jessica Salman, Dublin, OH

PREP: 20 MIN. • **BAKE:** 25 MIN. • **MAKES:** 2 SERVINGS

⅔ cup reduced-fat biscuit/baking mix
2 Tbsp. plus 1 tsp. water
2 cups fresh baby spinach, chopped
½ cup egg substitute
⅓ cup sour cream
⅓ cup shredded reduced-fat cheddar cheese
2 green onions, chopped
½ tsp. garlic powder
2 bacon strips, cooked and crumbled

1. In a small bowl, combine biscuit mix and water to form a soft dough. Press onto the bottom and up the side of a 7-in. pie plate coated with cooking spray.

2. Bake at 450° until golden brown, about 5 minutes. Remove from oven. Reduce heat to 375°.

3. In a small bowl, combine spinach, egg substitute, sour cream, cheese, onions and garlic powder. Pour into crust. Sprinkle with bacon. Bake for 25-30 minutes or until golden brown.

½ PIZZA: 365 cal., 16g fat (9g sat. fat), 45mg chol., 857mg sod., 34g carb. (6g sugars, 2g fiber), 18g pro.

SLOW-COOKER SPANAKOPITA
FRITTATA SANDWICHES

ENGLISH MUFFIN
BREAKFAST
BAKLAVA

ENGLISH MUFFIN BREAKFAST BAKLAVA

Classic baklava comes to breakfast courtesy of a lightly toasted cinnamon raisin English muffin and topped with a buttery baklava filling of pistachios and walnuts. First it's broiled then topped with a blend of mascarpone and fig preserves and lightly drizzled with honey. It's a delicious way to start the day and the perfect way to change up your breakfast routine. Serve with your choice of fresh fruit and lots of napkins.
—Sharyn LaPointe Hill, Las Cruces, NM

TAKES: 20 MIN. • **MAKES:** 8 SERVINGS

- ½ cup butter, softened
- ¼ cup shelled pistachios, coarsely chopped
- ¼ cup black walnuts, coarsely chopped
- 2 Tbsp. dark brown sugar
- 1 tsp. ground cinnamon
- ½ tsp. ground nutmeg
- ¼ tsp. ground cardamom
- 4 cinnamon raisin English muffins, split and lightly toasted
- ¼ cup mascarpone cheese
- ¼ cup fig preserves
- 2 Tbsp. honey

1. Preheat broiler. In a small bowl, mix butter, pistachios, walnuts, brown sugar and spices. Spread over split sides of muffin halves. Place on a baking sheet. Broil 3-4 in. from heat until just hot and bubbly, 1-2 minutes.

2. In another bowl, blend mascarpone cheese and fig preserves. Spread over muffin halves. Lightly drizzle each with honey; top with additional pistachios and walnuts.

1 MUFFIN HALF: 309 cal., 19g fat (9g sat. fat), 41mg chol., 202mg sod., 31g carb. (18g sugars, 1g fiber), 4g pro.

◇◇

51 CINNAMON-HONEY BROILED GRAPEFRUIT

Although grapefruit is naturally delicious, it gains even more flavor with this recipe. I often like to prepare this as a light breakfast, but it also makes an appealing addition to your morning meal.
—Carson Sadler, Souris, MB

TAKES: 10 MIN. • **MAKES:** 2 SERVINGS

- 1 medium grapefruit
- 2 tsp. honey
  Dash ground cinnamon

1. Cut grapefruit in half. With a sharp knife, cut around each section to loosen fruit. Place cut side up in a baking pan.

2. Drizzle each half with 1 tsp. honey; sprinkle with cinnamon. Broil 4 in. from heat for 2-3 minutes or until bubbly. Serve warm.

1 SERVING: 63 cal., 0 fat (0 sat. fat), 0 chol., 0 sod., 16g carb. (14g sugars, 1g fiber), 1g pro. **DIABETIC EXCHANGES:** ½ starch, ½ fruit.

FLORENCE-INSPIRED SOUFFLE

This light, beautiful and absolutely delicious souffle is sure to impress your brunch guests every time you serve it. They will be eager to grab their forks and dig into this little taste of Italy.
—Jenny Flake, Newport Beach, CA

PREP: 35 MIN. • **BAKE:** 35 MIN. • **MAKES:** 4 SERVINGS

- 6 egg whites
- ¾ cup onion and garlic salad croutons
- 1 small onion, finely chopped
- ¼ cup finely chopped sweet red pepper
- 2 oz. thinly sliced prosciutto, chopped
- 2 tsp. olive oil
- 2 cups fresh baby spinach
- 1 garlic clove, minced
- ⅓ cup all-purpose flour
- ½ tsp. salt
- ¼ tsp. pepper
- 1¼ cups fat-free milk
- 1 egg yolk, lightly beaten
- ¼ tsp. cream of tartar
- ¼ cup shredded Italian cheese blend

1. Place egg whites in a large bowl; let stand at room temperature for 30 minutes.

2. In a food processor, process croutons until ground. Sprinkle evenly onto the bottom and 1 in. up the side of a greased 2-qt. souffle dish; set aside.

3. In a large saucepan, saute onion, red pepper and prosciutto in oil until vegetables are crisp-tender, 3-5 minutes. Add spinach and garlic; cook just until spinach is wilted. Stir in flour, salt and pepper until blended. Gradually add milk. Bring to a boil; cook and stir 2 minutes or until thickened.

4. Transfer to a large bowl. Stir a small amount of hot mixture into egg yolk; return all to the bowl, stirring constantly. Cool slightly.

5. Add cream of tartar to egg whites; beat until stiff peaks form. Fold into vegetable mixture. Transfer to prepared dish; sprinkle with cheese.

6. Bake at 350° until top is puffed and center appears set, 35-40 minutes. Serve immediately.

1 SERVING: 223 cal., 9g fat (3g sat. fat), 73mg chol., 843mg sod., 20g carb. (6g sugars, 2g fiber), 16g pro. **DIABETIC EXCHANGES:** 2 lean meat, 1½ starch, ½ fat.

TOMATO-ONION QUICHE

This scaled-down quiche fills a 7-inch pie pan to the brim and is perfect for serving two or three. I think it's best fresh out of the oven when the cheese is wonderfully gooey.
—Sherri Crews, St. Augustine, FL

PREP: 20 MIN. • **BAKE:** 45 MIN. + STANDING • **MAKES:** 3 SERVINGS

1   sheet refrigerated pie crust
1   cup shredded part-skim
    mozzarella cheese
½   cup sliced sweet onion
2   small plum tomatoes, seeded
    and thinly sliced
3   medium fresh mushrooms,
    thinly sliced
¼   cup shredded Parmesan cheese
3   large eggs
½   cup half-and-half cream
½   tsp. ground mustard
½   tsp. dried basil
½   tsp. dried oregano
½   tsp. dried thyme

1. Cut crust sheet in half. Repackage and refrigerate half for another use. On a lightly floured surface, roll out remaining half into an 8-in. circle. Transfer to a 7-in. pie plate; flute edge.

2. Layer half the mozzarella cheese, onion and tomatoes in crust. Top with mushrooms; layer with remaining mozzarella cheese, onion and tomatoes. Sprinkle with Parmesan cheese. In a small bowl, combine eggs, cream, mustard and herbs; pour over top.

3. Bake at 350° for 45-55 minutes or until a knife inserted in center comes out clean. Let stand for 10 minutes before cutting.

1 PIECE: 436 cal., 26g fat (13g sat. fat), 265mg chol., 516mg sod., 26g carb. (7g sugars, 2g fiber), 22g pro.

---

⑤ᵢ YOGURT & HONEY FRUIT CUPS

A tasty combo of fresh fruit and creamy orange-kissed yogurt, this is guaranteed to disappear fast from your breakfast table.
—*Taste of Home* Test Kitchen

TAKES: 10 MIN. • **MAKES:** 6 SERVINGS

4½ cups cut-up fresh fruit (pears,
    apples, bananas, grapes, etc.)
¾   cup mandarin orange, vanilla
    or lemon yogurt
1   Tbsp. honey
½   tsp. grated orange zest
¼   tsp. almond extract

Divide fruit among 6 individual serving bowls. Combine yogurt, honey, orange zest and extract; spoon over the fruit.

¾ CUP: 97 cal., 0 fat (0 sat. fat), 2mg chol., 22mg sod., 23g carb. (9g sugars, 2g fiber), 2g pro.
DIABETIC EXCHANGES:
1 fruit, ½ starch.

GREEN SHAKSHUKA

This breakfast recipe is packed with healthy green vegetables as well as eggs and feta cheese for protein to start your day. The Italian parsley adds a lot of flavor to the fresh green vegetables. Make this dish with lemon-infused olive oil if you can find it in your grocery store.

—Carrie Dault, Baxter, TN

PREP: 20 MIN. • **COOK:** 20 MIN. • **MAKES:** 4 SERVINGS

1   Tbsp. olive oil
½   lb. fresh Brussels sprouts, quartered
1   medium green pepper, chopped
1   tsp. kosher salt, divided
¼   cup reduced-sodium chicken broth or vegetable broth, divided
3   garlic cloves, minced
1   small bunch kale, trimmed and chopped (about 8 cups)
9   oz. fresh baby spinach, chopped (about 7 cups)
¼   cup fresh parsley leaves, minced
4   large eggs
¼   cup crumbled feta cheese
1   tsp. grated lemon zest

1. In a large skillet, heat oil over medium-high heat. Add Brussels sprouts, green pepper and ½ tsp. salt; cook and stir until lightly browned, 10-12 minutes. Add 2 Tbsp. broth and garlic; cook 1 minute longer. In batches if needed, add kale, spinach and parsley; cook and stir until wilted, 3-4 minutes. Stir in the remaining 2 Tbsp. broth and ½ tsp. salt.

2. With back of spoon, make 4 wells in vegetable mixture; break an egg into each well. Sprinkle with feta and zest. Cook, covered, until egg whites are completely set and yolks begin to thicken but are not hard, 4-6 minutes.

1 EGG WITH 1 CUP VEGETABLE MIXTURE: 209 cal., 10g fat (3g sat. fat), 190mg chol., 756mg sod., 18g carb. (2g sugars, 6g fiber), 15g pro. **DIABETIC EXCHANGES:** 1 starch, 1 medium-fat meat, ½ fat.

🔟 DATE SMOOTHIE

Smoothies are a quick and easy way to start off your day. They also make healthy after-school snacks that older kids can make themselves or with some help from an adult. If you like your smoothies with more sweetness, add a drizzle of honey or maple syrup.
—*Taste of Home* Test Kitchen

TAKES: 10 MIN. • **MAKES:** 1 SERVING

1 cup unsweetened almond milk
2 pitted medjool dates
1 Tbsp. creamy peanut butter
1 medium ripe banana, sliced
 and frozen
4 ice cubes

In a blender, combine the first 3 ingredients; cover and process until blended. Add banana and ice cubes; cover and process until blended. Pour into chilled glasses; serve immediately.

1 SERVING: 271 cal., 11g fat (2g sat. fat), 0 chol., 241mg sod., 42g carb. (25g sugars, 6g fiber), 6g pro.

LATKES WITH LOX

Lox, a salty smoked salmon, is a year-round delicacy. This recipe, inspired by one from the Jewish Journal, *uses lox as a topping.*
—*Taste of Home* Test Kitchen

PREP: 20 MIN. • **COOK:** 5 MIN./BATCH • **MAKES:** 3 DOZEN

2 cups finely chopped onion
¼ cup all-purpose flour
6 garlic cloves, minced
2 tsp. salt
1 tsp. coarsely ground pepper
4 large eggs, lightly beaten
4 lbs. russet potatoes, peeled
 and shredded
¾ cup canola oil
TOPPINGS
4 oz. lox
 Optional: Sour cream and
 minced fresh chives

1. In a large bowl, combine first 5 ingredients. Stir in eggs until blended. Add potatoes; toss to coat.

2. Heat 2 Tbsp. oil in a large nonstick skillet over medium heat. Drop batter by ¼ cupfuls into oil; press lightly to flatten. Fry in batches until golden brown on both sides, using remaining oil as needed. Drain on paper towels. Serve with lox; top with sour cream and chives if desired.

3 LATKES WITH ⅓ OZ. LOX: 270 cal., 16g fat (2g sat. fat), 73mg chol., 610mg sod., 26g carb. (3g sugars, 2g fiber), 6g pro.

NICE AND SMOOTH

Soaking pitted medjool dates in a bowl of hot water for a few minutes will help soften them up. If you choose not to soak them first, just know that there may be a few small pieces of fruit in your smoothie as you sip.

ITALIAN BAKED EGGS & SAUSAGE

This isn't your typical egg bake! I serve this robust casserole of eggs, Italian sausage and fire-roasted tomatoes in bowls with warm, crusty rolls spread with butter.

—Shelly Bevington, Hermiston, OR

PREP: 15 MIN. • **BAKE:** 30 MIN. • **MAKES:** 8 SERVINGS

1   lb. bulk Italian sausage
1   jar (24 oz.) fire-roasted tomato and garlic pasta sauce
1   can (14½ oz.) fire-roasted diced tomatoes, drained
¾   cup part-skim ricotta cheese
8   large eggs
¼   tsp. salt
¼   tsp. pepper
¼   cup shredded Parmesan cheese
1   Tbsp. minced fresh basil
1   French bread demi-baguette (4 oz.), cut into 1-in. slices
¼   cup butter, softened

1. Preheat oven to 350°. In a large skillet over medium heat, cook sausage, crumbling meat, until no longer pink, 3-4 minutes; drain. Stir in pasta sauce and tomatoes. Transfer to a 13x9-in. baking dish.

2. Dollop ricotta cheese on top of meat mixture. Gently break an egg into a small bowl; slip egg onto meat mixture between dollops of ricotta. Repeat with remaining eggs. Sprinkle with salt, pepper and Parmesan cheese.

3. Bake until egg whites are completely set and yolks have begun to thicken but are not hard, 30-35 minutes. Remove from oven; sprinkle with basil.

4. Meanwhile, spread bread slices with butter; place on an ungreased baking sheet. Preheat broiler. Broil 3-4 in. from heat until golden brown, 1-2 minutes on each side. Serve immediately with baked eggs.

1 SERVING: 408 cal., 27g fat (11g sat. fat), 241mg chol., 1183mg sod., 22g carb. (8g sugars, 3g fiber), 19g pro.

VEGGIE FRITTATA

I was impressed with myself that I could omit dairy and still create something so good!
Use any vegetables in this recipe, then add a salad, fruit cup or yogurt on the side.
—Kizmet Byrd, Fort Wayne, IN

TAKES: 30 MIN. • **MAKES:** 6 SERVINGS

9   large eggs
½   tsp. salt, divided
¼   tsp. pepper, divided
1   Tbsp. olive oil
½   cup chopped carrot
½   cup chopped sweet red pepper
⅓   cup chopped red onion
½   cup sliced zucchini
2   Tbsp. chopped fresh basil, divided
2   garlic cloves, minced
½   cup grape tomatoes, halved

1. Preheat broiler. In a large bowl, whisk eggs, ¼ tsp. salt and ⅛ tsp. pepper until blended.

2. In a 10-in. broiler-safe skillet, heat oil over medium-high heat. Add carrot; cook and stir until crisp-tender, 4-5 minutes. Add red pepper and red onion; cook and stir until crisp-tender, 1-2 minutes. Add zucchini, 1 Tbsp. basil, garlic, and the remaining ¼ tsp. salt and ⅛ tsp. pepper; cook and stir until vegetables are tender.

3. Reduce heat to medium-low; pour in egg mixture. Cook, covered, until nearly set, 4-6 minutes. Add tomatoes; cook, uncovered, until edge begins to pull away from the pan, about 3 minutes.

4. Broil 3-4 in. from heat until eggs are completely set, 1-2 minutes. Let stand 5 minutes. Sprinkle with remaining 1 Tbsp. basil; cut into wedges.

1 WEDGE: 145 cal., 10g fat (3g sat. fat), 279mg chol., 313mg sod., 4g carb. (2g sugars, 1g fiber), 10g pro. **DIABETIC EXCHANGES:** 1 vegetable, 1 medium-fat meat, 1 fat.

READER REVIEW
"I love this recipe! I reduced it to make two servings and cooked it in my countertop convection oven instead of starting it on the stovetop. The cook time is about the same. I will definitely make it again!"
—ANNR, TASTEOFHOME.COM

BABA GANOUSH,
PAGE 59

MEZZE, SNACKS & DRINKS

Whether for a casual night at home or to surprise friends at a potluck, these appetizers and beverages elevate your snacking game. The vibrant colors and refreshing flavors of the Mediterranean are sure to liven up any occasion.

🍲 5i ORANGE BLOSSOM MINT REFRESHER

I came up with this recipe because I'm not a fan of regular iced tea. This version has the perfect combination of freshness and sweetness, and the orange blossom water gives the tea a distinctive flavor. People always request the recipe.
—Juliana Gauss, Centennial, CO

PREP: 10 MIN. + CHILLING • **COOK:** 6 HOURS • **MAKES:** 20 SERVINGS

20 cups water
1 bunch fresh mint (about 1 cup)
1 cup sugar
1 large navel orange
1 to 2 Tbsp. orange blossom water
  or 1½ to 2½ tsp. orange extract
  Optional: Orange slices and
  additional fresh mint

1. Place water and mint in a 6-qt. slow cooker. Cover and cook on high for 6 hours or until heated through. Strain mixture; discard mint.

2. Whisk in sugar until dissolved. Cut orange crosswise in half; squeeze juice from orange. Stir in juice and orange blossom water. Transfer to a pitcher. Refrigerate until cold, 4-6 hours. Serve over ice, with orange slices and additional mint if desired.

1 CUP: 43 cal., 0 fat (0 sat. fat), 0 chol., 0 sod., 11g carb. (11g sugars, 0 fiber), 0 pro.

INSIDE-OUT VEGGIE DIP

Cherry tomatoes and cucumber slices transform into these savory, bite-sized treats ideal for any gathering.
—Judie Thurstenson, Colcord, OK

PREP: 35 MIN. + CHILLING • **MAKES:** 3½ DOZEN

2 large cucumbers
16 cherry tomatoes
1 pkg. (8 oz.) cream cheese, softened
¼ cup finely chopped
  sweet red pepper
2 Tbsp. finely chopped celery
2 Tbsp. finely chopped green onion
1 Tbsp. finely chopped carrot
1 tsp. garlic powder
½ tsp. salt
½ tsp. onion powder

1. Peel strips from cucumbers to create decorative edges if desired; cut into ½-in. slices. Finely chop 2 slices; set aside. With a small spoon, scoop out some of the seeds from the remaining slices.

2. Cut a thin slice from the bottoms of tomatoes to allow them to rest flat. Cut a thin slice from the tops of tomatoes; scoop out pulp, leaving a ¼-in. shell. Invert onto paper towels to drain.

3. In a large bowl, combine cream cheese, red pepper, celery, onion, carrot, seasonings and chopped cucumber.

4. Fill tomatoes and cucumber slices with cream cheese mixture, about 1 tsp. in each. Refrigerate for at least 1 hour.

1 PIECE: 23 cal., 2g fat (1g sat. fat), 6mg chol., 45mg sod., 1g carb. (1g sugars, 0 fiber), 1g pro.

ORANGE BLOSSOM
MINT REFRESHER

51 SMOKED TROUT & HEARTS OF PALM BITES

I've had great luck finding hearts of palm in the canned vegetable section at the grocery store. In a pinch, you can use quartered artichoke hearts in place of the hearts of palms and still end up with a great tasting dish.
—Lori Stefanishion, Drumheller, AB

TAKES: 25 MIN. • **MAKES:** 2 DOZEN

1   can (14 oz.) hearts of palm, drained
24 bagel chips
4   oz. cream cheese, softened
6   oz. smoked trout, broken
    into 24 portions
3   Tbsp. capers, drained

Cut hearts of palm widthwise into thin slices. Spread bagel chips with cream cheese; layer with hearts of palm and trout. Garnish with capers.

1 APPETIZER: 86 cal., 3g fat (1g sat. fat), 7mg chol., 300mg sod., 11g carb. (0 sugars, 1g fiber), 3g pro.

BELLA BASIL RASPBERRY TEA

Give iced tea a grown-up twist. Fragrant basil lends flavor and the raspberries give it a bright red color. You'll love the fun fizz and make-ahead convenience!
—Laurie Bock, Lynden, WA

PREP: 45 MIN. • **MAKES:** 6 SERVINGS

3   cups fresh raspberries
1   cup sugar
1   cup packed fresh basil leaves,
    coarsely chopped
¼   cup lime juice
2   black tea bags
1   bottle (1 liter) carbonated water
    or 1 bottle (750 ml) sparkling rosé
    Ice cubes
    Optional: Fresh raspberries
    and basil leaves

1. In a large saucepan, combine the raspberries, sugar, basil and lime juice. Mash berries. Cook over medium heat until berries release juices, about 7 minutes.

2. Remove from heat; add tea bags. Cover and steep 20 minutes. Strain, discarding tea bags and raspberry seeds. Transfer tea to a 2-qt. pitcher. Cover and refrigerate until serving.

3. Just before serving, slowly add carbonated water or wine. Serve over ice. If desired, top with fresh raspberries and basil.

1 CUP: 281 cal., 0 fat (0 sat. fat), 0 chol., 9mg sod., 44g carb. (37g sugars, 4g fiber), 1g pro.

SPICY ROASTED CARROT HUMMUS

This is a wonderful appetizer for Easter, Mother's Day or any spring gathering. The roasted carrots give this hummus a bright, fresh flavor. Even those who don't like hummus end up loving this version.
—Anne Ormond, Dover, NH

PREP: 20 MIN. • **BAKE:** 15 MIN. • **MAKES:** 2 CUPS

1 cup chopped carrots
3 garlic cloves, peeled
3 Tbsp. olive oil, divided
1 can (15 oz.) garbanzo beans or chickpeas, rinsed and drained
2 Tbsp. lemon juice
2 Tbsp. tahini
1 Tbsp. water
1 tsp. hot pepper sauce, such as Tabasco
¼ tsp. sea salt
¼ tsp. ground turmeric
¼ tsp. ground cumin
⅛ tsp. cayenne pepper
¼ cup sunflower kernels
Assorted fresh vegetables and pita wedges

1. Preheat the oven to 400°. Place carrots and garlic in a rimmed baking sheet. Drizzle with 2 Tbsp. oil; toss to coat. Roast until carrots are soft, 15-20 minutes. Cool on a wire rack.

2. Transfer the carrot mixture to a food processor. Add garbanzo beans, lemon juice, tahini, water, hot sauce, salt and spices. While processing, add remaining 1 Tbsp. oil. Process until desired consistency is reached. Transfer to a serving dish. If desired, drizzle with additional oil and hot sauce. Top with sunflower kernels. Serve warm or chilled with vegetables and pita wedges.

¼ CUP: 155 cal., 11g fat (1g sat. fat), 0 chol., 175mg sod., 12g carb. (2g sugars, 3g fiber), 4g pro. **DIABETIC EXCHANGES:** 2 fat, 1 starch.

CARROT HUMMUS TIPS

What other toppings can you put on carrot hummus? *Toasted pumpkin seeds or pepitas would be delicious, and chopped, toasted walnuts would lend a bit of richness. For a juicy bite along with a snappy crunch, pomegranate arils look like little gems atop a fresh bowl of hummus.*

How long will carrot hummus last? *The carrot hummus will stay fresh for 5-7 days in an airtight container in the fridge, though it's likely you would have finished it by then.*

SANTORINI LAMB SLIDERS

I love lamb burgers, so I created a crowd-friendly slider version. The tzatziki sauce is best made a day or two in advance to allow the flavors to mingle.
—Cristina Certano, Colorado Springs, CO

PREP: 30 MIN. + CHILLING • **GRILL:** 10 MIN. • **MAKES:** 10 SERVINGS

1 cup plain Greek yogurt
½ cup shredded peeled cucumber
1¼ tsp. salt, divided
1 lb. ground lamb
1 Tbsp. grated lemon zest
4 garlic cloves, minced and divided
2 tsp. dried oregano
¼ tsp. plus ⅛ tsp. pepper, divided
1 tsp. lemon juice
1 tsp. dill weed
10 mini buns or mini ciabatta buns
10 Bibb lettuce leaves
or Boston lettuce leaves
1 medium red onion, thinly sliced
1 cup crumbled feta cheese

1. Line a strainer or colander with 4 layers of cheesecloth or 1 coffee filter; place over a bowl. Place yogurt in the prepared strainer; cover yogurt with sides of cheesecloth. Refrigerate for 2-4 hours. Meanwhile, place cucumber in a colander over a plate; sprinkle with ¼ tsp. salt and toss. Let stand for 30 minutes.

2. For burgers, in a large bowl, combine lamb, lemon zest, 2 garlic cloves, oregano, ¾ tsp. salt and ¼ tsp. pepper, mixing lightly but thoroughly. Shape into ten ½-in.-thick patties. Refrigerate for 30 minutes.

3. For sauce, remove yogurt from cheesecloth to a bowl; discard strained liquid. Squeeze cucumber and blot dry with paper towels. Add cucumber, lemon juice, dill, and the remaining 2 garlic cloves, ¼ tsp. salt and ⅛ tsp. pepper to yogurt, stirring until combined.

4. Grill burgers, covered, over medium heat 3-4 minutes on each side or until a thermometer reads 160°. Grill buns over medium heat, cut sides down, 30-60 seconds or until toasted. Serve burgers on buns with lettuce, red onion, feta and sauce.

1 SLIDER: 228 cal., 12g fat (5g sat. fat), 43mg chol., 531mg sod., 16g carb. (3g sugars, 1g fiber), 14g pro.

LIME-MARINATED SHRIMP SALAD

Ceviche is a seafood recipe of raw fish marinated in citrus juice, which cooks it without heat. This version starts with cooked shrimp and adds tomatoes, cucumbers and serrano peppers.
—Adan Franco, Milwaukee, WI

PREP: 25 MIN. + CHILLING • **MAKES:** 10 CUPS

1   large onion, quartered
2   to 4 serrano peppers, seeded and coarsely chopped
2   medium cucumbers, peeled, quartered and seeds removed
2   large tomatoes, cut into chunks
6   green onions, coarsely chopped (about ¾ cup)
2   lbs. peeled and deveined cooked shrimp (26-30 per lb.)
¾   cup lime juice
½   tsp. salt
¼   tsp. pepper
    Tortilla chips or tostada shells

1. Place onion and peppers in a food processor; pulse until finely chopped. Transfer to a large bowl. Place cucumbers, tomatoes and green onions in food processor; pulse until finely chopped. Add to bowl.

2. Place shrimp in food processor; pulse until chopped. Add shrimp, lime juice, salt and pepper to vegetable mixture; toss to coat. Refrigerate until cold. Serve with tortilla chips or tostada shells.

NOTE: Wear disposable gloves when cutting hot peppers; the oils can burn skin. Avoid touching your face.

½ CUP: 61 cal., 1g fat (0 sat. fat), 69mg chol., 128mg sod., 4g carb. (1g sugars, 1g fiber), 10g pro. **DIABETIC EXCHANGES:** 1 lean meat.

PISTACHIO &
DATE RICOTTA
CROSTINI

PISTACHIO & DATE RICOTTA CROSTINI

My husband and I regularly have date night at home where we make a four-course meal. For appetizers, I like to keep things simple but dressed up. I've found that making a special appetizer helps transform the atmosphere into a fancy meal. We've grown to really cherish these long and luxurious evenings together in our living room. Fresh figs can be used instead of dates if that's what you have on hand!
—Kristin Bowers, Gilbert, AZ

PREP: 20 MIN. • **BAKE:** 15 MIN. • **MAKES:** 3 DOZEN

36 slices French bread baguette
   (¼ in. thick)
2 Tbsp. olive oil
⅛ tsp. plus ¼ tsp. salt, divided
1 cup whole-milk ricotta cheese
4 oz. cream cheese, softened
3 Tbsp. honey, divided
4 tsp. grated lemon zest, divided
10 pitted medjool dates, chopped
   (about 1½ cups)
½ cup shelled pistachios,
   finely chopped

1. Preheat oven to 400°. Place bread slices on a large ungreased baking sheet. Brush tops with olive oil and sprinkle with ⅛ tsp. salt. Bake until golden brown, 12-15 minutes. Cool on baking sheet.

2. Meanwhile, place ricotta, cream cheese, 2 Tbsp. honey, 2 tsp. lemon zest and remaining ¼ tsp. salt in a food processor; process until almost smooth. Spread the mixture over bread slices. Top with dates and pistachios. Drizzle with remaining 1 Tbsp. honey and 2 tsp. lemon zest. Serve immediately.

1 PIECE: 57 cal., 3g fat (1g sat. fat), 6mg chol., 74mg sod., 6g carb. (3g sugars, 0 fiber), 1g pro.

🄵 REFRESHING BERRY WINE

This is an easy way to dress up wine for a party. Other fruit, like watermelon balls or sliced peaches, can be used in place of the strawberry slices.
—Laura Wilhelm, West Hollywood, CA

PREP: 35 MIN. + CHILLING • **MAKES:** 8 SERVINGS

1¼ cups frozen unsweetened
   raspberries
1 cup white grape juice
1 bottle (750 ml) dry rosé wine
2 cups sliced fresh strawberries
   Ice cubes
   Fresh mint or rosemary sprigs

In a small saucepan, combine raspberries and grape juice. Bring to a boil; reduce the heat. Cook and stir over medium heat 30 minutes or until liquid is almost evaporated. Remove from the heat. Press through a fine mesh strainer into a bowl; discard seeds. Transfer the puree to a pitcher. Stir in wine and strawberries. Refrigerate, covered, until chilled. Serve with ice; garnish with mint.

¾ CUP: 122 cal., 0 fat (0 sat. fat), 0 chol., 3mg sod., 14g carb. (7g sugars, 1g fiber), 0 pro.

ROASTED RED PEPPER HUMMUS

My son taught me how to make hummus, which is a tasty and healthy alternative to calorie-filled dips. Fresh roasted red bell peppers make it special.

—Nancy Watson-Pistole, Shawnee, KS

PREP: 30 MIN. + STANDING • **MAKES:** 3 CUPS

- 2 large sweet red peppers
- 2 cans (15 oz. each) garbanzo beans or chickpeas, rinsed and drained
- ⅓ cup lemon juice
- 3 Tbsp. tahini
- 1 Tbsp. olive oil
- 2 garlic cloves, peeled
- 1¼ tsp. salt
- 1 tsp. curry powder
- ½ tsp. ground coriander
- ½ tsp. ground cumin
- ½ tsp. pepper
  Optional: Fresh vegetables, pita bread or assorted crackers

1. Broil red peppers 4 in. from the heat until skins blister, about 5 minutes. With tongs, rotate peppers a quarter turn. Broil and rotate until all sides are blistered and blackened. Immediately place peppers in a bowl; cover and let stand for 15-20 minutes.

2. Peel off and discard charred skin. Remove stems and seeds. Place the peppers in a food processor. Add beans, lemon juice, tahini, oil, garlic and seasonings; cover and process until blended.

3. Transfer to a serving bowl. Serve with vegetables, pita bread or crackers as desired.

¼ CUP: 113 cal., 5g fat (1g sat. fat), 0 chol., 339mg sod., 14g carb. (3g sugars, 4g fiber), 4g pro. **DIABETIC EXCHANGES:** 1 fat, 1 starch.

READER REVIEW

"This is wonderful! It's so much better than store-bought hummus. I added a little real maple syrup and an 18-year-old balsamic vinegar to it, and it was perfect!"

— ZAMBONI_CHICK, TASTEOFHOME.COM

NANA'S DOLMADES WITH AVGOLEMONO SAUCE

This recipe is special to me because while I was growing up, our family always had dolmades for holidays and important events. They are fantastic for parties. You may also serve them as an entree.
—Elizabeth Latsis, Tacoma, WA

PREP: 45 MIN. • **COOK:** 45 MIN. • **MAKES:** ABOUT 6 DOZEN (2 CUPS SAUCE)

- 1 large sweet onion, finely chopped
- ¾ cup beef broth
- ½ cup uncooked long grain brown rice
- ½ cup chopped fresh parsley
- 1 large egg
- 3 Tbsp. tomato sauce
- 1 Tbsp. olive oil
- 1 Tbsp. butter, melted
- 2 tsp. minced fresh mint
- 2 tsp. kosher salt
- 2 tsp. pepper
- 1 lb. ground beef
- 1 jar (16 oz.) grape leaves, rinsed and drained

AVGOLEMONO SAUCE
- 2 cups beef broth
- 2 medium lemons
- 3 large eggs, beaten
  Dash kosher salt
  Dash pepper

1. In a large bowl, mix the first 11 ingredients; crumble beef over top and mix lightly but thoroughly. Pat grape leaves dry with paper towels.

2. Line bottom of a Dutch oven with 8 grape leaves. Place about 1 Tbsp. beef mixture on each remaining grape leaf, shiny side down. Fold in long sides over filling; roll up. Repeat. Arrange dolmades seam side down over grape leaves in Dutch oven. Place a heavy plate over dolmades. Add enough water just to cover plate. Bring to a boil; reduce heat. Cook, covered, until rice is tender, 45-50 minutes.

3. Meanwhile, for avgolemono sauce, in a small saucepan, bring broth to a boil. Reduce the heat to a simmer. Finely grate zest from lemons. Cut crosswise in half and squeeze juice from lemons. Transfer zest and juice to a small bowl. Whisk in eggs, salt and pepper until blended. Gradually whisk egg mixture into broth. Cook and stir over low heat until slightly thickened, 4-5 minutes (do not boil). Remove the plate from Dutch oven; remove dolmades with tongs, draining excess liquid. Serve with sauce.

1 DOLMA WITH 1½ TSP. SAUCE: 35 cal., 2g fat (1g sat. fat), 18mg chol., 237mg sod., 2g carb. (0 sugars, 1g fiber), 2g pro.

AIR-FRYER CALAMARI

KITCHEN TIP

The best dipping sauces to pair with calamari are marinara, ranch, chipotle ranch or garlic lemon.

AIR-FRYER CALAMARI

You can make crispy calamari just like your favorite Italian restaurant does thanks to the air fryer! A quick coat in crunchy panko bread crumbs and a few minutes in the air fryer are all it takes to make this special appetizer.
—Peggy Woodward, Shullsburg, WI

PREP: 20 MIN. • **COOK:** 10 MIN./BATCH • **MAKES:** 5 DOZEN

½ cup all-purpose flour
½ tsp. salt
1 large egg, lightly beaten
½ cup 2% milk
1 cup panko bread crumbs
½ tsp. seasoned salt
¼ tsp. pepper
8 oz. cleaned fresh or frozen calamari (squid), thawed and cut into ½-in. rings
Cooking spray

1. Preheat the air fryer to 400°. In a shallow bowl, combine flour and salt. In another shallow bowl, whisk egg and milk. In a third shallow bowl, combine bread crumbs, seasoned salt and pepper. Coat calamari with flour, then dip into egg mixture and coat with bread crumbs.

2. In batches, place calamari in a single layer on greased tray in air-fryer basket; spritz with cooking spray. Cook for about 4 minutes. Turn; spritz with cooking spray. Cook until golden brown, 3-5 minutes longer.

NOTE: In our testing, we find cook times vary dramatically among brands of air fryers. As a result, we give wider than normal ranges on suggested cook times. Begin checking at the first time listed and adjust as needed.

1 PIECE: 11 cal., 0 fat (0 sat. fat), 10mg chol., 28mg sod., 1g carb. (0 sugars, 0 fiber), 1g pro.

5i HONEY-ROSE PISTACHIOS

Crunch on a snack perfect to pop into your mouth while watching a game or as a pre-dinner fuel.
—Dana Swearengin, Forney, TX

TAKES: 15 MIN. • **MAKES:** 2 CUPS

3 Tbsp. honey
2 tsp. lemon juice
¼ tsp. rose water
2 cups shelled pistachios
2 tsp. dried rose petals, crumbled, optional

Preheat oven to 350°. In a large bowl, combine honey, lemon juice and rose water. Add pistachios; toss to coat. Spread mixture on a foil-lined baking sheet. Bake until fragrant and nuts start to brown, 8-10 minutes, stirring halfway. Toss with rose petals if desired. Cool on wire rack.

⅓ CUP: 266 cal., 19g fat (2g sat. fat), 0 chol., 176mg sod., 20g carb. (12g sugars, 4g fiber), 9g pro.

🍲 GREEK SHRIMP CANAPES

I grew up by the ocean and then moved to a landlocked state. I wanted to show people in my area how to easily cook seafood, and this is the recipe I came up with. I think it's safe to say it has become a neighborhood favorite.
—Amy Harris, Springville, UT

PREP: 15 MIN. + MARINATING • **COOK:** 65 MIN. • **MAKES:** 2½ DOZEN

1½ cups olive oil
¾ cup lemon juice
⅔ cup dry white wine
¼ cup Greek seasoning
4 garlic cloves, minced
1 lb. uncooked shrimp (31-40 per lb.), peeled and deveined
2 large cucumbers
1 pkg. (8 oz.) cream cheese, softened
Minced fresh parsley

1. In a large bowl, whisk the first 5 ingredients until blended. Pour 1½ cups marinade into a large bowl. Add the shrimp and stir to coat. Cover and refrigerate 45 minutes.

2. Meanwhile, pour remaining marinade into a 4- or 5-qt. slow cooker. Cook, covered, on high, 45 minutes. Drain shrimp, discarding marinade in bowl. Add shrimp to slow cooker. Cook, covered, on high until shrimp turn pink, about 20 minutes longer, stirring once; drain.

3. Cut each cucumber into ¼-in.-thick slices. Scoop out centers, leaving bottoms intact. Pipe cream cheese onto each cucumber slice; top with shrimp and parsley.

1 CANAPE: 68 cal., 6g fat (2g sat. fat), 26mg chol., 139mg sod., 1g carb. (1g sugars, 0 fiber), 3g pro.

🍲 5i SPICED APRICOT CIDER

You'll need just a few ingredients to simmer together this hot spiced beverage. Each delicious mugful is rich with apricot flavor.
—Connie Cummings, Gloucester, NJ

PREP: 5 MIN. • **COOK:** 2 HOURS • **MAKES:** 6 SERVINGS

2 cans (12 oz. each) apricot nectar
2 cups water
¼ cup lemon juice
¼ cup sugar
2 whole cloves
2 cinnamon sticks (3 in.)

In a 3-qt. slow cooker, combine all ingredients. Cover and cook on low until cider reaches the desired temperature, about 2 hours. Discard cloves and cinnamon sticks.

1 CUP: 70 cal., 0 fat (0 sat. fat), 0 chol., 2mg sod., 18g carb. (17g sugars, 0 fiber), 0 pro.

KITCHEN TIP

Instead of plain cream cheese, use your favorite variety of flavored cream cheese.

BABA GANOUSH

Baba ganoush (also spelled baba ghanoush or baba ghanouj) is a Lebanese dip made with roasted eggplant. It's typically served as a starter with pita bread or fresh vegetables.
—Nithya Narasimhan, Chennai, India

PREP: 15 MIN. • **BAKE:** 20 MIN. + COOLING • **MAKES:** 8 SERVINGS (1 CUP)

1 medium eggplant
2 Tbsp. olive oil, divided
1 tsp. salt, divided
½ tsp. paprika
2 Tbsp. tahini
1 garlic clove, minced
1 tsp. lemon juice
  Chopped fresh parsley

KITCHEN TIP
Baba ganoush is the perfect dip for pita bread, alongside other dips like hummus.

1. Preheat the oven to 450°. Cut eggplant in half lengthwise. Place cut side up on an ungreased baking sheet. Brush 1 Tbsp. olive oil over cut sides. Sprinkle with ½ tsp. salt and paprika. Bake until dark golden brown, 20-25 minutes. Remove eggplant from pan to a wire rack to cool completely.

2. Peel skin from eggplant; discard. Put flesh into a food processor and pulse to mash; transfer to bowl. Stir in tahini, garlic, lemon juice and remaining ½ tsp. salt. Spoon into serving dish. Drizzle with remaining 1 Tbsp. olive oil. Sprinkle with parsley and additional paprika.

2 TBSP.: 74 cal., 6g fat (1g sat. fat), 0 chol., 297mg sod., 5g carb. (2g sugars, 2g fiber), 1g pro.

FRUITY PEANUT BUTTER PITAS

My kids ask for these pita sandwiches all the time. They haven't noticed that as good as the pitas taste, they're good for them too.
—Kim Holmes, Emerald Park, SK

TAKES: 5 MIN. • **MAKES:** 2 SERVINGS

¼ cup peanut butter
⅛ tsp. each ground allspice, cinnamon and nutmeg
2 whole wheat pita pocket halves
½ medium apple, thinly sliced
½ medium firm banana, sliced

In a small bowl, blend peanut butter, allspice, cinnamon and nutmeg. Spread inside the pita bread halves; fill with apple and banana slices.

1 PITA HALF: 324 cal., 17g fat (4g sat. fat), 0 chol., 320mg sod., 36g carb. (13g sugars, 6g fiber), 12g pro. **DIABETIC EXCHANGES:** 3 fat, 1 starch, 1 fruit, 1 lean meat.

CLAMS CASINO

Your guests will be impressed with our version of this classic upscale appetizer. Cayenne pepper nicely seasons the bread crumb topping.
—*Taste of Home* Test Kitchen

PREP: 30 MIN. • **BAKE:** 15 MIN. • **MAKES:** 1 DOZEN

1 lb. rock or kosher salt
1 dozen fresh cherrystone clams
⅓ cup soft bread crumbs
3 Tbsp. minced fresh parsley, divided
2 Tbsp. olive oil
1 garlic clove, minced
⅛ tsp. cayenne pepper
⅛ tsp. coarsely ground pepper

1. Preheat the oven to 450°. Spread salt into an oven-safe metal serving platter or a 15x10x1-in. baking pan. Shuck clams, reserving the bottom shells; drain liquid (save for another use). Arrange clams in salt-lined pan.

2. Combine bread crumbs, 2 Tbsp. parsley, oil, garlic, cayenne and pepper; spoon over clams.

3. Bake until clams are firm and the bread crumb mixture is crisp and golden brown, 15-18 minutes. Sprinkle with remaining parsley. Serve immediately.

1 SERVING: 34 cal., 2g fat (0 sat. fat), 4mg chol., 16mg sod., 1g carb. (0 sugars, 0 fiber), 2g pro.

MEDITERRANEAN NACHOS

Make a Mediterranean version of nachos using crisped pita wedges topped with ground lamb or beef, feta cheese and a creamy cucumber sauce.

—Zaza Fullman-Kasl, Ventura, CA

PREP: 30 MIN. + STANDING • **COOK:** 15 MIN. • **MAKES:** 12 SERVINGS

- 2 medium cucumbers, peeled, seeded and grated
- 1½ tsp. salt, divided
- ½ tsp. ground cumin
- ½ tsp. ground coriander
- ½ tsp. paprika
- ¾ tsp. pepper, divided
- 6 whole pita breads
  Cooking spray
- 1 lb. ground lamb or beef
- 2 garlic cloves, minced
- 1 tsp. cornstarch
- ½ cup beef broth
- 2 cups plain Greek yogurt
- 2 Tbsp. lemon juice
- ¼ tsp. grated lemon zest
- 2 cups torn romaine
- 2 medium tomatoes, seeded and chopped
- ½ cup pitted Greek olives, sliced
- 4 green onions, thinly sliced
- ½ cup crumbled feta cheese

1. In a colander set over a bowl, toss cucumbers with ½ tsp. salt. Let stand for 30 minutes. Squeeze and pat dry. Set aside. In a small bowl, combine cumin, coriander, paprika, ½ tsp. pepper and ½ tsp. salt; set aside.

2. Cut each pita bread into 8 wedges; arrange in a singer layer on ungreased baking sheets. Spritz both sides of pitas with cooking spray; sprinkle with ¾ tsp. seasoning mix. Broil 3-4 in. from heat for 3-4 minutes on each side or until golden brown. Cool on wire racks.

3. In a large skillet, cook lamb with remaining seasoning mix over medium heat until lamb is no longer pink, 5-7 minutes, breaking into crumbles. Add garlic; cook 1 minute longer. Drain. Combine cornstarch and broth until smooth; gradually stir into the pan. Bring to a boil; cook and stir 2 minutes or until thickened.

4. In a small bowl, combine yogurt, lemon juice, lemon zest, cucumbers and remaining salt and pepper. Arrange pita wedges on a serving platter. Layer with lettuce, lamb mixture, tomatoes, olives, onions and cheese. Serve immediately with cucumber sauce.

1 SERVING: 253 cal., 12g fat (5g sat. fat), 37mg chol., 628mg sod., 23g carb. (4g sugars, 2g fiber), 12g pro.

READER REVIEW

"These were fantastic! I doubled the batch and we were able to eat them all week. The spices in the meat are spot on. We're thinking that we may use the ingredients to make Greek tacos. Bravo! This recipe is a keeper."

—BARKINMOONBAT, TASTEOFHOME.COM

SPINACH & FETA BOUREKAS

These pastries are light and soft with a bit of crunch, and are one of my favorite appetizers for the holidays. They can be filled with almost anything, but spinach and feta are my go-to fillings. Topped with everything seasoning, these little triangles are out of this world.

—Alex Stepanov, Matawan, NJ

PREP: 25 MIN. • **BAKE:** 25 MIN. • **MAKES:** 8 SERVINGS

1 Tbsp. olive oil or avocado oil
1 lb. fresh spinach, trimmed
½ cup chopped shallots
1 Tbsp. minced garlic
½ tsp. salt
¼ tsp. pepper
1 pkg. (17.3 oz.) frozen puff pastry, thawed
½ cup crumbled feta cheese
½ cup whole-milk ricotta cheese
1 large egg, beaten
1 Tbsp. everything seasoning blend

MIX IT UP

Other fillings, such as potato and dill or ricotta and caramelized onion, are tasty too! These can be made ahead and frozen; pull them out and bake them fresh at a moment's notice.

1. Preheat the oven to 400°. In a large skillet, heat oil over medium-high heat. Add spinach, shallots and garlic; cook and stir 2-3 minutes or until spinach is wilted. Remove from the heat; strain off any excess water. Stir in salt and pepper; set aside to cool to room temperature.

2. On a lightly floured surface, unfold puff pastry. Cut each sheet into 4 squares. In a small bowl, combine feta and ricotta; stir in the spinach mixture. Spoon cheese mixture diagonally over half of each square to within ½ in. of edges. Brush pastry edges with egg. Fold 1 corner over filling to the opposite corner, forming a triangle; press edges with a fork to seal. Place on parchment-lined baking sheets. Brush remaining egg over pastries; sprinkle with seasoning blend. Bake until golden brown, 25-30 minutes.

FREEZE OPTION: Freeze unbaked pastries on a parchment-lined baking sheet until firm. Transfer to an airtight container; return to freezer. To use, cook frozen pastries as directed until golden brown and heated through, increasing time to 30-32 minutes and covering with foil if pastries begin to brown too quickly.

1 PASTRY: 383 cal., 21g fat (6g sat. fat), 22mg chol., 635mg sod., 39g carb. (2g sugars, 6g fiber), 9g pro.

SPARKLING RED WINE SANGRIA

Sangria is a Spanish drink of wine mixed with spices, cut fruit and fruit juice, sherry or brandy. It's best to mix this and let it sit for an hour or more before serving so all the flavors of the fruit and wine blend together.
—*Taste of Home* Test Kitchen

TAKES: 5 MIN. • **MAKES:** 6 SERVINGS

- 1 **bottle (750 ml) dry red wine**
- 1 **cup sugar**
- ½ **cup orange liqueur**
- ½ **cup brandy**
- 3 **cups lemon-lime soda**
- 1 **cup sliced fresh strawberries**
- 1 **cup fresh blueberries**
- 1 **cup fresh raspberries**
- 1 **large navel orange, sliced**

In a pitcher, stir wine, sugar, orange liqueur and brandy until sugar dissolves. Stir in soda, berries and orange. Chill until ready to serve.

1 CUP: 448 cal., 0 fat (0 sat. fat), 0 chol., 18mg sod., 69g carb. (61g sugars, 3g fiber), 1g pro.

CHOCOLATE DATE ENERGY BALLS

Eating just one of these healthy treats satisfies my sweet tooth without added refined sugar. My recipe is a spinoff of an energy ball my daughter made for me when I was testing for my tae kwon do black belt.
—Barbara Estabrook, Appleton, WI

PREP: 20 MIN. + CHILLING • **MAKES:** 1 DOZEN

- 1¼ **cups pitted medjool dates, roughly chopped**
- 3 **oz. 60% bittersweet chocolate, coarsely chopped**
- ¼ **cup dried unsweetened tart cherries, chopped**
- ¼ **cup deluxe mixed nuts, coarsely chopped**
- 3 **Tbsp. unsweetened coconut flakes**
- 3 **Tbsp. sunflower kernels**
- 1½ **tsp. olive oil**
- 1 **tsp. vanilla extract**

Place dates, chocolate and cherries in a food processor; process until finely chopped, about 1 minute. Add nuts, coconut and sunflower kernels; process until blended. Add oil and vanilla; process until mixture comes together. Roll into 12 balls. Refrigerate, covered, at least 30 minutes before serving. Store in an airtight container in the refrigerator.

1 BALL: 125 cal., 6g fat (2g sat. fat), 0 chol., 25mg sod., 14g carb. (11g sugars, 2g fiber), 2g pro.

MARINATED OLIVES

These olives are nice to have for get-togethers because they're simple to make and they'll add a little zest to the buffet table offerings.
—Marguerite Shaeffer, Sewell, NJ

PREP: 10 MIN. + MARINATING • **MAKES:** 4 CUPS

2 cups large pimiento-stuffed olives, drained
1 cup pitted kalamata olives, drained
1 cup pitted medium ripe olives, drained
¼ cup olive oil
2 Tbsp. lemon juice
1 Tbsp. minced fresh thyme or 1 tsp. dried thyme
2 tsp. minced fresh rosemary or ½ tsp. dried rosemary, crushed
2 tsp. grated lemon zest
4 garlic cloves, slivered
Pepper to taste

1. Place olives in a bowl. Combine the remaining ingredients; pour over olives and stir. Cover and refrigerate for 1-2 days before serving, stirring several times each day.

2. Marinated olives may be refrigerated for up to 2 weeks. Serve with a slotted spoon.

¼ CUP: 98 cal., 10g fat (1g sat. fat), 0 chol., 572mg sod., 3g carb. (0 sugars, 0 fiber), 0 pro.

🟠 HONEY HYDRATOR

Stir up a pitcher of this refreshing drink, sweetened with honey.
—National Honey Board, Firestone, CO

TAKES: 5 MIN. • **MAKES:** 8 SERVINGS (2 QT.)

½ cup lukewarm water
½ cup honey
½ tsp. salt substitute or ¼ tsp. salt
2 cups cold orange juice
5 cups cold water

Place water, honey and salt substitute in a pitcher; stir until blended. Stir in juice and cold water. Refrigerate until serving.

NOTE: This recipe was tested with ½ tsp. Morton's Lite Salt.

1 CUP: 94 cal., 0 fat (0 sat. fat), 0 chol., 76mg sod., 24g carb. (23g sugars, 0 fiber), 0 pro. **DIABETIC EXCHANGES:** 1½ starch.

WATERMELON TAPAS

I start looking forward to biting into this summery treat when snow is still on the ground here! Whenever I make it for my friends, they swoon. It's also my secret for getting my kids to eat their fruit.
—Jami Geittmann, Greendale, WI

TAKES: 25 MIN. • **MAKES:** 8 SERVINGS

½ cup plain Greek yogurt
1 Tbsp. minced fresh mint
1 Tbsp. honey
8 wedges seedless watermelon, about 1 in. thick
1 medium kiwifruit, peeled and chopped
1 tangerine, sliced
½ cup sliced ripe mango
½ cup fresh raspberries
¼ cup fresh blueberries
¼ cup pomegranate seeds
2 Tbsp. pistachios, chopped

In a bowl, combine yogurt, mint and honey. Arrange watermelon wedges on a platter; top each with yogurt mixture, fruit and pistachios. If desired, top with additional honey and mint. Serve immediately.

1 WEDGE: 103 cal., 2g fat (1g sat. fat), 4mg chol., 18mg sod., 21g carb. (18g sugars, 2g fiber), 2g pro. **DIABETIC EXCHANGES:** 1½ fruit.

SPANAKOPITA PINWHEELS

I'm enthralled with spanakopita, and this spinach and feta pinwheel recipe was a quick and easy way to enjoy the pie. I have used it for get-togethers and family events with great success.
—Ryan Palmer, Windham, ME

PREP: 30 MIN. + COOLING • **BAKE:** 20 MIN. • **MAKES:** 2 DOZEN

1 medium onion, finely chopped
2 Tbsp. olive oil
1 tsp. dried oregano
1 garlic clove, minced
2 pkg. (10 oz. each) frozen chopped spinach, thawed and squeezed dry
2 cups crumbled feta cheese
2 large eggs, lightly beaten
1 pkg. (17.3 oz.) frozen puff pastry, thawed

1. In a small skillet, saute onion in oil until tender. Add oregano and garlic; cook 1 minute longer. Add spinach; cook until liquid is evaporated, about 3 minutes. Transfer spinach mixture to a large bowl; cool.

2. Add feta cheese and eggs to spinach mixture; mix well. Unfold puff pastry. Spread each sheet with half the spinach mixture to within ½ in. of edges. Roll up jelly-roll style. Cut each into twelve ¾-in. slices. Place cut side down on greased baking sheets.

3. Bake at 400° until golden brown, 18-22 minutes. Serve warm.

1 PINWHEEL: 197 cal., 13g fat (5g sat. fat), 39mg chol., 392mg sod., 14g carb. (1g sugars, 3g fiber), 7g pro.

WATERMELON
TAPAS

MOROCCAN SALMON,
PAGE 83

FISH & SEAFOOD

Quick, easy, delicious and packed with heart-healthy omega-3s, these catch-of-the-day selections will have you hooked.

SPINACH SHRIMP FETTUCCINE

*I experimented for a couple of years before perfecting this colorful dish,
and everyone raves about it. It is easy and light, and it fits into my busy schedule.*
—Kirstin Walker, Suffolk, VA

TAKES: 20 MIN. • **MAKES:** 8 SERVINGS

- 1 lb. uncooked fettuccine
- 1 pkg. (6 oz.) baby spinach
- 2 Tbsp. olive oil
- 4 garlic cloves, minced
- 1 lb. uncooked shrimp (31-40 per lb.), peeled and deveined
- 2 medium plum tomatoes, seeded and chopped
- ½ tsp. Italian seasoning
- ¼ tsp. salt
- ¼ cup shredded Parmesan cheese

1. Cook fettuccine according to package directions. Meanwhile, in a large skillet, saute spinach in oil 2 minutes or until leaves begins to wilt. Add garlic; cook 1 minute longer.

2. Add shrimp, tomatoes, Italian seasoning and salt; saute 2-3 minutes or until shrimp turn pink. Drain fettuccine and add to skillet; toss to coat. Sprinkle with Parmesan cheese.

1¼ CUPS: 283 cal., 5g fat (1g sat. fat), 85mg chol., 209mg sod., 41g carb. (2g sugars, 3g fiber), 17g pro. **DIABETIC EXCHANGES:** 2 starch, 2 vegetable, 1½ lean meat.

⑤ PESTO FISH WITH PINE NUTS

I love fish, and Italian flavors are my favorite. This is a tasty way to get more healthy fish into your diet.
—Valery Anderson, Sterling Heights, MI

TAKES: 15 MIN. • **MAKES:** 4 SERVINGS

- 2 envelopes pesto sauce mix, divided
- 4 cod fillets (6 oz. each)
- ¼ cup olive oil
- ½ cup shredded Parmesan or Romano cheese
- ½ cup pine nuts, toasted

1. Prepare 1 envelope pesto sauce mix according to package directions. Sprinkle fillets with remaining pesto mix, patting to help adhere.

2. In a large skillet, heat oil over medium heat. Add fillets; cook until fish just begins to flake easily with a fork, 4-5 minutes on each side. Remove from heat. Sprinkle with cheese and pine nuts. Serve with pesto sauce.

NOTE: To toast nuts, bake in a shallow pan in a 350° oven for 5-10 minutes or cook in a skillet over low heat until lightly browned, stirring occasionally.

1 FILLET WITH SCANT 3 TBSP. PESTO SAUCE: 560 cal., 39g fat (5g sat. fat), 72mg chol., 1522mg sod., 17g carb. (7g sugars, 1g fiber), 35g pro.

PESTO CHICKEN WITH PINE NUTS: Substitute 4 boneless skinless chicken breasts (6 oz. each) for cod. Cook 6-8 minutes on each side or until a thermometer reads 165°.

SPINACH SHRIMP
FETTUCCINE

GREEK TILAPIA

*While on a trip through the Greek islands, my husband and I had a dish that we loved.
I tried to duplicate it by combining several different recipes and came up with this.*
—Sally Burrell, Idaho Falls, ID

PREP: 30 MIN. • **BAKE:** 10 MIN. • **MAKES:** 4 SERVINGS

- 4 tilapia fillets (4 oz. each)
- 4 tsp. butter
- 1 large egg
- ¾ cup crumbled tomato and basil feta cheese
- ¼ cup fat-free milk
- ¼ tsp. cayenne pepper
- 1 large tomato, seeded and chopped
- ¼ cup chopped ripe olives
- ¼ cup pine nuts, toasted
- 1 Tbsp. minced fresh parsley
- 1 Tbsp. lemon juice
- ⅛ tsp. pepper

1. In a large cast-iron or other ovenproof skillet, brown fish in butter.

2. In a small bowl, combine egg, cheese, milk and cayenne; spoon over fish. Sprinkle with tomato, olives and pine nuts. Bake, uncovered, at 425° until fish just begins to flake easily with a fork, 10-15 minutes.

3. In a small bowl, combine parsley, lemon juice and pepper; drizzle over fish.

1 FILLET: 279 cal., 16g fat (6g sat. fat), 123mg chol., 362mg sod., 5g carb. (2g sugars, 2g fiber), 29g pro.

READER REVIEW

"I first saw this recipe in Taste of Home *print edition. I made it and loved it! It's so easy and full of flavor. Even my husband went back for seconds! I used toasted almonds instead of pine nuts. I have made it twice already and added it to my favorites. It's also a great recipe for those on the South Beach Diet."*
—WRITER2, TASTEOFHOME.COM

🍲 RED CLAM SAUCE

This recipe tastes as if it's taken a whole day's work. What a classy way to jazz up pasta sauce!
—JoAnn Brown, Latrobe, PA

PREP: 25 MIN. • **COOK:** 3 HOURS • **MAKES:** 4 SERVINGS

1 medium onion, chopped
1 Tbsp. canola oil
2 garlic cloves, minced
2 cans (6½ oz. each) chopped clams, undrained
1 can (14½ oz.) diced tomatoes, undrained
1 can (6 oz.) tomato paste
¼ cup minced fresh parsley
1 bay leaf
1 tsp. sugar
1 tsp. dried basil
½ tsp. dried thyme
6 oz. linguine, cooked and drained
Additional minced fresh parsley, optional

1. In a small skillet, saute the onion in oil until tender. Add garlic; cook for 1 minute longer.

2. Transfer to a 1½- or 2-qt. slow cooker. Stir in clams, tomatoes, tomato paste, parsley, bay leaf, sugar, basil and thyme.

3. Cover and cook on low until heated through, 3-4 hours. Discard bay leaf. Serve with linguine. If desired, sprinkle with additional parsley.

FREEZE OPTION: Omit additional parsley. Cool before placing in a freezer container. Cover and freeze for up to 3 months. To use, thaw in the refrigerator overnight. Place in a large saucepan; heat through, stirring occasionally. Serve with linguine and, if desired, minced parsley.

1 CUP SAUCE WITH ¾ CUP COOKED LINGUINE: 305 cal., 5g fat (0 sat. fat), 15mg chol., 553mg sod., 53g carb. (14g sugars, 7g fiber), 15g pro.

STOVETOP RED CLAM SAUCE: Saute onion and garlic as directed in a large saucepan. Add the diced tomatoes, tomato paste, parsley, bay leaf, sugar, basil and thyme. Bring to a boil. Reduce heat; cover and simmer 45 minutes, stirring occasionally. Stir in clams; heat through. Serve as directed.

KITCHEN TIP

To keep parsley fresh for up to a month, trim the ends of the stems and place the bunch in a tumbler with an inch of water. Be sure no loose leaves are in the water. Tie a produce bag around the tumbler to trap humidity; store in the refrigerator.

BROILED PARMESAN TILAPIA

Even picky eaters will find a way to love fish when you plate up this toasty Parmesan-coated entree. I serve it with mashed cauliflower and a green salad for a low-calorie meal everyone can enjoy.
—Trisha Kruse, Eagle, ID

TAKES: 20 MIN. • **MAKES:** 6 SERVINGS

6 tilapia fillets (6 oz. each)
¼ cup grated Parmesan cheese
¼ cup reduced-fat mayonnaise
2 Tbsp. lemon juice
1 Tbsp. butter, softened
1 garlic clove, minced
1 tsp. minced fresh basil or
   ¼ tsp. dried basil
½ tsp. seafood seasoning

1. Place fillets on a broiler pan coated with cooking spray. In a small bowl, combine the remaining ingredients; spread over fillets.

2. Broil 3-4 in. from heat until fish flakes easily with a fork, 10-12 minutes.

1 FILLET: 207 cal., 8g fat (3g sat. fat), 94mg chol., 260mg sod., 2g carb. (1g sugars, 0 fiber), 33g pro. **DIABETIC EXCHANGES:** 5 lean meat, 1 fat.

---

51 LEMON SALMON WITH BASIL

At our house we opt for healthy foods, and this lemony salmon with basil is a knockout in the good-for-you category. We have it with asparagus or zucchini.
—Shanna Belz, Prineville, OR

TAKES: 25 MIN. • **MAKES:** 4 SERVINGS

4 salmon fillets (6 oz. each)
2 tsp. olive oil
1 Tbsp. grated lemon zest
½ tsp. salt
¼ tsp. pepper
2 Tbsp. thinly sliced fresh basil
2 medium lemons, thinly sliced
   Additional fresh basil

1. Preheat the oven to 375°. Place salmon in a greased 15x10x1-in. baking pan. Drizzle with oil; sprinkle with lemon zest, salt, pepper and 2 Tbsp. basil; top with lemon slices.

2. Bake 15-20 minutes or until fish just begins to flake easily with a fork. If desired, top with additional basil.

1 SALMON FILLET: 294 cal., 18g fat (3g sat. fat), 85mg chol., 381mg sod., 3g carb. (1g sugars, 1g fiber), 29g pro. **DIABETIC EXCHANGES:** 5 lean meat, ½ fat.

SPANISH FISH

These flaky fish fillets get plenty of fresh flavor from onions and tomato, plus a little zip from cayenne pepper. This recipe is a particular favorite of my family's. The fish doesn't get dry ... it's moist and delicious.
—Pix Stidham, Exeter, CA

PREP: 10 MIN. • **BAKE:** 40 MIN. • **MAKES:** 6 SERVINGS

1	Tbsp. olive oil
1	large onion, thinly sliced
2	Tbsp. diced pimientos
6	sea bass or halibut fillets (6 oz. each)
1¼	tsp. salt
¼	tsp. ground mace
¼	tsp. cayenne pepper
¼	tsp. pepper
6	thick slices tomato
1	cup thinly sliced fresh mushrooms
3	Tbsp. chopped green onions
¼	cup white wine or chicken broth
4½	tsp. butter
½	cup dry bread crumbs

1. Brush oil onto the bottom of a 13x9-in. baking dish; top with onion and pimientos. Pat fish dry. Combine salt, mace, cayenne and pepper; sprinkle over both sides of fish.

2. Arrange fish over onion and pimientos. Top each fillet with a tomato slice; sprinkle with mushrooms and green onions. Pour wine over fish and vegetables.

3. In a nonstick skillet, melt butter; add bread crumbs. Cook and stir over medium heat until lightly browned. Sprinkle over fish.

4. Cover and bake at 350° for 20 minutes. Uncover and bake until fish flakes easily with a fork, 20-25 minutes longer.

1 SERVING: 251 cal., 9g fat (3g sat. fat), 68mg chol., 700mg sod., 11g carb. (0 sugars, 1g fiber), 29g pro. **DIABETIC EXCHANGES:** 4 lean meat, 1 vegetable, 1 fat, ½ starch.

LAUREN'S BOUILLABAISSE

This golden-colored soup is brimming with an assortment of seafood and is paired with savory, colorful sourdough toast with spread.

—Lauren Covas, New Brunswick, NJ

PREP: 30 MIN. • **COOK:** 20 MIN. • **MAKES:** 12 SERVINGS (5 QT.)

⅔ cup chopped roasted sweet red pepper, drained
¼ cup reduced-fat mayonnaise

TOASTS

6 slices sourdough bread
1 garlic clove, halved

BOUILLABAISSE

1 medium onion, chopped
1 Tbsp. olive oil
2 garlic cloves, minced
2 plum tomatoes, chopped
½ tsp. saffron threads or 2 tsp. ground turmeric
3½ cups cubed red potatoes
2½ cups thinly sliced fennel bulb
1 carton (32 oz.) reduced-sodium chicken broth
3 cups clam juice
2 tsp. dried tarragon
24 fresh littleneck clams
24 fresh mussels, scrubbed and beards removed
1 lb. red snapper fillet, cut into 2-in. pieces
¾ lb. uncooked shrimp (26-30 per lb.), peeled and deveined
¼ cup minced fresh parsley

1. Place red pepper and mayonnaise in a food processor; cover and process until smooth. Refrigerate until serving.

2. For toasts, rub 1 side of each bread slice with garlic; discard garlic. Cut bread slices in half. Place on an ungreased baking sheet. Bake at 400° for 4-5 minutes on each side or until lightly browned.

3. In a stockpot, saute onion in oil until tender. Add garlic; cook 1 minute longer. Reduce heat; stir in tomatoes and saffron. Add potatoes, fennel, broth, clam juice and tarragon. Bring to a boil. Reduce heat; simmer, uncovered, 10-12 minutes or until potatoes are almost tender.

4. Add clams, mussels, snapper and shrimp. Cook, stirring occasionally, 10-15 minutes or until clams and mussels open and fish flakes easily with a fork. Discard any unopened clams or mussels. Spoon into bowls; sprinkle with parsley. Spread pepper mayo over toasts; serve with bouillabaisse.

1⅔ CUPS WITH 2 TSP. SPREAD ON ½ PIECE OF BREAD: 239 cal., 5g fat (1g sat. fat), 70mg chol., 684mg sod., 23g carb. (3g sugars, 2g fiber), 24g pro. **DIABETIC EXCHANGES:** 3 lean meat, 1½ starch, ½ fat.

MOROCCAN
SALMON

MOROCCAN SALMON

If you're trying to add more fish to your diet, here's a deliciously simple recipe for baked salmon. Here, the salmon is topped with sauteed onion, tomatoes, golden raisins and spices, transforming an ordinary weeknight meal into a culinary adventure.
—*Taste of Home* Test Kitchen

PREP: 15 MIN. • **BAKE:** 25 MIN. • **MAKES:** 4 SERVINGS

2   cups sliced onions, separated
    into rings
1   Tbsp. canola oil
4   garlic cloves, minced
2   cups sliced plum tomatoes
¼   cup golden raisins
½   tsp. salt
½   tsp. ground cumin
½   tsp. ground turmeric
⅛   tsp. ground cinnamon
4   salmon fillets (4 oz. each)
    Hot cooked couscous, optional

1. Preheat oven to 375°. In a large nonstick skillet, saute onions in oil until tender, about 5 minutes. Add garlic; cook 1 minute longer. Add tomatoes, raisins and seasonings; cook and stir 5 minutes longer.

2. Place salmon in a 13x9-in. baking dish coated with cooking spray. Top with the onion mixture.

3. Cover and bake 25-30 minutes or until fish just begins to flake easily with a fork. If desired, serve with couscous.

1 SERVING: 311 cal., 16g fat (3g sat. fat), 67mg chol., 374mg sod., 17g carb. (12g sugars, 3g fiber), 24g pro.

HEARTY SHRIMP RISOTTO

Given the white wine, goat cheese and fresh spinach, guests will think you picked up this dish from an Italian restaurant!
—Lydia Jensen, Kansas City, MO

PREP: 15 MIN. • **COOK:** 35 MIN. • **MAKES:** 4 SERVINGS

4   cups reduced-sodium
    chicken broth
1   small onion, finely chopped
1   Tbsp. olive oil
1   cup uncooked arborio rice
1   fresh thyme sprig
1   bay leaf
¼   tsp. pepper
¾   cup white wine or additional
    reduced-sodium chicken broth
1   lb. uncooked shrimp (31-40 per lb.),
    peeled and deveined
2   cups chopped fresh spinach
4   oz. fresh goat cheese, crumbled

1. In a small saucepan, heat broth and keep warm. In a large nonstick skillet, saute onion in oil until tender. Add rice, thyme, bay leaf and pepper; cook and stir 2-3 minutes. Reduce heat; stir in wine. Cook and stir until all of the liquid is absorbed.

2. Add heated broth, ½ cup at a time, stirring constantly. Allow the liquid to absorb between additions. Cook just until risotto is creamy and rice is almost tender. (Cooking time is about 20 minutes.) Add shrimp and spinach; cook until shrimp turn pink and spinach is wilted.

3. Stir in cheese. Discard thyme and bay leaf. Serve immediately.

1¼ CUPS: 405 cal., 9g fat (3g sat. fat), 157mg chol., 832mg sod., 45g carb. (2g sugars, 1g fiber), 28g pro. **DIABETIC EXCHANGES:** 3 lean meat, 2½ starch, 1 fat.

CIOPPINO

Using prepared pasta sauce makes this hearty and hot one-pot dinner a cinch.
—Jeff Mancini, Eagle River, WA

PREP: 25 MIN. • **COOK:** 25 MIN. • **MAKES:** 8 SERVINGS (3 QT.)

5 garlic cloves, minced
2 Tbsp. olive oil
1 jar (24 oz.) tomato basil pasta sauce
1 bottle (8 oz.) clam juice
1 cup dry white wine or chicken broth
¼ cup water
1 tsp. salt
1 tsp. sugar
1 tsp. crushed red pepper flakes
1 tsp. minced fresh basil
1 tsp. minced fresh thyme
1 lb. fresh littleneck clams
1 lb. fresh mussels, scrubbed and beards removed
1 lb. uncooked shrimp (31-40 per lb.), peeled and deveined
1 lb. bay scallops
1 pkg. (6 oz.) fresh baby spinach

1. In a Dutch oven, saute garlic in oil until tender. Add pasta sauce, clam juice, wine, water and seasonings. Bring to a boil. Reduce heat; simmer, uncovered, about 10 minutes.

2. Add clams, mussels and shrimp. Bring to a boil. Reduce heat; simmer, uncovered, about 10 minutes, stirring occasionally.

3. Stir in scallops and spinach; cook 5-7 minutes longer or until clams and mussels open, shrimp turn pink and scallops are opaque. Discard any unopened clams or mussels.

NOTE: A part of the bivalve mollusk family, scallops are commonly found in 2 groups—the sea scallop, yielding 10-20 per lb., or the much smaller bay scallop, yielding 60-90 per lb. Scallops are usually available shucked and sold fresh or frozen, and they range in color from pale beige to creamy pink. Scallops can be broiled, grilled, pan-fried or deep-fried, and they cook in a matter of minutes.

1½ CUPS: 259 cal., 7g fat (1g sat. fat), 108mg chol., 1057mg sod., 15g carb. (7g sugars, 3g fiber), 29g pro.

READER REVIEW

"I just finished making this dish, and it did not disappoint! My hubby had three bowls and, with every mouthful, was praising how much he was enjoying it. It's so yummy and I wouldn't change a thing. This is definitely a keeper."

—JANNINE, TASTEOFHOME.COM

SALMON WITH BALSAMIC-HONEY GLAZE

Look no further—you've just found the first, last and only way you'll ever want to fix salmon again. The sweet and tangy flavors blend beautifully in this easy-to-remember recipe.
—Mary Lou Timpson, Colorado City, AZ

TAKES: 30 MIN. • MAKES: 8 SERVINGS

½ cup balsamic vinegar
2 Tbsp. white wine or chicken broth
2 Tbsp. Dijon mustard
2 Tbsp. honey
5 garlic cloves, minced
1 Tbsp. olive oil
8 salmon fillets (6 oz. each)
½ tsp. salt
½ tsp. pepper
1 Tbsp. minced fresh oregano

1. Combine the first 6 ingredients in a small saucepan. Bring to a boil; cook and stir 4-5 minutes or until thickened.

2. Place salmon skin side down on a greased 15x10x1-in. baking pan. Sprinkle with salt and pepper. Spoon glaze over salmon; top with oregano.

3. Bake, uncovered, at 400° until fish flakes easily with a fork, 12-15 minutes.

1 FILLET: 319 cal., 17g fat (3g sat. fat), 85mg chol., 323mg sod., 9g carb. (8g sugars, 0 fiber), 29g pro. **DIABETIC EXCHANGES:** 4 lean meat, ½ starch, ½ fat.

◇◇

5i PESTO HALIBUT

The mildness of halibut contrasts perfectly with the robust flavor of pesto in this recipe. It takes only minutes to get the fish ready for the oven, so you can start quickly on your side dishes. Nearly everything goes well with this entree.
—April Showalter, Indianapolis, IN

TAKES: 20 MIN. • MAKES: 6 SERVINGS

2 Tbsp. olive oil
1 envelope pesto sauce mix
1 Tbsp. lemon juice
6 halibut fillets (4 oz. each)

1. Preheat oven to 450°. In a small bowl, combine oil, sauce mix and lemon juice; brush over both sides of fillets. Place in a greased 13x9-in. baking dish.

2. Bake, uncovered, until fish just begins to flake easily with a fork, 12-15 minutes.

1 FILLET: 188 cal., 7g fat (1g sat. fat), 36mg chol., 481mg sod., 5g carb. (2g sugars, 0 fiber), 24g pro. **DIABETIC EXCHANGES:** 3 lean meat, 1 fat.

SEARED SCALLOPS WITH MINTED PEA PUREE

I'm always in the mood for mint, whether it's in a mojito or alongside a roasted leg of lamb. As a seafood lover, I came up with this blend of my favorite herb and shellfish.
—Teerawat Wiwatpanit, Chicago, IL

PREP: 20 MIN. • **COOK:** 15 MIN. • **MAKES:** 4 SERVINGS

4   cups fresh or frozen peas, thawed
    (about 16 oz.)
½   cup vegetable broth or water
3   Tbsp. sherry
2   garlic cloves, minced
½   tsp. salt, divided
¼   tsp. pepper, divided
⅓   cup minced fresh mint
¼   cup half-and-half cream
16 sea scallops (about 2 lbs.)
1   tsp. smoked paprika
1   Tbsp. canola oil
    Optional: Sliced fresh sugar snap
    peas and pea sprouts

1. In a large saucepan, cook peas and broth over medium-high heat until peas are bright green and tender, 3-4 minutes. Drain, reserving the cooking liquid. Set aside 1 cup peas; keep warm. Transfer remaining peas to a blender. Add sherry, garlic, ¼ tsp. salt, ⅛ tsp. pepper and reserved cooking liquid. Puree until smooth. Cool. Add mint and cream; puree until smooth.

2. Pat scallops dry with paper towels; sprinkle with paprika and remaining ¼ tsp. salt and ⅛ tsp. pepper. In a large nonstick skillet, heat the oil over medium-high heat. Add scallops in batches; cook until golden brown and firm, 2-3 minutes on each side. Serve with pea puree and reserved peas. Top with additional mint and, if desired, sugar snap peas and pea sprouts.

4 SCALLOPS WITH ½ CUP PEA PUREE: 351 cal., 7g fat (2g sat. fat), 62mg chol., 1355mg sod., 32g carb. (9g sugars, 9g fiber), 36g pro.

GRILLED CHORIZO & SHRIMP PAELLA

This shrimp paella recipe is not only healthy but satisfying too! It has vitamin C from the sweet red pepper, fiber from the rice and lean protein from the chicken sausage.

—Daniel Bartholomay, Fargo, ND

PREP: 25 MIN. • **GRILL:** 10 MIN. • **MAKES:** 8 SERVINGS

1 medium sweet red pepper, chopped
1 medium onion, chopped
2 Tbsp. olive oil
4 cups instant brown rice
4 garlic cloves, minced
1 chipotle pepper in adobo sauce, chopped
6 cups reduced-sodium chicken broth
1 can (14½ oz.) no-salt-added diced tomatoes
1 tsp. saffron threads or 4 tsp. ground turmeric
1 lb. uncooked shrimp (31-40 per lb.), peeled and deveined
1 pkg. (12 oz.) fully cooked chorizo chicken sausage or flavor of your choice, cut into ¼-in. slices
1 medium mango, coarsely chopped
2 Tbsp. lime juice
¼ tsp. cayenne pepper
1 medium lime, cut into wedges
2 Tbsp. minced fresh cilantro

1. In a Dutch oven, saute red pepper and onion in oil until tender. Add rice, garlic and chipotle pepper; saute 2 minutes longer. Add broth, tomatoes and saffron. Bring to a boil. Reduce heat; cover and simmer until liquid is absorbed, about 5 minutes. Let stand 5 minutes.

2. Meanwhile, in a large bowl, combine shrimp, sausage and mango; sprinkle with lime juice and cayenne. Transfer to a grill wok or basket. Grill, covered, over medium heat until shrimp turn pink, 5-8 minutes, stirring occasionally.

3. Add the shrimp mixture to Dutch oven; toss to combine. Garnish with lime wedges and cilantro.

NOTE: If you do not have a grill wok or basket, use a disposable foil pan. Poke holes in the bottom of the pan with a meat fork to allow liquid to drain.

1½ CUPS: 388 cal., 9g fat (2g sat. fat), 101mg chol., 787mg sod., 55g carb. (11g sugars, 4g fiber), 24g pro.

DID YOU KNOW?

Saffron, the stigmas of a tiny fall-flowering crocus, is the most expensive spice in the world. It grows mainly in a belt that runs from Morocco and Spain in the west to Tajikistan and India in the east. Each flower makes just 3 stigmas, which are gathered by hand. A gram of good-quality saffron costs around $13; and that works out to $6,000 a pound! Luckily, a little bit goes a long way.

TUNA STEAK ON FETTUCCINE

For something new to try with tuna, I suggest this tangy dish. Although I prefer the marinade on tuna or mahi mahi, it's great on any fish, grilled, baked or broiled.
—Caren Stearns, Austin, TX

PREP: 10 MIN. + MARINATING • **COOK:** 20 MIN. • **MAKES:** 2 SERVINGS

8   Tbsp. white wine or chicken broth, divided
3   Tbsp. olive oil, divided
1   tsp. dried basil, divided
1   tsp. dried oregano, divided
¼   tsp. salt, divided
⅛   tsp. pepper, divided
1   tuna, swordfish or halibut steak (about 10 oz.), cut in half
½   cup thinly sliced sweet onion
1   cup canned diced tomatoes, undrained
¼   tsp. brown sugar
3   oz. uncooked fettuccine

1. In a shallow bowl, combine 2 Tbsp. wine, 2 Tbsp. oil, ¼ tsp. basil, ¼ tsp. oregano, and half the salt and pepper; add tuna. Turn to coat; cover and refrigerate 1 hour.

2. In a large skillet, saute onion in remaining oil until tender. Add tomatoes, brown sugar and remaining wine, basil, oregano, salt and pepper. Bring to a boil. Reduce heat; simmer, uncovered, until bubbly and slightly thickened, 4-6 minutes. Meanwhile, cook fettuccine according to package directions.

3. Drain tuna, discarding marinade. Place tuna over tomato mixture; return to a boil. Reduce heat; simmer, covered, until fish just begins to flake easily with a fork, about 6 minutes. Remove tuna and keep warm. Drain fettuccine; add to tomato mixture and toss to coat. Divide between 2 plates; top with tuna.

1 SERVING: 505 cal., 17g fat (3g sat. fat), 55mg chol., 518mg sod., 41g carb. (8g sugars, 5g fiber), 42g pro.

MEDITERRANEAN BAKED FISH

The mouthwatering aroma of this herbed dish baking is sure to lure guests to your kitchen. It makes a colorful presentation for company. In a pinch, you can use dried herbs and canned diced tomatoes to replace the fresh ingredients.
—Ellen De Munnik, Chesterfield, MI

TAKES: 30 MIN. • **MAKES:** 4 SERVINGS

1   cup thinly sliced leeks
     (white portion only)
2   garlic cloves, minced
2   tsp. olive oil
12   large fresh basil leaves
1½   lbs. tilapia or cod fillets
1   tsp. salt
2   plum tomatoes, sliced
1   can (2¼ oz.) sliced ripe olives,
     drained
1   medium lemon
⅛   tsp. pepper
4   fresh rosemary sprigs

1. In a nonstick skillet, saute leeks and garlic in oil until tender; set aside. Coat a 13x9-in. baking dish with cooking spray. Arrange basil in dish in a single layer; top with fish fillets. Sprinkle with salt. Top with leek mixture.

2. Arrange tomatoes and olives over fish. Thinly slice half of the lemon; place over top. Squeeze juice from remaining lemon over all. Sprinkle with pepper.

3. Cover and bake at 425° until fish flakes easily with a fork, 15-20 minutes. Garnish with rosemary.

4½ OZ.: 180 cal., 5g fat (1g sat. fat), 34mg chol., 844mg sod., 7g carb. (3g sugars, 1g fiber), 26g pro. **DIABETIC EXCHANGES:** 3 lean meat, 1 vegetable.

READER REVIEW

"It's a nice recipe. I add a small can of artichokes."
—NIKMYOWN, TASTEOFHOME.COM

🏵 LEMON-PARSLEY TILAPIA

I like to include seafood in our weekly dinner rotation but don't want to bother with anything complicated. My family adores this dish, and it's a breeze to prepare. Cod and snapper work well here too—simply adjust the cooking time if needed.
—Trisha Kruse, Eagle, ID

TAKES: 20 MIN. • **MAKES:** 4 SERVINGS

4   tilapia fillets (about 4 oz. each)
2   Tbsp. lemon juice
1   Tbsp. butter, melted
2   Tbsp. minced fresh parsley
2   garlic cloves, minced
2   tsp. grated lemon zest
½   tsp. salt
¼   tsp. pepper

1. Preheat oven to 375°. Place tilapia in a parchment-lined 15x10x1-in. pan. Drizzle with lemon juice, then melted butter.

2. Bake for 11-13 minutes or until fish just begins to flake easily with a fork. Meanwhile, mix remaining ingredients. Remove fish from oven; sprinkle with parsley mixture.

1 FILLET: 124 cal., 4g fat (2g sat. fat), 63mg chol., 359mg sod., 1g carb. (0 sugars, 0 fiber), 21g pro. **DIABETIC EXCHANGES:** 3 lean meat, 1 fat.

PESTO SHRIMP PASTA

A dash of red pepper puts zip in this lively main dish.
—Gloria Jones Grenga, Newnan, GA

TAKES: 30 MIN. • **MAKES:** 4 SERVINGS

8   oz. uncooked spaghetti
3   Tbsp. olive oil, divided
1   cup loosely packed
    fresh basil leaves
¼   cup lemon juice
2   garlic cloves, peeled
½   tsp. salt
1   lb. fresh asparagus, trimmed
    and cut into 2-in. pieces
¾   lb. uncooked shrimp (31-40 per lb.),
    peeled and deveined
⅛   tsp. crushed red pepper flakes

1. Cook spaghetti according to the package directions. Meanwhile, in a blender, combine 1 Tbsp. oil, basil, lemon juice, garlic and salt; cover and process until smooth.

2. In a large skillet, saute asparagus in remaining oil until crisp-tender. Add the shrimp and pepper flakes. Cook and stir until shrimp turn pink, 2-4 minutes.

3. Drain spaghetti; place in a large bowl. Add basil mixture; toss to coat. Add shrimp mixture and mix well.

1 CUP: 393 cal., 12g fat (2g sat. fat), 103mg chol., 406mg sod., 47g carb. (3g sugars, 3g fiber), 23g pro.

FRA DIAVOLO

Meaning "brother devil" in Italian, fra diavolo describes a variety of seafood dishes in spicy tomato sauce.

SPINACH & SHRIMP FRA DIAVOLO

This quick dish is spicy, garlicky, saucy and loaded with delicious shrimp. Plus, with the addition of spinach, you're also getting a serving of veggies. When you need a perfect low-fat weeknight meal that is easy to pull together, this is it. You can substitute arugula or kale for the spinach if you'd like.
—Julie Peterson, Crofton, MD

TAKES: 30 MIN. • **MAKES:** 4 SERVINGS

2 Tbsp. olive oil
1 medium onion, chopped
5 garlic cloves, minced
½ to 1 tsp. crushed red pepper flakes
1 cup dry white wine
1 can (14½ oz.) diced tomatoes, undrained
1 can (8 oz.) tomato sauce
3 Tbsp. minced fresh basil or 1 Tbsp. dried basil
1 tsp. dried oregano
¼ tsp. salt
¼ tsp. pepper
1 lb. uncooked shrimp (26-30 per lb.), peeled and deveined
3 cups finely chopped fresh spinach
   Grated Parmesan cheese, optional

1. In a large skillet, heat oil over medium-high heat. Add onion; cook and stir until tender, 5-7 minutes. Add garlic and pepper flakes; cook 1 minute longer. Stir in wine. Bring to a boil; cook until liquid is reduced by half. Stir in tomatoes, tomato sauce, basil, oregano, salt and pepper. Cook and stir until sauce is slightly thickened, about 10 minutes.

2. Add shrimp and spinach; cook and stir until shrimp turn pink and spinach is wilted, 3-5 minutes. If desired, sprinkle with cheese.

1½ CUPS: 235 cal., 9g fat (1g sat. fat), 138mg chol., 727mg sod., 14g carb. (6g sugars, 4g fiber), 22g pro. **DIABETIC EXCHANGES:** 3 lean meat, 2 vegetable, 1½ fat.

TILAPIA WITH LEMON CAPER SAUCE

My husband and I are trying to increase the amount of fish we eat. This recipe is fast and tasty, even for non-fish eaters.
—Catherine Jensen, Blytheville, AR

TAKES: 25 MIN. • **MAKES:** 4 SERVINGS

4 tilapia fillets (6 oz. each)
½ tsp. salt
¼ tsp. pepper
1 Tbsp. all-purpose flour
1 Tbsp. olive oil
½ cup reduced-sodium chicken broth
2 Tbsp. lemon juice
1 Tbsp. butter
1 Tbsp. drained capers
   Optional: Lemon wedges and
   hot cooked pasta

1. Sprinkle tilapia with salt and pepper. Dust lightly with flour.

2. In a large skillet, heat oil over medium heat. Add tilapia; cook until lightly browned and fish just begins to flake easily with a fork, 3-5 minutes per side. Remove from pan; keep warm.

3. Add broth, lemon juice, butter and capers to the same skillet; cook and stir until mixture is reduced by half, about 5 minutes. Spoon over tilapia. If desired, serve with lemon wedges and pasta.

1 FILLET WITH 1 TBSP. SAUCE: 207 cal., 8g fat (3g sat. fat), 90mg chol., 500mg sod., 2g carb. (0 sugars, 0 fiber), 32g pro. **DIABETIC EXCHANGES:** 5 lean meat, ½ fat.

---

⑤i CAESAR SALMON WITH ROASTED TOMATOES & ARTICHOKES

This is my go-to recipe for quick dinners, family or guests. This dish is colorful, healthy, easy to prepare and absolutely delicious. It's hard to believe it is only five ingredients!
—Mary Hawkes, Prescott, AZ

TAKES: 25 MIN. • **MAKES:** 4 SERVINGS

4 salmon fillets (5 oz. each)
5 Tbsp. reduced-fat
   Caesar vinaigrette, divided
¼ tsp. pepper, divided
2 cups grape tomatoes
1 can (14 oz.) water-packed artichoke
   hearts, drained and quartered
1 medium sweet orange or yellow
   pepper, cut into 1-in. pieces

1. Preheat oven to 425°. Place salmon on half of a 15x10x1-in. baking pan coated with cooking spray. Brush with 2 Tbsp. vinaigrette; sprinkle with ⅛ tsp. pepper.

2. In a large bowl, combine tomatoes, artichoke hearts and sweet pepper. Add remaining vinaigrette and pepper; toss to coat. Place tomato mixture on remaining half of the pan. Roast until fish just begins to flake easily with a fork and vegetables are tender, 12-15 minutes.

1 FILLET WITH ¾ CUP TOMATO MIXTURE: 318 cal., 16g fat (3g sat. fat), 73mg chol., 674mg sod., 12g carb. (4g sugars, 2g fiber), 28g pro. **DIABETIC EXCHANGES:** 4 lean meat, 1 vegetable, 1 fat.

TILAPIA WITH
LEMON CAPER SAUCE

KITCHEN TIP

We recommend soaking wooden skewers for at least 30 minutes before using them. This helps prevent the wood from burning or catching fire while grilling. If you plan to bake these shrimp kabobs in the oven, you may not need to soak the skewers as they will not have direct access to a heat source.

SHRIMP KABOBS

Marinating the shrimp in Italian dressing adds wonderful flavor to these colorful kabobs.
—Sharon Aweau, Kapolei, HI

PREP: 35 MIN. + MARINATING • **GRILL:** 10 MIN. • **MAKES:** 4 SERVINGS

- 1 cup Italian salad dressing, divided
- 1½ lbs. uncooked shrimp (16-20 per lb.), peeled and deveined
- 2 large onions, cut into 8 wedges each
- 16 large fresh mushrooms
- 2 large green peppers, cut into 1½-in. pieces
- 16 cherry tomatoes

1. In a shallow dish, combine ½ cup salad dressing and shrimp. In another shallow dish, combine vegetables and remaining ½ cup dressing. Cover and refrigerate for 2 hours, stirring occasionally.

2. Drain shrimp, discarding marinade. On 8 metal or soaked wooden skewers, alternately thread the shrimp and vegetables. Grill kabobs, covered, over medium heat or broil 4 in. from the heat for 6 minutes or until shrimp turn pink, turning occasionally.

2 KABOBS: 260 cal., 6g fat (1g sat. fat), 207mg chol., 416mg sod., 19g carb. (8g sugars, 3g fiber), 31g pro. **DIABETIC EXCHANGES:** 4 lean meat, 1 starch, 1 vegetable.

🍲 SPICY SEAFOOD STEW

The hardest part of this quick and easy recipe is peeling and dicing the potatoes— and you can even do that the night before. Just place the potatoes in water and store them in the refrigerator overnight to speed up assembly the next day.
—Bonnie Marlow, Ottoville, OH

PREP: 30 MIN. • **COOK:** 4¾ HOURS • **MAKES:** 9 SERVINGS (2¼ QT.)

- 2 lbs. potatoes, peeled and diced
- 1 lb. carrots, sliced
- 1 jar (24 oz.) pasta sauce
- 2 jars (6 oz. each) sliced mushrooms, drained
- 1½ tsp. ground turmeric
- 1½ tsp. minced garlic
- 1 tsp. cayenne pepper
- ¼ tsp. salt
- 1½ cups water
- 1 lb. sea scallops
- 1 lb. uncooked shrimp (31-40 per lb.), peeled and deveined

In a 5-qt. slow cooker, combine first 8 ingredients. Cook, covered, on low heat 4½-5 hours or until potatoes are tender. Stir in water, scallops and shrimp. Cook, covered, until scallops are opaque and shrimp turn pink, 15-20 minutes longer.

1 CUP: 229 cal., 2g fat (0 sat. fat), 73mg chol., 803mg sod., 34g carb. (10g sugars, 6g fiber), 19g pro.

NICOISE SALAD

This garden-fresh salad is a feast for the eyes as well as the palate.
Add some crusty bread and you have a mouthwatering meal.
—Marla Fogderud, Mason, MI

PREP: 40 MIN. • **MAKES:** 2 SERVINGS

⅓ cup olive oil
3 Tbsp. white wine vinegar
1½ tsp. Dijon mustard
⅛ tsp. each salt, onion powder
  and pepper
SALAD
2 small red potatoes
½ cup cut fresh green beans
3½ cups torn Bibb lettuce
½ cup cherry tomatoes, halved
10 Greek olives, pitted and halved
2 hard-boiled large eggs, quartered
1 can (5 oz.) albacore white tuna in
  water, drained and flaked

1. In a small bowl, whisk oil, vinegar, mustard, salt, onion powder and pepper; set aside.

2. Place potatoes in a small saucepan and cover with water. Bring to a boil. Reduce heat; cover and simmer until tender, 15-20 minutes. Drain and cool; cut into quarters.

3. Place beans in another saucepan and cover with water. Bring to a boil. Cover and cook until crisp-tender, 3-5 minutes; drain and rinse in cold water.

4. Divide lettuce between 2 salad plates; top with potatoes, beans, tomatoes, olives, eggs and tuna. Drizzle with the dressing.

1 SALAD: 613 cal., 49g fat (8g sat. fat), 242mg chol., 886mg sod., 18g carb. (3g sugars, 3g fiber), 26g pro.

READER REVIEW
"This is my second time making this dish. I used leftover fresh tuna and added a few more veggies to the plate—Kirby cucumbers, pickled beets and marinated mushrooms. I also put some fresh herbs in the vinaigrette."
—ANNR, TASTEOFHOME.COM

PISTACHIO-CRUSTED
FRIED FISH

PISTACHIO-CRUSTED FRIED FISH

This nut-crusted fish is so novel compared to standard breaded fillets. Plus, the pistachios give it a lovely color.
—*Taste of Home* Test Kitchen

TAKES: 30 MIN. • **MAKES:** 6 SERVINGS

½ cup dry bread crumbs
½ cup chopped pistachios
½ tsp. seafood seasoning
¼ tsp. salt
¼ tsp. garlic powder
¼ tsp. pepper
½ cup all-purpose flour
½ cup 2% milk
1½ lbs. whitefish or cod fillets
3 Tbsp. canola oil

1. In a shallow bowl, combine the first 6 ingredients. Place flour and milk in separate shallow bowls. Dip fish fillets in flour, then in milk; coat with pistachio mixture.

2. In a large nonstick skillet, heat oil over medium heat; add fish. Cook until fish just begins to flake easily with a fork, 4-5 minutes on each side.

3 OZ. COOKED FISH: 325 cal., 18g fat (2g sat. fat), 71mg chol., 260mg sod., 14g carb. (2g sugars, 1g fiber), 26g pro. **DIABETIC EXCHANGES:** 3 lean meat, 3 fat, 1 starch.

GRAPEFRUIT GREMOLATA SALMON

If you're looking for a simple fish dish, make this Italian-inspired recipe that combines salmon, broiled grapefruit and a fragrant gremolata. Halibut may be substituted for the salmon.
—Gilda Lester, Millsboro, DE

TAKES: 30 MIN. • **MAKES:** 4 SERVINGS

2 medium grapefruit
¼ cup minced fresh parsley
1 garlic clove, minced
1 Tbsp. plus 1 tsp. brown sugar, divided
4 salmon fillets (6 oz. each)
1 Tbsp. cumin seeds, crushed
½ tsp. salt
½ tsp. coarsely ground pepper

1. Preheat broiler. Finely grate enough zest from grapefruit to measure 2 Tbsp. In a small bowl, mix parsley, garlic and grapefruit zest. Set aside.

2. Cut a thin slice from the top and bottom of each grapefruit; stand grapefruit upright on a cutting board. With a knife, cut off the peel and outer membrane from grapefruit. Cut along the membrane of each segment to remove fruit. Arrange sections in a single layer on half of a foil-lined 15x10x1-in. baking pan. Sprinkle with 1 Tbsp. brown sugar.

3. Place salmon on other half of the pan. Mix cumin seeds, salt, pepper and remaining 1 tsp. brown sugar; sprinkle over salmon.

4. Broil 3-4 in. from heat until fish just begins to flake easily with a fork and grapefruit is lightly browned, 8-10 minutes. Sprinkle salmon with parsley mixture; serve with grapefruit.

1 SERVING: 332 cal., 16g fat (3g sat. fat), 85mg chol., 387mg sod., 16g carb. (13g sugars, 2g fiber), 30g pro. **DIABETIC EXCHANGES:** 4 lean meat, 1 starch.

TILAPIA FLORENTINE

Get a little more heart-healthy fish into your weekly diet with this quick and easy entree.
Topped with fresh spinach and a splash of lime, it's sure to become a favorite!
—Melanie Bachman, Ulysses, PA

TAKES: 30 MIN. • **MAKES:** 4 SERVINGS

1 pkg. (6 oz.) fresh baby spinach
6 tsp. canola oil, divided
4 tilapia fillets (4 oz. each)
2 Tbsp. lemon juice
2 tsp. garlic-herb seasoning blend
1 large egg, lightly beaten
½ cup part-skim ricotta cheese
¼ cup grated Parmesan cheese
   Optional: Lemon wedges and
   additional grated Parmesan cheese

1. Preheat oven to 375°. In a large nonstick skillet, cook spinach in 4 tsp. oil until wilted; drain. Meanwhile, place tilapia in a greased 13x9-in. baking dish. Drizzle with lemon juice and remaining 2 tsp. oil. Sprinkle with the seasoning blend.

2. In a small bowl, combine egg, ricotta cheese and spinach; spoon over fillets. Sprinkle with Parmesan cheese.

3. Bake until fish just begins to flake easily with a fork, 15-20 minutes. If desired, serve with lemon wedges and additional Parmesan cheese.

1 FILLET WITH ⅓ CUP SPINACH MIXTURE: 249 cal., 13g fat (4g sat. fat), 122mg chol., 307mg sod., 4g carb. (1g sugars, 1g fiber), 29g pro.

GARLIC-LEMON SHRIMP LINGUINE

The Cheesecake Factory has an extensive menu, but I always seem to order their delicious fresh and citrusy Lemon Shrimp Linguine. I'd enjoyed it enough times that I was confident I could reproduce it to share with friends and family. I think I hit it spot on! When I have fresh basil from the garden, I use that instead of parsley.
—Trisha Kruse, Eagle, ID

TAKES: 30 MIN. • **MAKES:** 4 SERVINGS

8 oz. uncooked linguine
2 Tbsp. olive oil
1 Tbsp. butter
1 lb. uncooked shrimp (26-30 per lb.),
   peeled and deveined
3 garlic cloves, minced
1 Tbsp. grated lemon zest
1 Tbsp. lemon juice
1 tsp. lemon-pepper seasoning
2 Tbsp. minced fresh parsley

1. Cook linguine according to package directions for al dente. Meanwhile, in a large skillet, heat oil and butter over medium-high heat. Add shrimp; cook and stir 3 minutes. Add garlic, lemon zest and juice, and lemon pepper; cook and stir until shrimp turn pink, 2-3 minutes longer. Stir in parsley.

2. Drain linguine, reserving ⅓ cup pasta water. Add enough reserved pasta water to shrimp mixture to achieve desired consistency. Serve with linguine.

1 SERVING: 387 cal., 12g fat (3g sat. fat), 146mg chol., 239mg sod., 43g carb. (2g sugars, 2g fiber), 26g pro.

TILAPIA FLORENTINE TIPS

Can you use other types of fish instead of tilapia? *Yes, you can use other types of fish—any lean white fish will work, such as cod, sole, swai or snapper.*

Can you use frozen spinach instead of fresh spinach to make Tilapia Florentine? *Frozen spinach can be used in place of fresh! Just make sure you thaw and squeeze most of the liquid from frozen spinach before proceeding with the recipe.*

What's the best way to reheat leftovers of Tilapia Florentine? *Reheating in your microwave is probably your best bet, to prevent the fish from drying out. Placing a damp towel or microwave-safe lid over the dish when reheating can help prevent dryness.*

TILAPIA FLORENTINE

CHICKEN SOUVLAKI PITAS,
PAGE 123

CHICKEN & TURKEY

Indulge in the flavors of classic Mediterranean ingredients such as artichokes, olives, fresh herbs, lemon and feta when you enjoy these light and lively chicken and turkey entrees.

EASY MEDITERRANEAN CHICKEN

Everyone I know loves this special chicken recipe. I changed a few things to make it healthier, but it tastes just as good.
—Kara Zilis, Oak Forest, IL

TAKES: 30 MIN. • **MAKES:** 4 SERVINGS

4   boneless skinless chicken breast
     halves (4 oz. each)
1   Tbsp. olive oil
1   can (14½ oz.) no-salt-added
     stewed tomatoes
1   cup water
1   tsp. dried oregano
¼   tsp. garlic powder
1½   cups instant brown rice
1   pkg. (12 oz.) frozen cut green beans
12   pitted Greek olives, halved
½   cup crumbled feta cheese

1. In a large nonstick skillet, brown chicken in oil on each side. Stir in the tomatoes, water, oregano and garlic powder. Bring to a boil; reduce heat. Cover and simmer 10 minutes.

2. Stir in rice and green beans. Return to a boil. Cover and simmer until a thermometer reads 165° and rice is tender, 8-10 minutes longer. Stir in olives; sprinkle with cheese.

1 SERVING: 417 cal., 12g fat (3g sat. fat), 70mg chol., 386mg sod., 44g carb. (6g sugars, 6g fiber), 31g pro. **DIABETIC EXCHANGES:** 3 lean meat, 2 starch, 2 vegetable, 1 fat.

🍲 ITALIAN CHICKEN & PEPPERS

I put this chicken recipe together one day when I had leftover peppers and wanted something easy. To my delight, the taste reminded me of pizza—something I love but can no longer eat! It pairs well with steamed broccoli.
—Brenda Nolen, Simpsonville, SC

PREP: 20 MIN. • **COOK:** 3 HOURS • **MAKES:** 6 SERVINGS

1   jar (24 oz.) garden-style
     spaghetti sauce
1   medium onion, sliced
¼   cup grated Parmesan cheese
2   garlic cloves, minced
1   tsp. dried oregano
1   tsp. dried basil
½   tsp. salt
¼   tsp. pepper
½   each small green, sweet yellow and
     red peppers, julienned
6   boneless skinless chicken breast
     halves (4 oz. each)
     Hot cooked pasta
     Shaved Parmesan cheese, optional

1. Mix first 8 ingredients; stir in peppers. Place chicken in a 3-qt. slow cooker. Top with sauce mixture.

2. Cook, covered, on low 3-4 hours or until a thermometer inserted in chicken reads 165°. Serve with pasta; if desired, top with shaved cheese.

1 SERVING: 221 cal., 6g fat (1g sat. fat), 66mg chol., 738mg sod., 16g carb. (9g sugars, 3g fiber), 26g pro. **DIABETIC EXCHANGES:** 3 lean meat, 1 starch.

MAKE IT YOUR OWN

Add ingredients or seasonings you love to this recipe instead. Use fresh tomatoes and minced garlic instead of canned, and add any fresh vegetable instead of frozen green beans.

EASY MEDITERRANEAN CHICKEN

TURKEY GYRO PIZZA

With toppings similar to a Greek salad, this veggie pizza reminds us of the Mediterranean. Want some extra protein? Add a little deli turkey.
—Angela Robinson, Findlay, OH

TAKES: 30 MIN. • **MAKES:** 4 SERVINGS

2 cups biscuit/baking mix
6 Tbsp. cold water
¼ tsp. dried oregano
¼ cup Greek vinaigrette
½ cup pitted Greek olives, sliced
½ cup thinly sliced roasted sweet red pepper
1½ cups shredded part-skim mozzarella cheese
½ cup crumbled feta cheese
½ cup chopped cucumber
1 small tomato, chopped
Additional Greek vinaigrette, optional

1. Preheat oven to 425°. In a small bowl, combine biscuit mix, water and oregano to form a soft dough. Press dough to fit a greased 12-in. pizza pan; pinch edge to form a rim. Bake 10-12 minutes or until lightly browned.

2. Brush ¼ cup vinaigrette over crust; top with olives, red pepper and cheeses. Bake 8-10 minutes or until cheese is melted and crust is lightly browned.

3. Sprinkle with cucumber and tomato before serving. If desired, drizzle with additional vinaigrette.

1 PIECE: 524 cal., 28g fat (10g sat. fat), 35mg chol., 1716mg sod., 48g carb. (4g sugars, 3g fiber), 18g pro.

ARUGULA PESTO CHICKEN

We had an abundance of arugula in our garden, so I turned it into pesto. The bold green color reminds my son of something the Hulk would eat.
—Courtney Stultz, Weir, KS

TAKES: 25 MIN. • **MAKES:** 4 SERVINGS

4 cups fresh arugula or spinach
1 cup fresh basil leaves
¼ cup pine nuts
1 garlic clove, minced
1½ tsp. sea salt, divided
¼ cup plus 1 Tbsp. olive oil, divided
4 medium zucchini
1 rotisserie chicken, skin removed, shredded
2 plum tomatoes, chopped
¼ tsp. pepper
Grated Parmesan cheese, optional

1. Pulse arugula, basil, pine nuts, garlic and 1 tsp. salt in a food processor until chopped. While processing, gradually add ¼ cup oil in a steady stream until mixture is smooth. Using a shredder or spiralizer, shred zucchini lengthwise into long strands.

2. In a large skillet, heat remaining oil over medium heat. Add zucchini strands and chicken. Cook and stir until zucchini is crisp-tender, about 4 minutes.

3. Remove from heat. Add tomatoes, pesto, pepper and remaining salt; toss to coat. If desired, sprinkle with Parmesan cheese. Serve using a slotted spoon.

1½ CUPS: 488 cal., 32g fat (5g sat. fat), 110mg chol., 836mg sod., 10g carb. (6g sugars, 3g fiber), 41g pro.

🍲 CORSICAN CHICKEN

Moist and tender chicken thighs make a delicious hot entree for winter months. Just add a salad and a lemon dessert.
I set the table with warm, sunny Mediterranean shades and patterns that look gorgeous with this colorful meal.
—Mary Bergfeld, Eugene, OR

PREP: 20 MIN. • **COOK:** 4½ HOURS • **MAKES:** 8 SERVINGS

- 3 Tbsp. butter, softened
- 2 Tbsp. herbes de Provence
- 1 tsp. salt
- 2 garlic cloves, minced
- ½ tsp. coarsely ground pepper
- 2 lbs. boneless skinless chicken thighs
- 1 large onion, chopped
- ½ cup oil-packed sun-dried tomatoes, julienned
- 1 can (10½ oz.) condensed beef consomme, undiluted
- ½ cup dry vermouth or orange juice
- ½ cup pitted Greek olives, quartered
- 1 tsp. grated orange zest
- 2 tsp. cornstarch
- 1 Tbsp. cold water
  Optional: 2 Tbsp. minced fresh parsley or basil, or drained and diced pimientos

1. In a small bowl, combine butter, herbes de Provence, salt, garlic and pepper; rub over chicken.

2. Place in a 5-qt. slow cooker. Add the onion, tomatoes, consomme and vermouth. Cover and cook on low for 4-5 hours or until chicken is no longer pink. Add olives and orange zest. Cover and cook on high for 30 minutes.

3. Remove chicken and vegetables to a serving platter; keep warm. Skim fat from cooking juices; transfer to a small saucepan. Bring liquid to a boil.

4. Combine cornstarch and water until smooth. Gradually stir into the pan. Bring to a boil; cook and stir 2 minutes or until thickened. Pour over chicken. If desired, sprinkle with parsley, basil or pimientos.

NOTE: Look for herbes de Provence in the spice aisle.

3 OZ. COOKED CHICKEN WITH 3 TBSP. OLIVE MIXTURE: 287 cal., 16g fat (5g sat. fat), 89mg chol., 808mg sod., 8g carb. (4g sugars, 1g fiber), 23g pro.

MEDITERRANEAN BRAISED
CHICKEN THIGHS

MEDITERRANEAN BRAISED CHICKEN THIGHS

This chicken and artichoke dish was inspired by a once-in-a-lifetime trip to Santorini for my parents' 40th anniversary. It's cooked in a big skillet until the chicken basically falls off the bone and all the flavors meld together into a sauce that will have you spooning it into your mouth. It's really a showstopper!
—Grace Vallo, Salem, NH

PREP: 15 MIN. • **COOK:** 30 MIN. • **MAKES:** 6 SERVINGS

2 Tbsp. butter
2 Tbsp. olive oil
6 bone-in chicken thighs (about 2 lbs.)
1 can (14 oz.) water-packed small artichoke hearts, drained
3 shallots, halved
⅓ cup dry white wine
½ cup pitted Greek olives
⅓ cup reduced-sodium chicken broth
1 Tbsp. lemon juice
1 garlic clove, thinly sliced
1 Tbsp. drained capers
1 tsp. ground sumac or za'atar seasoning

1. Preheat oven to 375°. In a 12-in. cast-iron or other ovenproof skillet, heat butter and oil over medium-high heat. Brown chicken, skin side down. Turn thighs over; arrange artichokes and shallots around chicken. Cook 1 minute longer. Add wine to pan; cook 1 minute longer, stirring to loosen browned bits from pan.

2. Add remaining ingredients to pan. Bake 15-20 minutes or until a thermometer inserted in chicken reads 170°-175°.

1 CHICKEN THIGH WITH ⅓ CUP ARTICHOKE MIXTURE: 378 cal., 26g fat (7g sat. fat), 91mg chol., 551mg sod., 10g carb. (1g sugars, 0 fiber), 25g pro.

🍲 CHICKEN ATHENA

With olives, sun-dried tomatoes, lemon juice and garlic, Greek flavors abound in my easy chicken dish that's prepared in the slow cooker. Serve it with orzo or couscous for a tasty accompaniment.
—Radelle Knappenberger, Oviedo, FL

PREP: 15 MIN. • **COOK:** 4 HOURS • **MAKES:** 6 SERVINGS

6 boneless skinless chicken breast halves (6 oz. each)
2 medium onions, chopped
⅓ cup sun-dried tomatoes (not packed in oil), chopped
⅓ cup pitted Greek olives, chopped
2 Tbsp. lemon juice
1 Tbsp. balsamic vinegar
3 garlic cloves, minced
½ tsp. salt

Place chicken in a 3-qt. slow cooker. Add the remaining ingredients. Cover and cook on low for 4 hours or until a thermometer reads 170°.

1 CHICKEN BREAST HALF: 237 cal., 6g fat (1g sat. fat), 94mg chol., 467mg sod., 8g carb. (5g sugars, 1g fiber), 36g pro. **DIABETIC EXCHANGES:** 4 lean meat, 1 vegetable, 1 fat.

MOROCCAN APRICOT CHICKEN

Chili sauce, apricots and Moroccan seasoning create an incredible sauce for slow-cooked chicken thighs. Traditional Moroccan apricot chicken typically includes chili pepper paste, but I use chili sauce in my version.
—Arlene Erlbach, Morton Grove, IL

PREP: 25 MIN. • **COOK:** 4¼ HOURS • **MAKES:** 6 SERVINGS

1 tsp. olive oil
½ cup slivered almonds
6 bone-in chicken thighs (about 2¼ lbs.)
¾ cup chili sauce
½ cup apricot preserves
½ cup dried apricots, quartered
4 tsp. Moroccan seasoning (ras el hanout)
1 Tbsp. vanilla extract
1½ tsp. garlic powder
1 can (15 oz.) garbanzo beans or chickpeas, rinsed and drained
¼ cup orange juice
Chopped fresh parsley, optional

1. In a large skillet, heat oil over medium heat. Add almonds; cook and stir until lightly browned, 2-3 minutes. Remove with a slotted spoon; drain on paper towels. In the same skillet, brown chicken on both sides. Remove from heat. Transfer chicken to a 4- or 5-qt. slow cooker. Stir chili sauce, preserves, apricots, Moroccan seasoning, vanilla and garlic powder into drippings. Pour over chicken.

2. Cook, covered, on low 4-4½ hours or until a thermometer inserted in chicken reads 170°-175°. Stir in garbanzo beans and orange juice. Cook, covered, on low until heated through, 15-30 minutes longer. Serve with almonds. If desired, sprinkle with parsley.

1 CHICKEN THIGH WITH ¾ CUP GARBANZO BEAN MIXTURE: 482 cal., 21g fat (4g sat. fat), 81mg chol., 633mg sod., 47g carb. (27g sugars, 5g fiber), 28g pro.

READER REVIEW
"Winner, winner, chicken dinner! This was so good! And it was easy to make. The toasted almonds add the icing on the cake. I used boneless thighs and it was very juicy. I love the sweetness, and I don't love chickpeas but I didn't mind them here."
—SUSAN6540, TASTEOFHOME.COM

MEDITERRANEAN
TURKEY PANINI

MEDITERRANEAN TURKEY PANINI

The word panini refers to sandwiches that are pressed and toasted. I make panini for my fellow teachers and friends. For potlucks, make several and cut them into fourths.
—Martha Muellenberg, Vermillion, SD

TAKES: 25 MIN. • **MAKES:** 4 SERVINGS

4   ciabatta rolls, split
1   jar (24 oz.) marinara or spaghetti sauce, divided
1   container (4 oz.) crumbled feta cheese
1   jar (7½ oz.) marinated quartered artichoke hearts, drained and chopped
2   plum tomatoes, sliced
1   lb. sliced deli turkey

1. Spread each ciabatta bottom with 2 Tbsp. marinara sauce. Top with half the cheese; add the artichokes, tomatoes, turkey and remaining cheese. Spread each ciabatta top with 2 Tbsp. marinara sauce; place over turkey.

2. Cook on a panini maker or indoor grill until cheese is melted, 4-5 minutes. Place remaining marinara sauce in a small microwave-safe bowl; cover and microwave on high until heated through. Serve with sandwiches.

1 SANDWICH WITH ⅓ CUP SAUCE: 701 cal., 18g fat (5g sat. fat), 55mg chol., 2314mg sod., 98g carb. (18g sugars, 8g fiber), 40g pro.

TURKEY & BULGUR SALAD

Cranberry juice concentrate gives this wonderful luncheon salad a burst of flavor. I like to line a serving platter with lettuce leaves and mound the salad in the center for a pretty presentation.
—Carole Resnick, Cleveland, OH

PREP: 25 MIN. + STANDING • **MAKES:** 6 SERVINGS

1½   cups reduced-sodium chicken broth
½   cup water
1   cup bulgur
2   cups cubed cooked turkey breast
1   small cucumber, finely chopped
1   cup canned garbanzo beans or chickpeas, rinsed and drained
3   green onions, thinly sliced
¼   cup sliced ripe olives
3   Tbsp. dried cranberries
¼   cup olive oil
3   Tbsp. lime juice
2   Tbsp. thawed cranberry juice concentrate
1   cup cherry tomatoes, halved
3   Tbsp. minced fresh parsley

1. In a small saucepan, bring broth and water to a boil. Place bulgur in a large bowl. Stir in broth mixture. Cover and let stand for 30 minutes or until most of the liquid is absorbed. Drain. Stir in turkey, cucumber, beans, onions, olives and cranberries.

2. In a small bowl, whisk oil, lime juice and cranberry juice concentrate. Stir into bulgur mixture. Add tomatoes and parsley; gently toss to coat. Serve at room temperature or chilled.

1½ CUPS: 302 cal., 11g fat (2g sat. fat), 40mg chol., 283mg sod., 32g carb. (6g sugars, 7g fiber), 20g pro. **DIABETIC EXCHANGES:** 2 starch, 2 lean meat, 2 fat.

TURKEY MEATBALL GYROS

My whole family loves these gyros, and I appreciate how quick and easy they are. The meatballs can be made the night before or made in a big batch to freeze and use as needed.
—Jennifer Coduto, Kent, OH

TAKES: 30 MIN. • **MAKES:** 4 SERVINGS

½ cup seasoned bread crumbs
1 large egg
1 tsp. garlic powder
½ tsp. salt
¼ tsp. pepper
1 lb. lean ground turkey
¾ cup reduced-fat plain yogurt
½ cup finely chopped peeled cucumber
2 Tbsp. finely chopped onion
1½ tsp. lemon juice
8 whole wheat pita pocket halves
2 cups shredded lettuce
1 cup chopped tomatoes

1. In a large bowl, combine the bread crumbs, egg and seasonings. Crumble turkey over mixture and mix lightly but thoroughly. Shape into 16 balls.

2. Place meatballs on a rack coated with cooking spray in a shallow baking pan. Bake, uncovered, at 400° until no longer pink, 15-20 minutes.

3. Meanwhile, in a small bowl, combine yogurt, cucumber, onion and lemon juice. Line pitas with lettuce and tomatoes; add meatballs and drizzle with yogurt sauce.

2 FILLED PITA POCKET HALVES: 439 cal., 14g fat (4g sat. fat), 145mg chol., 975mg sod., 48g carb. (6g sugars, 6g fiber), 32g pro.

TARA'S SPANISH CHICKEN

This recipe has simple flavors that take me back to Grandma's house. She knew a million ways to cook a chicken, but this was my favorite.
—Tara Imig, Fort Worth, TX

PREP: 25 MIN. • **BAKE:** 55 MIN. • **MAKES:** 6 SERVINGS

1 broiler/fryer chicken (3 to 4 lbs.), cut up
1 large sweet red pepper, sliced
1 medium lemon, sliced
¼ cup sliced pimiento-stuffed olives
2 Tbsp. capers, drained
¼ cup olive oil
2 Tbsp. dried oregano
1 Tbsp. smoked paprika
1 tsp. salt
½ tsp. pepper

1. Preheat oven to 350°. Place the first 5 ingredients in a large bowl. Combine the remaining ingredients; drizzle over chicken mixture. Toss to coat. Transfer to a 15x10x1-in. baking pan.

2. Bake, uncovered, until chicken juices run clear, 55-60 minutes.

4 OZ. COOKED CHICKEN: 402 cal., 27g fat (6g sat. fat), 104mg chol., 673mg sod., 5g carb. (2g sugars, 2g fiber), 34g pro.

LEMON-ROASTED CHICKEN WITH OLIVE COUSCOUS

If you can find preserved lemons, use them instead of the plain lemons for an even more authentic flavor in this North African-inspired recipe.

—David Feder, Buffalo Grove, IL

PREP: 20 MIN. • **BAKE:** 1½ HOURS + STANDING • **MAKES:** 8 SERVINGS (4 CUPS COUSCOUS)

1 roasting chicken (5 to 6 lbs.)
1 medium lemon, thinly sliced
1 tsp. fennel seeds, crushed
1 Tbsp. olive oil
¾ tsp. coarsely ground pepper
¼ tsp. salt

OLIVE COUSCOUS
1 cup uncooked whole wheat couscous
½ tsp. dried thyme
¼ tsp. salt
½ cup coarsely chopped pitted green olives
1 Tbsp. pine nuts

1. Place chicken on a rack in a shallow roasting pan, breast side up.

2. Tuck wings under chicken; tie drumsticks together.

3. With fingers, carefully loosen skin from chicken breast; place lemon slices and fennel under the skin. Secure skin to underside of breast with toothpicks. Rub skin with oil; sprinkle with pepper and salt.

4. Roast at 350° for 1½-2 hours or until a thermometer inserted in thigh reads 180°, basting occasionally with pan drippings. Remove chicken from the oven; cover loosely with foil and let stand for 15 minutes before carving.

5. Meanwhile, prepare couscous according to package directions, adding thyme and salt to water before heating. Stir in olives and pine nuts during the last minute of cooking. Serve with chicken.

7 OZ. COOKED CHICKEN WITH ½ CUP COUSCOUS:: 456 cal., 24g fat (6g sat. fat), 112mg chol., 435mg sod., 20g carb. (1g sugars, 3g fiber), 39g pro.

CHICKEN SOUVLAKI PITAS

This is a favorite at our house, especially in summer. A quick trip to the market for a few ingredients results in gourmet-style Greek sandwiches that we often enjoy outdoors by the grill. Of course, a simple Greek salad on the side is a nice addition.
—Becky A. Drees, Pittsfield, MA

PREP: 20 MIN. + MARINATING • **GRILL:** 10 MIN. • **MAKES:** 6 SERVINGS

5   medium lemons, divided
4   Tbsp. olive oil
4   garlic cloves, minced
2   tsp. dried oregano
½   tsp. salt
¼   tsp. pepper
2   lbs. boneless skinless chicken
     breasts, cut into 1-in. pieces
6   whole pita breads
1   carton (8 oz.) refrigerated
     tzatziki sauce
     Optional toppings: Chopped
     tomatoes, chopped cucumber,
     sliced red onion and fresh
     dill sprigs

1. Cut 3 lemons crosswise in half; squeeze juice from lemons. Transfer juice to a large bowl or shallow dish. Whisk in oil, garlic, oregano, salt and pepper. Add chicken; turn to coat. Refrigerate 1 hour.

2. Drain chicken, discarding marinade. Thinly slice remaining lemons. On 12 metal or soaked wooden skewers, alternately thread chicken and lemon slices. Grill kabobs, covered, over medium heat (or broil 4 in. from heat) until chicken is no longer pink, about 10 minutes, turning occasionally. Serve with pita bread, tzatziki sauce and toppings as desired.

1 PITA: 369 cal., 8g fat (2g sat. fat), 90mg chol., 462mg sod., 34g carb. (2g sugars, 1g fiber), 37g pro. **DIABETIC EXCHANGES:** 5 lean meat, 2 starch, 1 fat.

GREEK CHICKEN SHEET-PAN DINNER

I love roasted vegetables and keeping things simple. One bowl and one sheet pan, that's it. You could certainly use boneless chicken and add other veggies. Serve it with cucumber salad.
—Sara Martin, Whitefish, MT

PREP: 10 MIN. • **BAKE:** 40 MIN. • **MAKES:** 4 SERVINGS

- 4 bone-in chicken thighs, skin removed
- ½ cup Greek vinaigrette
- 8 small red potatoes, quartered
- 1 medium sweet red pepper, cut into ½-in. strips
- 1 can (14 oz.) water-packed artichoke hearts, drained and halved
- ¾ cup pitted ripe olives, drained
- 1 small red onion, cut into 8 wedges
- ¼ tsp. pepper
- ⅓ cup crumbled feta cheese

1. Preheat oven to 375°. Spray a 15x10x1-in. baking pan with cooking spray; set aside.

2. In a large bowl, combine the first 7 ingredients; toss to coat. Place chicken and vegetables in a single layer on baking pan; sprinkle with pepper. Bake until a thermometer inserted in chicken reads 170°- 175° and vegetables are tender, 30-35 minutes.

3. If desired, preheat broiler. Broil chicken and vegetables 3-4 in. from heat until lightly browned, 2-3 minutes. Remove from oven, cool slightly. Sprinkle with feta cheese.

1 SERVING: 481 cal., 24g fat (5g sat. fat), 92mg chol., 924mg sod., 31g carb. (3g sugars, 4g fiber), 31g pro.

SHEET-PAN DINNER TIPS

Can you use different cuts of chicken to make Greek sheet-pan chicken? *While this recipe uses bone-in chicken thighs, you can easily swap in other cuts. It's important to use cuts of chicken that will cook in a similar time frame, so the veggies don't over- or under-cook. If you're using thicker chicken breasts, consider pounding them flatter. If you have chicken tenders or smaller pieces, keep an eye on them and remove if they're done before the potatoes or veggies.*

Can you use a baking sheet instead of a sheet pan to make this recipe? *Sheet-pan dinners allow you to cook everything on one pan, so cleanup is a snap. Make sure to use a sheet pan with a lip so the juices don't run over and burn on the bottom of your oven. If you have a pan without a lip, get creative with some aluminum foil and make a boat of sorts by folding the edges to create a barrier at least 1 in. high.*

SPANISH-STYLE PAELLA

If you enjoy cooking ethnic foods, this hearty rice dish is wonderful.
It's brimming with generous chunks of sausage, shrimp and veggies.
—*Taste of Home* Test Kitchen

PREP: 10 MIN. • **COOK:** 35 MIN. • **MAKES:** 8 SERVINGS

¾ lb. boneless skinless chicken breasts, cubed
½ lb. Spanish chorizo links, sliced
1 Tbsp. olive oil
1 garlic clove, minced
1 cup uncooked short grain rice
1 cup chopped onion
1½ cups chicken broth
1 can (14½ oz.) stewed tomatoes, undrained
½ tsp. paprika
¼ tsp. ground cayenne pepper
¼ tsp. salt
10 strands saffron, crushed or ⅛ tsp. ground saffron
½ lb. uncooked shrimp (31 to 40 per lb.), peeled and deveined
½ cup sweet red pepper strips
½ cup green pepper strips
½ cup frozen peas
Optional: Minced fresh parsley and lemon wedges

1. In a large saucepan or skillet over medium-high heat, cook chicken and sausage in oil for 5 minutes or until sausage is lightly browned and chicken is no longer pink, stirring frequently. Add garlic; cook 1 minute longer. Drain if necessary.

2. Stir in rice and onion. Cook until onion is tender and rice is lightly browned, stirring frequently. Add broth, tomatoes, paprika, cayenne, salt and saffron. Bring to a boil. Reduce heat to low; cover and cook for 10 minutes.

3. Stir in shrimp, peppers and peas. Cover and cook 10 minutes longer or until rice is tender, shrimp turn pink and liquid is absorbed. Top with fresh parsley and lemon wedges if desired.

1 CUP: 237 cal., 7g fat (2g sat. fat), 62mg chol., 543mg sod., 27g carb. (5g sugars, 2g fiber), 16g pro.

⑤ⁱ BROILED CHICKEN & ARTICHOKES

My wife and I first made this chicken entree as newlyweds, and we have been hooked on it ever since.
We make it almost weekly now. It's so simple and affordable, yet delicious and healthy. You can't beat that!
—Chris Koon, Midlothian, VA

TAKES: 15 MIN. • **MAKES:** 8 SERVINGS

8 boneless skinless chicken thighs
   (about 2 lbs.)
2 jars (7½ oz. each) marinated
   quartered artichoke hearts,
   drained
2 Tbsp. olive oil
1 tsp. salt
½ tsp. pepper
¼ cup shredded Parmesan cheese
2 Tbsp. minced fresh parsley

1. Preheat broiler. In a large bowl, toss chicken and artichokes with oil, salt and pepper. Transfer to a broiler pan.

2. Broil 3 in. from heat 8-10 minutes or until a thermometer inserted in chicken reads 170°, turning chicken and artichokes halfway through cooking. Sprinkle with cheese. Broil 1-2 minutes longer or until cheese is melted. Sprinkle with parsley.

1 SERVING: 288 cal., 21g fat (5g sat. fat), 77mg chol., 584mg sod., 4g carb. (0 sugars, 0 fiber), 22g pro.

MARSALA TURKEY BREAST

Every home cook has a go-to party dish; this one is mine. The only prep is popping everything in to marinate.
—Johnna Johnson, Scottsdale, AZ

PREP: 20 MIN. + MARINATING • **BAKE:** 35 MIN. • **MAKES:** 8 SERVINGS

2 skin-on boneless turkey breast
   halves (about 2 lbs. each)
1 cup pitted dates, quartered
½ cup pitted green olives, halved
½ cup red wine vinegar
½ cup olive oil
1 jar (3½ oz.) capers, drained
1 whole garlic bulb, cloves
   separated, peeled and minced
   (about ¼ cup)
¼ cup dried oregano
6 bay leaves
½ tsp. salt
1 cup packed brown sugar
1 cup Marsala wine

1. Cut each turkey breast half crosswise iin half; place in a bowl or shallow dish. Add dates, olives, vinegar, oil, capers, garlic, oregano, bay leaves and salt. Turn turkey to coat; cover and refrigerate 3-4 hours.

2. Preheat oven to 350°. Place turkey in a single layer in a large shallow roasting pan; top with marinade mixture. Sprinkle brown sugar over turkey. Pour wine around turkey. Bake, uncovered, until a thermometer inserted in turkey reads 165°, basting turkey occasionally with pan juices, 35-45 minutes.

3. Remove from oven; let turkey stand for 5 minutes before slicing. Discard bay leaves. Serve turkey with date-olive mixture and pan juices.

NOTE: If skin-on boneless turkey breast halves are not available, ask your butcher to debone a 5-pound bone-in turkey breast, leaving the skin attached.

8 OZ. COOKED TURKEY WITH 2 TBSP. OLIVE MIXTURE AND ¼ CUP PAN JUICES: 661 cal., 29g fat (6g sat. fat), 132mg chol., 793mg sod., 47g carb. (39g sugars, 3g fiber), 52g pro.

BROILED CHICKEN
& ARTICHOKES

CILANTRO & LEMON MARINATED CHICKEN KABOBS

Cook the onions first so there's plenty of room on the grill for the chicken skewers. Before serving, give the whole platter a spritz of lemon for a sunshiny delight.
—Moumita Ghosh, Kolkata, West Bengal

PREP: 40 MIN. + MARINATING • **GRILL:** 20 MIN. • **MAKES:** 6 SERVINGS

1½ lbs. boneless skinless chicken breasts, cut into 1-in. pieces
3 Tbsp. lemon juice
1½ tsp. salt
½ cup water
¼ cup plain yogurt
1 cup fresh cilantro leaves
⅓ cup fresh mint leaves
2 serrano peppers, sliced
1 piece fresh gingerroot (1 in.), coarsely chopped
4 garlic cloves, sliced
3 medium sweet onions, cut crosswise into ½-in. slices
4 Tbsp. canola oil, divided
Lemon wedges

1. In a large bowl, toss chicken with lemon juice and salt; let stand for 15 minutes. Meanwhile, place water, yogurt, herbs, peppers, ginger and garlic in a blender; cover and process until smooth. Stir into chicken mixture; refrigerate, covered, 2 hours.

2. Brush onions with 2 Tbsp. oil. On a lightly oiled rack, grill, covered, over medium heat or broil 4 in. from heat 10-12 minutes or until tender, turning occasionally.

3. Remove chicken from marinade; discard marinade. Thread chicken onto 6 metal or soaked wooden skewers. Grill, covered, over medium heat or broil 4 in. from heat 10-12 minutes or until chicken is no longer pink, turning occasionally and brushing with remaining oil during the last 4 minutes. Serve with grilled onions and lemon wedges.

NOTE: Wear disposable gloves when cutting hot peppers; the oils can burn skin. Avoid touching your face.

1 KABOB WITH ½ GRILLED ONION: 224 cal., 12g fat (2g sat. fat), 63mg chol., 651mg sod., 4g carb. (3g sugars, 1g fiber), 24g pro. **DIABETIC EXCHANGES:** 3 lean meat, 2 fat, 1 vegetable.

ITALIAN SAUSAGE-STUFFED ZUCCHINI

I've always had to be creative when getting my family to eat vegetables, so I decided to make stuffed zucchini using the pizza flavors that everyone loves. It worked! We like to include sausage for a main dish but it could be a meatless side too.
—Donna Marie Ryan, Topsfield, MA

PREP: 35 MIN. • **BAKE:** 15 MIN. • **MAKES:** 6 SERVINGS

6 medium zucchini (about 8 oz. each)
1 lb. Italian turkey sausage links, casings removed
2 medium tomatoes, seeded and chopped
1 cup panko bread crumbs
⅓ cup grated Parmesan cheese
⅓ cup minced fresh parsley
2 Tbsp. minced fresh oregano or 2 tsp. dried oregano
2 Tbsp. minced fresh basil or 2 tsp. dried basil
¼ tsp. pepper
¾ cup shredded part-skim mozzarella cheese
Additional minced fresh parsley, optional

1. Preheat oven to 350°. Cut each zucchini lengthwise in half. Scoop out flesh, leaving a ¼-in. shell; chop flesh. Place zucchini shells in a large microwave-safe dish. In batches, microwave, covered, on high until crisp-tender, 2-3 minutes.

2. In a large skillet, cook sausage and zucchini flesh over medium heat 6-8 minutes or until sausage is no longer pink, breaking sausage into crumbles; drain. Stir in tomatoes, bread crumbs, Parmesan cheese, herbs and pepper. Spoon into zucchini shells.

3. Place in 2 ungreased 13x9-in. baking dishes. Bake, covered, 15-20 minutes or until zucchini is tender. Sprinkle with mozzarella cheese. Bake, uncovered, 5-8 minutes longer or until the cheese is melted. If desired, sprinkle with additional minced parsley.

2 STUFFED ZUCCHINI HALVES: 206 cal., 9g fat (3g sat. fat), 39mg chol., 485mg sod., 16g carb. (5g sugars, 3g fiber), 17g pro. **DIABETIC EXCHANGES:** 2 vegetable, 2 lean meat, ½ starch.

READER REVIEW

"I made this recipe last night, and it was delicious! I used a small melon scooper to remove the flesh, which worked out great. And there's so much moisture in the flesh that it made sense to cook it with the sausage and then drain. This recipe is a keeper!"
—DEBBIEHIGGINS, TASTEOFHOME.COM

🍲 GARDEN CHICKEN CACCIATORE

Treat company to this perfect Italian meal. You will have time to visit with your guests while it simmers, and it often earns rave reviews. I serve it with couscous, green beans and a dry red wine. Mangia!
—Martha Schirmacher, Sterling Heights, MI

PREP: 15 MIN. • **COOK:** 8½ HOURS • **MAKES:** 12 SERVINGS

12 boneless skinless chicken thighs
    (about 3 lbs.)
 2 medium green peppers, chopped
 1 can (14½ oz.) diced tomatoes
    with basil, oregano and
    garlic, undrained
 1 can (6 oz.) tomato paste
 1 medium onion, chopped
 ½ cup reduced-sodium chicken broth
 ¼ cup dry red wine or additional
    reduced-sodium chicken broth
 3 garlic cloves, minced
 ¾ tsp. salt
 ⅛ tsp. pepper
 2 Tbsp. cornstarch
 2 Tbsp. cold water
    Minced fresh parsley, optional

1. Place chicken in a 4- or 5-qt. slow cooker. In a medium bowl, combine green peppers, tomatoes, tomato paste, onion, broth, wine, garlic, salt and pepper; pour over chicken. Cook, covered, on low until chicken is tender, 8-10 hours.

2. In a small bowl, mix cornstarch and water until smooth; gradually stir into slow cooker. Cook, covered, on high 30 minutes or until sauce is thickened. If desired, sprinkle with parsley before serving.

3 OZ. COOKED CHICKEN WITH ABOUT ½ CUP SAUCE: 207 cal., 9g fat (2g sat. fat), 76mg chol., 410mg sod., 8g carb. (4g sugars, 1g fiber), 23g pro. **DIABETIC EXCHANGES:** 3 lean meat, 1 vegetable, ½ fat.

GREEK CHICKEN
MEAT LOAF

GREEK CHICKEN MEAT LOAF

I love this recipe. It's so easy to put together and lighter than most other meat loaves.
—Maria Romaine, West Babylon, NY

PREP: 20 MIN. • **BAKE:** 1 HOUR + STANDING • **MAKES:** 8 SERVINGS

1 pkg. (10 oz.) frozen chopped spinach, thawed and squeezed dry
1 cup seasoned bread crumbs
1 large egg, room temperature, lightly beaten
1 Tbsp. lemon juice
2 garlic cloves, minced
1½ tsp. Italian seasoning
1 tsp. garlic powder
¾ tsp. salt
½ tsp. pepper
1 cup crumbled feta cheese, divided
2 lbs. ground chicken
1 green onion, finely chopped

1. Preheat oven to 350°. In a large bowl, combine the first 9 ingredients. Reserve 1 Tbsp. feta for topping. Add remaining feta to spinach mixture. Add chicken; mix lightly but thoroughly. Transfer to a greased 9x5-in. loaf pan.

2. Bake 60-70 minutes or until a thermometer reads 165°. Let stand for 10 minutes before slicing. Serve with green onion and remaining 1 Tbsp. feta.

FREEZE OPTION: Shape meat loaf in greased loaf pan; cover and freeze until firm. Remove from pan and wrap securely in foil; return to freezer. To use, unwrap meat loaf and bake in pan as directed, increasing time as necessary for a thermometer inserted in center to read 165°.

1 PIECE: 263 cal., 13g fat (4g sat. fat), 106mg chol., 662mg sod., 12g carb. (1g sugars, 3g fiber), 25g pro. **DIABETIC EXCHANGES:** 3 medium-fat meat.

5i BRUSCHETTA-TOPPED CHICKEN & SPAGHETTI

I'm always on the lookout for healthy recipes for my family. If you find yourself craving Italian food, this delicious 30-minute meal hits the spot.
—Susan Wholley, Fairfield, CT

TAKES: 30 MIN. • **MAKES:** 4 SERVINGS

8 oz. uncooked whole wheat spaghetti
4 boneless skinless chicken breast halves (5 oz. each)
½ tsp. pepper
1 Tbsp. olive oil
1 cup prepared bruschetta topping
⅓ cup shredded Italian cheese blend
2 Tbsp. grated Parmesan cheese

1. Preheat broiler. Cook spaghetti according to package directions; drain. Pound chicken breasts with a meat mallet to ½-in. thickness. Sprinkle with pepper. In a large nonstick skillet, heat oil over medium heat; cook chicken until no longer pink, 5-6 minutes on each side.

2. Transfer to an 8-in. square baking pan. Spoon bruschetta topping over chicken; sprinkle with cheeses. Broil 3-4 in. from heat until cheese is golden brown, 5-6 minutes. Serve with spaghetti.

1 CHICKEN BREAST HALF WITH 1 CUP COOKED SPAGHETTI : 431 cal., 10g fat (4g sat. fat), 87mg chol., 641mg sod., 47g carb. (4g sugars, 8g fiber), 40g pro. **DIABETIC EXCHANGES:** 4 lean meat, 3 starch, ½ fat.

SKILLET-ROASTED LEMON CHICKEN WITH POTATOES

This is a meal I have my students make in our nutrition unit. It has a delicious lemon-herb flavor and is simple to make.
—Mindy Rottmund, Lancaster, PA

PREP: 20 MIN. • **BAKE:** 25 MIN. • **MAKES:** 4 SERVINGS

1   Tbsp. olive oil, divided
1   medium lemon, thinly sliced
4   garlic cloves, minced and divided
¼ tsp. grated lemon zest
½ tsp. salt, divided
¼ tsp. pepper, divided
8   boneless skinless chicken thighs
      (4 oz. each)
¼ tsp. dried rosemary, crushed
1   lb. fingerling potatoes,
      halved lengthwise
8   cherry tomatoes
      Minced fresh parsley, optional

1. Preheat oven to 450°. Grease a 10-in. cast-iron or other ovenproof skillet with 1 tsp. oil. Arrange lemon slices in a single layer in skillet.

2. Combine 1 tsp. oil, 2 minced garlic cloves, lemon zest, ¼ tsp. salt and ⅛ tsp. pepper; rub over chicken. Place over lemon.

3. In a large bowl, combine rosemary and the remaining oil, garlic, salt and pepper. Add potatoes and tomatoes; toss to coat. Arrange over chicken. Bake, uncovered, 25-30 minutes or until chicken is no longer pink and potatoes are tender. If desired, sprinkle with minced parsley before serving.

2 CHICKEN THIGHS WITH 4 OZ. POTATOES AND 2 TOMATOES: 446 cal., 20g fat (5g sat. fat), 151mg chol., 429mg sod., 18g carb. (2g sugars, 3g fiber), 45g pro.

ALMOND-APRICOT CHICKEN SALAD

Here's a one-of-a-kind pasta salad that combines tender chicken, sweet apricots and crunchy vegetables. Plus, the lemony dressing can't be beat.

—Susan Voigt, Plymouth, MN

PREP: 20 MIN. + CHILLING • **MAKES:** 10 SERVINGS

1 pkg. (8 oz.) spiral pasta
1 pkg. (6 oz.) dried apricots, thinly sliced
3 cups coarsely chopped fresh broccoli
2½ cups diced cooked chicken
½ cup chopped green onions
½ cup chopped celery
1 cup sour cream
¾ cup mayonnaise
1 Tbsp. lemon juice
2 tsp. grated lemon zest
2 tsp. Dijon mustard
1½ tsp. salt
¾ tsp. dried savory
½ tsp. pepper
¾ cup sliced almonds, toasted

1. Cook pasta according to package directions, adding apricots during the last 4 minutes. Drain and rinse with cold water; place in a large bowl. Add broccoli, chicken, onions and celery.

2. In a small bowl, combine the next 8 ingredients. Pour over salad and toss to coat. Cover and chill until serving; fold in almonds.

1 SERVING: 411 cal., 24g fat (6g sat. fat), 52mg chol., 524mg sod., 31g carb. (10g sugars, 4g fiber), 17g pro.

51 GRILLED BASIL CHICKEN & TOMATOES

Relax after work with a cold drink while this savory chicken marinates in an herby tomato blend for an hour, then toss it on the grill. It tastes just like summer.
—Laura Lunardi, West Chester, PA

PREP: 15 MIN. + MARINATING • **GRILL:** 10 MIN. • **MAKES:** 4 SERVINGS

- ¾ cup balsamic vinegar
- ¼ cup tightly packed fresh basil leaves
- 2 Tbsp. olive oil
- 1 garlic clove, minced
- ½ tsp. salt
- 8 plum tomatoes
- 4 boneless skinless chicken breast halves (4 oz. each)

1. For marinade, place the first 5 ingredients in a blender. Cut 4 tomatoes into quarters and add to blender; cover and process until blended. Halve remaining tomatoes for grilling.

2. In a bowl, combine chicken and ⅔ cup marinade; refrigerate, covered, 1 hour, turning occasionally. Reserve remaining marinade for serving.

3. Drain chicken, discarding marinade. Place chicken on an oiled grill rack over medium heat. Grill chicken, covered, until a thermometer reads 165°, 4-6 minutes per side. Grill tomatoes, covered, over medium heat until lightly browned, 2-4 minutes per side. Serve chicken and tomatoes with reserved marinade.

1 SERVING: 177 cal., 5g fat (1g sat. fat), 63mg chol., 171mg sod., 8g carb. (7g sugars, 1g fiber), 24g pro. **DIABETIC EXCHANGES:** 3 lean meat, 1 vegetable, ½ fat.

READER REVIEW
"This is the best marinade for chicken! I think it is the balsamic vinegar that makes it different than the rest. Every time I make it, people ask me for the recipe. I usually grill more than I need and have the leftovers on a salad the next day. Delicious!"
—JOYCERM53, TASTEOFHOME.COM

FALAFEL,
PAGE 175

VEGETARIAN MAINS

Whether you follow a strict vegetarian lifestyle or just enjoy a meatless dinner now and again, you'll love these tantalizing veggie-filled entrees.

FOUR-CHEESE STUFFED SHELLS

More cheese, please! You'll get your fill from saucy jumbo pasta shells loaded with four kinds—mozzarella, Asiago, ricotta and cottage cheese. Do the prep work, and then freeze according to the recipe directions to have a ready-to-bake meal for a future busy night.
—Taste of Home Test Kitchen

PREP: 20 MIN. • **BAKE:** 25 MIN. • **MAKES:** 2 SERVINGS

6 uncooked jumbo pasta shells
½ cup shredded part-skim mozzarella cheese, divided
¼ cup shredded Asiago cheese
¼ cup ricotta cheese
¼ cup 4% cottage cheese
1 Tbsp. minced chives
1 pkg. (10 oz.) frozen chopped spinach, thawed and squeezed dry
1 cup meatless spaghetti sauce

1. Preheat oven to 350°. Cook pasta according to package directions. Meanwhile, in a small bowl, combine ¼ cup mozzarella cheese, Asiago cheese, ricotta cheese, cottage cheese, chives and ½ cup spinach (save the remaining spinach for another use).

2. Spread ½ cup spaghetti sauce into a shallow 1½-qt. baking dish coated with cooking spray. Drain pasta; stuff with cheese mixture. Arrange in prepared dish. Top with remaining spaghetti sauce and mozzarella.

3. Cover and bake until heated through, 25-30 minutes.

FREEZE OPTION: Cover and freeze unbaked casserole. To use, partially thaw in refrigerator overnight. Remove from refrigerator 30 minutes before baking. Preheat oven to 350°. Bake as directed, increasing time as necessary to heat through and for a thermometer inserted in the center of 2 or 3 shells to read 165°.

3 STUFFED SHELLS: 376 cal., 14g fat (9g sat. fat), 49mg chol., 959mg sod., 39g carb. (13g sugars, 4g fiber), 25g pro.

WILD MUSHROOM PIZZA

What's great about this wild mushroom pizza is you don't need to worry about finding the right toppings. Whatever wild mushrooms are in season or at your market will work beautifully. I like to get as many different ones as possible.

—James Schend, Pleasant Prairie, WI

PREP: 30 MIN. + RISING • **BAKE:** 15 MIN. • **MAKES:** 6 SERVINGS

1 pkg. (¼ oz.) active dry yeast
¾ cup warm water (110° to 115°)
1 tsp. olive oil
½ tsp. sugar
½ cup whole wheat flour
½ tsp. salt
1½ cups all-purpose flour

TOPPINGS
2 tsp. olive oil, divided
1 lb. sliced fresh wild mushrooms
¼ cup chopped shallot
4 garlic cloves, minced
2 oz. cream cheese, softened
1½ tsp. salt
½ cup shredded Gruyere cheese
¼ cup shredded Parmesan cheese
6 fresh thyme sprigs, stems removed
Fresh basil, optional

1. In a bowl, dissolve yeast in warm water. Add oil and sugar; mix well. Combine whole wheat flour and salt; stir into yeast mixture until smooth. Stir in enough all-purpose flour to form a soft dough.

2. Turn onto a floured surface; knead until smooth and elastic, 6-8 minutes. Place in a bowl coated with cooking spray, turning once to coat top. Cover and let rise in a warm place until doubled, about 1½ hours. Preheat oven to 425°.

3. Punch down dough; press onto a 12-in. pizza pan coated with cooking spray. Prick dough several times with a fork. Bake until edges are light golden brown, 10-12 minutes.

4. Meanwhile, in a large skillet, heat 1 tsp. oil over medium-high heat; saute mushrooms in a single layer, in batches, until golden brown, about 8 minutes. Add onion and garlic; cook until onion is tender.

5. In a food processor, process half of sauteed mushrooms with cream cheese, remaining olive oil and salt. Spread on crust. Top with remaining mushroom mixture, cheeses and thyme. Bake until crust is golden brown and cheese is melted, 12-14 minutes. If desired, garnish with additional fresh thyme and basil.

1 PIECE: 284 cal., 10g fat (5g sat. fat), 22mg chol., 357mg sod., 37g carb. (3g sugars, 3g fiber), 12g pro. **DIABETIC EXCHANGES:** 2½ starch, 2 medium-fat meat, ½ fat.

CUMIN-SPICED LENTIL BURGERS

I adapted my Turkish daughter-in-law's traditional recipe for lentil logs—typically wrapped in a lettuce leaf and served with a lemon wedge—into vegan burgers. If you prefer a spicier version, add hot chili powder or crushed red chile peppers.
—Sheila Joan Suhan, Scottdale, PA

PREP: 30 MIN. + STANDING • **COOK:** 10 MIN./BATCH • **MAKES:** 8 SERVINGS

2¼ cups water, divided
1   cup dried red lentils, rinsed
1   cup bulgur (fine grind)
1½ tsp. salt, divided
6   Tbsp. canola oil, divided
1   large onion, chopped
1   Tbsp. ground cumin
1   Tbsp. chili powder
1   large egg, lightly beaten
6   green onions, sliced
3   Tbsp. chopped fresh parsley
8   flatbread wraps
8   Tbsp. Sriracha mayonnaise
    Optional toppings: Lettuce leaves, sliced tomato and sliced onions

KITCHEN TIP

If the burger mixture is too dry and does not stick together, add 1-2 Tbsp. water to it to soften.

1. Place 2 cups water and lentils in a large saucepan. Bring to a boil. Reduce heat; simmer, uncovered, until lentils are tender, 15-20 minutes, stirring occasionally. Remove from heat; stir in bulgur and 1 tsp. salt. Cover and let stand until bulgur is tender and liquid is absorbed, 15-20 minutes.

2. Meanwhile, in a large nonstick skillet, heat 2 Tbsp. oil over medium-high heat. Add onion; cook and stir until tender, 5-7 minutes. Add cumin and chili powder; cook 1 minute longer. Remove from heat. Add onion mixture to lentil mixture. Stir in egg, green onions, parsley and remaining ½ tsp. salt, mixing lightly but thoroughly. If needed, add remaining ¼ cup water, 1 Tbsp. at a time, to help mixture stay together when squeezed; shape into eight ½-in.-thick patties.

3. In the same skillet, heat remaining 4 Tbsp. oil over medium-high heat. Add burgers in batches; cook until golden brown, 3-5 minutes on each side. Serve in wraps with Sriracha mayonnaise and, if desired, toppings of your choice.

1 BURGER: 434 cal., 23g fat (2g sat. fat), 1mg chol., 780mg sod., 54g carb. (2g sugars, 16g fiber), 16g pro.

EASY VEGETABLE LASAGNA

Bursting with garden favorites, this lasagna is a vegetable lover's dream. The pasta layers are generously stuffed with roasted zucchini, mushrooms, peppers and onion in homemade tomato sauce.
—Susanne Ebersol, Bird-in-Hand, PA

PREP: 45 MIN. • **BAKE:** 20 MIN. + STANDING • **MAKES:** 12 SERVINGS

1 large onion, chopped
1 Tbsp. olive oil
6 garlic cloves, minced
1 can (28 oz.) tomato puree
1 can (8 oz.) tomato sauce
3 Tbsp. minced fresh basil
3 Tbsp. minced fresh oregano
1 tsp. sugar
½ tsp. crushed red pepper flakes

ROASTED VEGETABLES

4 cups sliced zucchini
3 cups sliced fresh mushrooms
2 medium green peppers, cut into 1-in. pieces
1 medium onion, cut into 1-in. pieces
½ tsp. salt
¼ tsp. pepper
6 lasagna noodles, cooked, rinsed and drained
4 cups shredded part-skim mozzarella cheese
1 cup shredded Parmesan cheese
   Additional minced fresh oregano, optional

1. Preheat oven to 450°. In a saucepan, saute onion in oil over medium heat until tender; add garlic and cook 1 minute longer. Stir in the next 6 ingredients. Bring to a boil. Reduce heat; simmer, uncovered, for 20-25 minutes or until slightly thickened.

2. Meanwhile, in a large bowl, combine the vegetables, salt and pepper. Transfer to two 15x10x1-in. baking pans coated with cooking spray. Bake 15-18 minutes or until golden brown. Reduce oven temperature to 400°.

3. Spread ½ cup sauce into a 13x9-in. baking dish coated with cooking spray. Layer with 3 noodles, 1¾ cups sauce, and half the roasted vegetables and cheeses. Repeat the layers.

4. Cover and bake 10 minutes. Uncover and bake 10-15 minutes longer or until bubbly and golden brown. Let stand for 10 minutes before serving. If desired, garnish with additional fresh oregano.

1 PIECE: 258 cal., 11g fat (6g sat. fat), 29mg chol., 571mg sod., 23g carb. (6g sugars, 3g fiber), 16g pro. **DIABETIC EXCHANGES:** 2 vegetable, 2 medium-fat meat, ½ starch.

HEARTY TOMATO-OLIVE PENNE

Who needs meat when you have a pasta dish loaded with tomatoes, olives and Havarti cheese?
I often assemble it in advance and bake it the next day, adding a few minutes to the cooking time.
—Jacqueline Frank, Green Bay, WI

PREP: 50 MIN. • **BAKE:** 25 MIN. • **MAKES:** 8 SERVINGS

2 large onions, chopped
6 Tbsp. olive oil
3 garlic cloves, minced
3 lbs. plum tomatoes, seeded and chopped (about 10 tomatoes)
1 cup vegetable or chicken broth
1 Tbsp. dried basil
1 tsp. crushed red pepper flakes
½ tsp. salt
¼ tsp. pepper
1 pkg. (16 oz.) uncooked penne pasta
1 block (24 oz.) Havarti cheese, cut into ½-in. cubes
1 cup pitted Greek olives
⅓ cup grated Parmesan cheese

1. In a Dutch oven over medium-high heat, saute onions in oil until tender. Add garlic; cook 1 minute longer. Stir in tomatoes, broth, basil, pepper flakes, salt and pepper. Bring to a boil. Reduce heat; cover and simmer 25-30 minutes or until sauce is slightly thickened.

2. Meanwhile, cook penne according to package directions; drain.

3. Preheat oven to 375°. Stir Havarti cheese, olives and cooked penne into the sauce. Transfer to a greased 13x9-in. baking dish; sprinkle with Parmesan.

4. Cover and bake 20 minutes. Uncover; bake 5 minutes longer or until cheese is melted.

1½ CUPS: 719 cal., 43g fat (19g sat. fat), 83mg chol., 1082mg sod., 56g carb. (10g sugars, 5g fiber), 31g pro.

ZUCCHINI ROLL-UPS

We love lasagna, but these zucchini roll-ups are a little healthier and a lot quicker! Using zucchini pasta also makes the dish gluten free and grain free. To make zucchini strips, use a box grater or mandoline to get even slices.
—Courtney Stultz, Weir, KS

PREP: 15 MIN. • **BAKE:** 20 MIN. • **MAKES:** 3 SERVINGS

1 cup part-skim ricotta cheese
1½ tsp. Italian seasoning, divided
¼ tsp. salt
¼ tsp. pepper
2 medium zucchini
4 plum tomatoes, seeded and chopped
1 can (8 oz.) tomato sauce
1 Tbsp. tomato paste
   Shredded Parmesan cheese, optional

1. Preheat oven to 425°. In a small bowl, combine ricotta, ½ tsp. Italian seasoning, salt and pepper. Slice zucchini lengthwise into twelve ⅛-in.-thick slices. Top each slice with 1 rounded Tbsp. cheese mixture. Roll up and secure with toothpicks; place seam side down in an ungreased 8-in. baking dish.

2. Combine tomatoes, tomato sauce, tomato paste and remaining 1 tsp. Italian seasoning; pour over rolls. Cover and bake until bubbly, 20-25 minutes. Remove toothpicks before serving. If desired, sprinkle with Parmesan cheese.

4 ROLL-UPS: 175 cal., 8g fat (4g sat. fat), 26mg chol., 643mg sod., 16g carb. (7g sugars, 4g fiber), 13g pro. **DIABETIC EXCHANGES:** 2 vegetable, 1 medium-fat meat.

HEARTY
TOMATO-OLIVE
PENNE

🍲 VEGETARIAN STUFFED PEPPERS

These filling and flavorful peppers are an updated version of my mom's stuffed peppers, which were a favorite when I was growing up in upstate New York. Whenever I make them, I'm reminded of home.
—Melissa McCabe, Victor, NY

PREP: 30 MIN. • **COOK:** 3½ HOURS • **MAKES:** 6 SERVINGS

- 2 cups cooked brown rice
- 3 small tomatoes, chopped
- 1 cup frozen corn, thawed
- 1 small sweet onion, chopped
- ¾ cup cubed Monterey Jack cheese
- ⅓ cup chopped ripe olives
- ⅓ cup canned black beans, rinsed and drained
- ⅓ cup canned red beans, rinsed and drained
- 4 fresh basil leaves, thinly sliced
- 3 garlic cloves, minced
- 1 tsp. salt
- ½ tsp. pepper
- 6 large sweet peppers
- ¾ cup meatless spaghetti sauce
- ½ cup water
- 4 Tbsp. grated Parmesan cheese, divided

1. Place the first 12 ingredients in a large bowl; mix lightly to combine. Cut and discard tops from sweet peppers; remove seeds. Fill peppers with rice mixture.

2. In a small bowl, mix spaghetti sauce and water; pour half the mixture into an oval 5-qt. slow cooker. Add filled peppers. Top with remaining sauce. Sprinkle with 2 Tbsp. Parmesan cheese.

3. Cook, covered, on low 3½-4 hours or until heated through and peppers are tender. Sprinkle with remaining 2 Tbsp. Parmesan cheese.

1 STUFFED PEPPER: 261 cal., 8g fat (4g sat. fat), 18mg chol., 815mg sod., 39g carb. (9g sugars, 7g fiber), 11g pro. **DIABETIC EXCHANGES:** 2 starch, 1 vegetable, 1 lean meat, 1 fat.

BAKED VEGETARIAN STUFFED PEPPERS: Preheat oven to 350°. Fill peppers as directed. Spoon half of the sauce mixture into an ungreased 3-qt. baking dish. Add peppers; top with remaining sauce mixture. Sprinkle with cheese as directed. Bake, covered, 30-35 minutes or until heated through and peppers are tender.

READER REVIEW
"I baked the peppers instead. I used plain tomato sauce the second time I made it and froze the leftover stuffing (we are only two) and used it as a side dish another time."
—DSTLAURENT, TASTEOFHOME.COM

GNOCCHI WITH WHITE BEANS

Here's one of those no-fuss recipes you can toss together and cook in one skillet. Ideal for a busy weeknight, it's also good with crumbled Italian chicken sausage if you need to please meat lovers.
—Juli Meyers, Hinesville, GA

TAKES: 30 MIN. • **MAKES:** 6 SERVINGS

1 Tbsp. olive oil
1 medium onion, chopped
2 garlic cloves, minced
1 pkg. (16 oz.) potato gnocchi
1 can (15 oz.) cannellini beans, rinsed and drained
1 can (14½ oz.) Italian diced tomatoes, undrained
1 pkg. (6 oz.) fresh baby spinach
¼ tsp. pepper
½ cup shredded part-skim mozzarella cheese
3 Tbsp. grated Parmesan cheese

1. In a large skillet, heat oil over medium-high heat. Add onion; cook and stir until tender. Add garlic; cook 1 minute longer. Add gnocchi; cook and stir until golden brown, 5-6 minutes. Stir in beans, tomatoes, spinach and pepper; heat through.

2. Sprinkle with cheeses; cover and remove from heat. Let stand until cheese is melted, 3-4 minutes.

NOTE: Look for potato gnocchi in the pasta or frozen foods section.

1 CUP: 307 cal., 6g fat (2g sat. fat), 13mg chol., 789mg sod., 50g carb. (10g sugars, 6g fiber), 13g pro.

GREEK BROWN & WILD RICE BOWLS

This fresh rice dish tastes like the Mediterranean in a bowl! It is short on ingredients but packs in so much flavor. For a hand-held version, leave out the rice and tuck the rest of the ingredients in a pita pocket.
—Darla Andrews, Boerne, TX

TAKES: 15 MIN. • **MAKES:** 2 SERVINGS

1 pkg. (8½ oz.) ready-to-serve whole grain brown and wild rice medley
¼ cup Greek vinaigrette, divided
½ medium ripe avocado, peeled and sliced
¾ cup cherry tomatoes, halved
¼ cup crumbled feta cheese
¼ cup pitted Greek olives, sliced
Minced fresh parsley, optional

In a microwave-safe bowl, combine the rice mix and 2 Tbsp. vinaigrette. Cover and cook on high until heated through, about 2 minutes. Divide between 2 bowls. Top with avocado, tomatoes, cheese, olives, remaining dressing and, if desired, parsley.

1 SERVING: 433 cal., 25g fat (4g sat. fat), 8mg chol., 1355mg sod., 44g carb. (3g sugars, 6g fiber), 8g pro.

FESTIVE FALL FALAFEL

Falafel is the ultimate Israeli street food. Pumpkin adds a light sweetness and keeps the patties moist while baking. Top these beauties with maple tahini sauce. You can serve them sandwich-style, as an appetizer over a bed of greens, or with soup and salad.
—Julie Peterson, Crofton, MD

PREP: 20 MIN. • **BAKE:** 30 MIN. • **MAKES:** 4 SERVINGS

1 cup canned garbanzo beans or chickpeas, rinsed and drained
½ cup canned pumpkin
½ cup fresh cilantro leaves
¼ cup chopped onion
1 garlic clove, halved
¾ tsp. salt
½ tsp. ground ginger
½ tsp. ground cumin
¼ tsp. ground coriander
¼ tsp. cayenne pepper

MAPLE TAHINI SAUCE
½ cup tahini
¼ cup water
2 Tbsp. maple syrup
1 Tbsp. cider vinegar
½ tsp. salt
8 pita pocket halves
Optional: Sliced cucumber, onions and tomatoes

1. Preheat oven to 400°. Place the first 10 ingredients in a food processor; pulse until combined. Drop by tablespoonfuls onto a greased baking sheet. Bake until firm and golden brown, 30-35 minutes.

2. Meanwhile, in a small bowl, combine tahini, water, syrup, vinegar and salt. Serve falafel in pita pocket with maple tahini sauce and optional toppings as desired.

2 FILLED PITA HALVES: 469 cal., 21g fat (3g sat. fat), 0 chol., 1132mg sod., 57g carb. (10g sugars, 8g fiber), 14g pro.

MEDITERRANEAN COBB SALAD

I'm a huge fan of taking classic dishes and adding some flair to them. I also like to change up heavier dishes, like the classic Cobb salad. I've replaced typical chicken with crunchy falafel that's just as satisfying.
—Jenn Tidwell, Fair Oaks, CA

PREP: 1 HOUR • **COOK:** 5 MIN./BATCH • **MAKES:** 10 SERVINGS

1 pkg. (6 oz.) falafel mix
½ cup sour cream or plain yogurt
¼ cup chopped seeded peeled cucumber
¼ cup 2% milk
1 tsp. minced fresh parsley
¼ tsp. salt
4 cups torn romaine
4 cups fresh baby spinach
3 hard-boiled large eggs, chopped
2 medium tomatoes, seeded and finely chopped
1 medium ripe avocado, peeled and finely chopped
¾ cup crumbled feta cheese
8 bacon strips, cooked and crumbled
½ cup pitted Greek olives, finely chopped

1. Prepare and cook falafel according to package directions. When cool enough to handle, crumble or coarsely chop falafel.

2. In a small bowl, mix sour cream, cucumber, milk, parsley and salt. In a large bowl, combine romaine and spinach; transfer to a platter. Arrange crumbled falafel and remaining ingredients over greens. Drizzle with dressing.

1 CUP: 258 cal., 18g fat (5g sat. fat), 83mg chol., 687mg sod., 15g carb. (3g sugars, 5g fiber), 13g pro.

READER REVIEW

"What a refreshing and delicious salad. I prepared it for my husband and daughter and they loved! I have never seen them so excited about a salad. I wanted to make it an entree so I added cubed turkey to it as well. I substituted garbanzo beans for the falafel mix. I also added chopped green onions and cucumbers."
—PDARWIN, TASTEOFHOME.COM

ZUCCHINI RICOTTA BAKE

I have made this lasagna-like zucchini casserole frequently over the years and shared the recipe with many people. It's a little bit lighter than other layered casseroles, making it an amazing choice for anyone trying to eat right.
—Eleanor Hauserman, Huntsville, AL

PREP: 15 MIN. • **BAKE:** 1 HOUR + STANDING • **MAKES:** 12 SERVINGS

- 2 lbs. zucchini
- 1 carton (15 oz.) reduced-fat ricotta cheese
- ½ cup egg substitute
- ½ cup dry bread crumbs, divided
- 5 Tbsp. grated Parmesan cheese, divided
- 1 Tbsp. minced fresh parsley
- ¼ tsp. dried oregano
- ¼ tsp. dried basil
- ⅛ tsp. pepper
- 1 jar (28 oz.) meatless pasta sauce
- 1½ cups shredded reduced-fat mozzarella cheese
   Fresh basil leaves, optional

1. Preheat oven to 350°. Cut zucchini lengthwise into ¼-in. slices. Place in a basket over 1 in. boiling water. Cover and steam until just tender, 5-6 minutes. Drain; pat dry.

2. In a large bowl, combine ricotta, egg substitute, 3 Tbsp. bread crumbs, 3 Tbsp. Parmesan, parsley, oregano, basil and pepper; set aside.

3. Spread a third of the spaghetti sauce in a 13x9-in. baking dish coated with cooking spray. Sprinkle with 2 Tbsp. bread crumbs. Cover with half each zucchini, ricotta mixture and mozzarella. Repeat layers of sauce, zucchini, ricotta mixture and mozzarella. Cover with remaining sauce.

4. Combine remaining 3 Tbsp. crumbs and 2 Tbsp. Parmesan; sprinkle over top. Cover and bake 45 minutes. Uncover; bake until golden brown, 15 minutes longer. Let stand 15 minutes before cutting. Sprinkle with fresh basil if desired.

1 PIECE: 150 cal., 5g fat (3g sat. fat), 20mg chol., 513mg sod., 14g carb. (8g sugars, 2g fiber), 11g pro. **DIABETIC EXCHANGES:** 1 vegetable, 1 lean meat, 1 fat, ½ starch.

WEEKNIGHT SKILLET SPINACH PIE

I love sneaking extra veggies into my kids' dinners. Because of this pie's flaky crust and extra cheese, the kids never know they're eating a vitamin-rich dish. Plus, I'm not hovering over an oven for hours. Put the spinach and phyllo sheets in the refrigerator the night before or early in the morning for thawing.

—Kristyne Mcdougle Walter, Lorain, OH

PREP: 35 MIN. • **BAKE:** 35 MIN. + COOLING • **MAKES:** 8 SERVINGS

- 2 large eggs, lightly beaten
- 3 pkg. (10 oz. each) frozen chopped spinach, thawed and squeezed dry
- 2 cups (8 oz.) crumbled feta cheese
- 1½ cups shredded part-skim mozzarella cheese
- ¼ cup chopped walnuts, toasted
- 1½ tsp. dried oregano
- 1½ tsp. dill weed
- ½ tsp. pepper
- ¼ tsp. salt
- ¼ cup julienned soft sun-dried tomatoes (not packed in oil), optional
- ⅓ cup canola oil
- 12 sheets phyllo dough (14x9-in. size)

1. Preheat oven to 375°. In a large bowl, combine eggs, spinach, cheeses, walnuts, seasonings and, if desired, tomatoes; set aside. Brush a 10-in. cast-iron or other ovenproof skillet with some of the oil; set aside.

2. Unroll phyllo dough. Place 1 sheet of phyllo dough on a work surface; brush with oil. (Keep remaining phyllo covered with a damp towel to prevent it from drying out.) Place in prepared skillet, letting edges of phyllo hang over side. Repeat with an additional 5 sheets of phyllo, again brushing with oil and rotating sheets to cover the skillet.

3. Spread spinach mixture over phyllo in skillet. Top with an additional 6 sheets of phyllo, again brushing with oil and rotating sheets. Fold ends of phyllo up over top of pie; brush with oil.

4. Using a sharp knife, cut into 8 wedges. Bake on a lower oven rack until top is golden brown, 35-40 minutes. Cool on a wire rack. Refrigerate leftovers.

1 PIECE: 334 cal., 23g fat (7g sat. fat), 75mg chol., 649mg sod., 17g carb. (2g sugars, 5g fiber), 18g pro.

HOMEMADE MEATLESS SPAGHETTI SAUCE

(PICTURED ON PAGE 5)

When my tomatoes ripen, the first things I make are BLTs and this homemade spaghetti sauce.
—Sondra Bergy, Lowell, MI

PREP: 20 MIN. • **COOK:** 3¼ HOURS • **MAKES:** 2 QT.

4   medium onions, chopped
½   cup canola oil
12 cups chopped peeled fresh
    tomatoes
4   garlic cloves, minced
3   bay leaves
4   tsp. salt
2   tsp. dried oregano
1¼ tsp. pepper
½   tsp. dried basil
2   cans (6 oz. each) tomato paste
⅓   cup packed brown sugar
    Hot cooked pasta
    Minced fresh basil, optional

1. In a Dutch oven, saute onions in oil until tender. Add tomatoes, garlic, bay leaves, salt, oregano, pepper and dried basil. Bring to a boil. Reduce heat; cover and simmer for 2 hours, stirring occasionally.

2. Add the tomato paste and brown sugar; simmer, uncovered, for 1 hour. Discard bay leaves. Serve with pasta and, if desired, minced fresh basil.

½ CUP: 133 cal., 7g fat (1g sat. fat), 0 chol., 614mg sod., 17g carb. (12g sugars, 3g fiber), 2g pro.

GRILLED GREEK PITA PIZZAS

This easy flatbread pizza captures classic Mediterranean flavors in every bite. It works equally well as a speedy main dish or an appetizer.
—Kristen Heigl, Staten Island, NY

TAKES: 20 MIN. • **MAKES:** 4 SERVINGS

1   jar (12 oz.) marinated quartered
    artichoke hearts, drained and
    chopped
1   cup grape tomatoes, halved
½   cup pitted Greek olives, halved
⅓   cup chopped fresh parsley
2   Tbsp. olive oil
¼   tsp. pepper
¾   cup hummus
4   whole pita breads
1   cup crumbled feta cheese

Place first 6 ingredients in a bowl; toss to combine. Spread hummus over pita breads. Top with artichoke mixture; sprinkle with cheese. Grill pizzas, covered, over medium heat 4-5 minutes or until bottoms are golden brown.

1 PIZZA: 585 cal., 34g fat (8g sat. fat), 15mg chol., 1336mg sod., 50g carb. (7g sugars, 6g fiber), 15g pro.

SLOW-COOKER VEGGIE LASAGNA

This veggie-licious alternative to traditional lasagna makes use of slow-cooker convenience. I suggest using chunky spaghetti sauce.
—Laura Davister, Little Suamico, WI

PREP: 25 MIN. • **COOK:** 3½ HOURS • **MAKES:** 2 SERVINGS

½ cup shredded part-skim
  mozzarella cheese
3 Tbsp. 1% cottage cheese
2 Tbsp. grated Parmesan cheese
2 Tbsp. egg substitute
½ tsp. Italian seasoning
⅛ tsp. garlic powder
¾ cup meatless spaghetti sauce,
  divided
½ cup sliced zucchini, divided
2 no-cook lasagna noodles
4 cups fresh baby spinach
½ cup sliced fresh mushrooms

1. Cut two 18x3-in. strips of heavy-duty foil; crisscross so they resemble an "X." Place strips on bottom and up side of a 1½-qt. slow cooker. Coat strips with cooking spray.

2. In a small bowl, combine the first 6 ingredients. Spread 1 Tbsp. spaghetti sauce on bottom of the prepared slow cooker. Top with half of the zucchini and a third of the cheese mixture.

3. Break noodles into 1-in. pieces; sprinkle half of the noodles over cheese mixture. Spread with 1 Tbsp. sauce. Top with half of the spinach and half of the mushrooms. Repeat layers. Top with remaining cheese mixture and remaining spaghetti sauce.

4. Cover and cook on low for 3½-4 hours or until noodles are tender.

1 SERVING: 259 cal., 8g fat (4g sat. fat), 23mg chol., 859mg sod., 29g carb. (9g sugars, 4g fiber), 19g pro. **DIABETIC EXCHANGES:** 2 lean meat, 2 medium-fat meat, 1½ starch, 1 vegetable, ½ fat.

READER REVIEW

"I love this recipe. Perfect for the two of us. Pick your favorite sauce, and it's fast and easy to make. Rarely any leftovers, which is good because my husband won't eat anything left over."
—RLSHEEHAN55, TASTEOFHOME.COM

GARDEN HARVEST SPAGHETTI SQUASH

I was in the grocery store and spotted a perfectly ripe spaghetti squash. I knew I had to try it, so I cooked it according to the label. I topped it with my favorite vegetables for pasta, and it was an instant family favorite.
—Veronica McCann, Columbus, OH

PREP: 30 MIN. • **BAKE:** 35 MIN. • **MAKES:** 4 SERVINGS

1   medium spaghetti squash
     (about 4 lbs.)
1   medium sweet red pepper,
     chopped
1   medium red onion, chopped
1   small zucchini, chopped
1   cup chopped fresh mushrooms
½   cup chopped leek (white portion
     only)
½   cup shredded carrots
1   Tbsp. olive oil
1   garlic clove, minced
1   can (14½ oz.) stewed tomatoes
½   cup tomato paste
¼   cup V8 juice
1   tsp. pepper
½   tsp. salt
2   cups fresh baby spinach
1   Tbsp. minced fresh basil
2   tsp. minced fresh oregano
2   tsp. minced fresh thyme
1   tsp. minced fresh rosemary
¼   cup grated Parmesan and
     Romano cheese blend

1. Cut squash in half lengthwise; discard seeds. Place squash cut side down in a 15x10x1-in. baking pan; add ½ in. hot water. Bake, uncovered, at 375° until squash is easily pierced with a fork, 30-40 minutes. Drain water from pan; turn squash cut side up. Bake 5 minutes longer or until squash is tender.

2. Meanwhile, in a Dutch oven, saute red pepper, onion, zucchini, mushrooms, leek and carrots in oil until tender. Add garlic; cook 1 minute longer. Add the stewed tomatoes, tomato paste, V8 juice, pepper and salt; bring to a boil. Reduce heat; cover and simmer for 15 minutes. Stir in spinach and herbs; heat through.

3. When squash is cool enough to handle, use a fork to separate strands. Serve with sauce; sprinkle with cheese.

1¼ CUPS SQUASH WITH 1 CUP SAUCE: 224 cal., 7g fat (2g sat. fat), 8mg chol., 732mg sod., 37g carb. (18g sugars, 7g fiber), 10g pro. **DIABETIC EXCHANGES:** 3 starch, ½ fat.

GREEK SALAD RAVIOLI

Turn the fresh flavors of a Greek salad into a warm dish for cold winter nights. I like to make a large batch, freeze it, then simply drop ravioli into simmering water for dinner in five minutes!
—Carla Mendres, Winnipeg, MB

PREP: 45 MIN. • **COOK:** 5 MIN./BATCH • **MAKES:** 8 SERVINGS

10 oz. (about 12 cups) fresh baby spinach
½ cup finely chopped roasted sweet red peppers
½ cup pitted and finely chopped ripe olives
½ cup crumbled feta cheese
3 Tbsp. snipped fresh dill
2 to 3 tsp. dried oregano
2 Tbsp. butter
3 Tbsp. all-purpose flour
2 cups whole milk
96 pot sticker or gyoza wrappers
Additional snipped fresh dill, optional
Sauce of your choice

KITCHEN TIP

Wonton wrappers may be substituted for pot sticker or gyoza wrappers. Stack 2 or 3 wonton wrappers on a work surface; cut into circles with a 3½-in. biscuit or round cookie cutter. Fill and wrap as directed.

1. In a large skillet over medium heat, cook and stir spinach in batches until wilted, 3-4 minutes. Drain on paper towels. In a bowl, combine spinach with next 5 ingredients.

2. In a small saucepan, melt butter over medium heat. Stir in flour until smooth; gradually whisk in milk. Bring to a boil, stirring constantly, until sauce thickens and coats a spoon, 2-3 minutes. Stir into spinach mixture.

3. Place 1 Tbsp. spinach mixture in center of a pot sticker wrapper. (Cover remaining wrappers with a damp paper towel until ready to use.) Moisten wrapper edge with water, and place another wrapper on top. Press edges to seal. Repeat with remaining wrappers.

4. Fill a Dutch oven two-thirds full with water; bring to a boil. Reduce heat; drop ravioli in batches into simmering water 3-4 minutes or until cooked through. If desired, sprinkle with additional dill. Serve with sauce of your choice.

FREEZE OPTION: Cover and freeze uncooked ravioli on waxed paper-lined baking sheets until firm. Transfer to freezer containers; return to freezer. To use, cook as directed, increasing time to 6 minutes.

6 RAVIOLI: 283 cal., 8g fat (4g sat. fat), 22mg chol., 442mg sod., 44g carb. (4g sugars, 2g fiber), 10g pro. **DIABETIC EXCHANGES:** 3 starch, 1 high-fat meat, 1 fat.

PESTO VEGETABLE PIZZA

PESTO VEGETABLE PIZZA

My family loves pizza night, but we have rarely ordered takeout since I created this fresh and flavorful version. Always a winner in my house, it is a fast and delicious meal.
—Kate Selner, Lino Lakes, MN

TAKES: 30 MIN. • **MAKES:** 6 SERVINGS

1 prebaked 12-in. thin pizza crust
2 garlic cloves, halved
½ cup pesto sauce
¾ cup packed fresh spinach, chopped
2 large portobello mushrooms, thinly sliced
1 medium sweet yellow pepper, julienned
2 plum tomatoes, seeded and sliced
⅓ cup packed fresh basil, chopped
1 cup shredded part-skim mozzarella cheese
¼ cup grated Parmesan cheese
½ tsp. fresh or dried oregano

1. Preheat oven to 450°. Place crust on an ungreased 12-in. pizza pan. Rub cut side of garlic cloves over crust; discard garlic. Spread pesto sauce over crust. Top with spinach, mushrooms, yellow pepper, tomatoes and basil. Sprinkle with cheeses and oregano.

2. Bake until pizza is heated through and cheese is melted, 10-15 minutes.

1 PIECE: 310 cal., 15g fat (4g sat. fat), 15mg chol., 707mg sod., 31g carb. (4g sugars, 2g fiber), 13g pro. **DIABETIC EXCHANGES:** 2 starch, 2 fat, 1 lean meat, 1 medium-fat meat.

ROASTED BUTTERNUT LINGUINE

Squash is one of our favorite vegetables, and this is my husband's preferred fall dish. He looks forward to it all year!
—Kim Caputo, Cannon Falls, MN

PREP: 20 MIN. • **BAKE:** 45 MIN. • **MAKES:** 4 SERVINGS

4 cups cubed peeled butternut squash
1 medium red onion, chopped
3 Tbsp. olive oil
¼ tsp. crushed red pepper flakes
½ lb. uncooked linguine
2 cups julienned Swiss chard
1 Tbsp. minced fresh sage
½ tsp. salt
¼ tsp. pepper

1. Preheat oven to 350°. Place squash and onion in a 15x10x1-in. baking pan coated with cooking spray. Combine oil and pepper flakes; drizzle over vegetables and toss to coat.

2. Bake, uncovered, 45-50 minutes or until tender, stirring occasionally.

3. Meanwhile, cook linguine according to package directions; drain and place in a large bowl. Add squash mixture, Swiss chard, sage, salt and pepper; toss to combine.

1½ CUPS: 384 cal., 12g fat (2g sat. fat), 0 chol., 344mg sod., 64g carb. (7g sugars, 6g fiber), 10g pro.

GARDEN BOUNTY PASTA SAUCE

I came up with this recipe after planting too many zucchini plants in our vegetable garden. My husband loved it the first time I served it and now we make it quite often.
—Joy Turner, Amherst, OH

PREP: 20 MIN. • **COOK:** 1 HOUR • **MAKES:** 5 CUPS

2 Tbsp. butter
2 Tbsp. canola oil
2 medium onions, chopped
8 large tomatoes, chopped
2 medium zucchini, cut into ½-in. pieces
4 garlic cloves, minced
2 tsp. dried oregano
1 tsp. salt
½ tsp. pepper
Hot cooked pasta

In a large saucepan, melt butter with oil over medium heat. Add onions, cook and stir until tender, 5-7 minutes. Stir in tomatoes, zucchini, garlic, oregano, salt and pepper; bring to a boil. Reduce heat; simmer, uncovered, until zucchini is tender and sauce reaches desired consistency, 50-60 minutes. Serve with pasta.

½ CUP SAUCE: 89 cal., 6g fat (2g sat. fat), 6mg chol., 266mg sod., 10g carb. (6g sugars, 3g fiber), 2g pro. **DIABETIC EXCHANGES:** 2 vegetable, 1 fat.

MEDITERRANEAN BULGUR SALAD

Whether it's nutrition or taste you're after, it doesn't get any better than this. Bulgur, beans, tomatoes, pine nuts and olive oil team up in this vegetarian main dish salad.
—*Taste of Home* Test Kitchen

PREP: 15 MIN. • **COOK:** 20 MIN. • **MAKES:** 9 SERVINGS

3 cups vegetable broth
1½ cups uncooked bulgur
6 Tbsp. olive oil
2 Tbsp. lemon juice
2 Tbsp. minced fresh parsley
½ tsp. salt
¼ tsp. pepper
1 can (15 oz.) garbanzo beans or chickpeas, rinsed and drained
2 cups halved cherry tomatoes
1 cup chopped cucumber
8 green onions, sliced
1 pkg. (4 oz.) crumbled feta cheese
½ cup pine nuts, toasted

1. In a large saucepan, bring broth and bulgur to a boil over high heat. Reduce heat; cover and simmer for 20 minutes or until tender and broth is almost absorbed. Remove from the heat; let stand at room temperature, uncovered, until broth is absorbed.

2. In a small bowl, whisk oil, lemon juice, parsley, salt and pepper.

3. In a large serving bowl, combine bulgur, beans, tomatoes, cucumber and onions. Drizzle with dressing; toss to coat. Sprinkle with cheese and pine nuts.

1 CUP: 298 cal., 17g fat (3g sat. fat), 7mg chol., 657mg sod., 31g carb. (4g sugars, 8g fiber), 10g pro.

GARDEN BOUNTY
PASTA SAUCE

FALAFEL

FALAFEL TIPS

How do you make the falafel mixture easy to shape? Chilling the falafel mixture for an hour in the fridge makes it easier to shape, so make sure you don't skip that step!

What are some variations of this falafel recipe? Replace mint with parsley for a more traditional take on this falafel recipe, or try pan-frying, baking or air-frying your falafel.

How do you serve falafel? Serve falafel in or alongside pita bread with plenty of fresh veggies and your favorite sauce.

FALAFEL

Falafel is a common street food in the Middle East. They are gluten free, crunchy on the outside, tender on the inside, and full of flavor from cilantro, mint, coriander and nutty sesame seeds. Parsley can be added or used instead of mint. The classic version is deep-fried, but they can also be pan-fried, baked or cooked in an air fryer. Serve in or alongside pita bread with red onion, tomato, pickled cucumber and tahini sauce.
—Nithya Narasimhan, Chennai, India

PREP: 10 MIN. + STANDING • **COOK:** 15 MIN. • **MAKES:** 4 SERVINGS

1 cup dried garbanzo beans
  or chickpeas
½ tsp. baking soda
1 cup fresh cilantro leaves
½ cup fresh mint leaves
5 garlic cloves
1 tsp. salt
½ tsp. pepper, optional
1 tsp. ground coriander
1 tsp. chili powder
1 tsp. sesame seeds
1 tsp. baking powder
  Oil for deep-fat frying

1. In a large bowl, cover beans with water. Stir in baking soda. Cover and let stand overnight. Drain beans; rinse and pat dry.

2. In a food processor, pulse cilantro and mint until finely chopped. Add beans, garlic, salt, pepper if desired, coriander and chili powder. Pulse until mixture is blended and the texture of coarse meal. Transfer to a large bowl. Cover and refrigerate at least 1 hour.

3. Stir in sesame seeds and baking powder. Shape into sixteen 2-in. balls. In an electric skillet or a deep-fat fryer, heat oil to 375°. Fry falafel balls, a few at a time, until golden brown, about 2 minutes, turning occasionally. Drain on paper towels.

4 PIECES: 224 cal., 13g fat (1g sat. fat), 0 chol., 760mg sod., 32g carb. (1g sugars, 16g fiber), 9g pro.

MARGHERITA PITA PIZZAS

My husband plants the garden, and I harvest and cook the fruits of his labor. My favorite way to use plum tomatoes is with this easy pizza. It is so good!
—Rosemarie Weleski, Natrona Heights, PA

TAKES: 20 MIN. • **MAKES:** 4 SERVINGS

4 pita breads (6 in.)
2 tsp. olive oil
2 garlic cloves, minced
2 cups shredded part-skim
  mozzarella cheese
3 plum tomatoes, thinly sliced
¼ tsp. garlic powder
1 tsp. Italian seasoning
  Thinly sliced fresh basil, optional

1. Place pita breads on an ungreased baking sheet; brush with oil. Top with garlic, 1 cup cheese, tomatoes, garlic powder and remaining cheese; sprinkle with Italian seasoning.

2. Bake at 425° until cheese is melted, 10-12 minutes. Top with basil.

1 SERVING: 340 cal., 12g fat (6g sat. fat), 33mg chol., 588mg sod., 38g carb. (4g sugars, 2g fiber), 20g pro. **DIABETIC EXCHANGES:** 2 starch, 2 medium-fat meat, ½ fat.

CREAMY AVOCADO MANICOTTI

I am always looking for creative ways to make vegetarian dinners a little different. I grow my own basil, and avocados are a versatile favorite, so this recipe is a fantastic way to make manicotti that's a little unusual.
—Jennifer Coduto, Kent, OH

PREP: 25 MIN. • **BAKE:** 45 MIN. • **MAKES:** 7 SERVINGS

1   pkg. (8 oz.) manicotti shells
1   small onion, finely chopped
1   Tbsp. olive oil
2   garlic cloves, minced
1   can (28 oz.) crushed tomatoes
½   cup minced fresh basil
     or 3 Tbsp. dried basil
⅓   cup dry red wine or vegetable broth
1   Tbsp. brown sugar
½   tsp. salt
½   tsp. pepper

FILLING
1   carton (15 oz.) reduced-fat
     ricotta cheese
1   medium ripe avocado, peeled
     and mashed
½   cup grated Parmesan cheese
¼   tsp. salt
¼   tsp. pepper
1   cup shredded part-skim
     mozzarella cheese
1   medium ripe avocado, sliced,
     optional

1. Cook manicotti according to package directions. Meanwhile, in a large skillet, saute onion in oil until tender. Add garlic; cook 1 minute longer. Stir in the tomatoes, basil, wine, brown sugar, salt and pepper. Bring to a boil. Reduce heat; simmer, uncovered, 10-15 minutes, stirring occasionally.

2. Drain manicotti. In a small bowl, combine the ricotta cheese, avocado, Parmesan cheese, salt and pepper. Stuff cheese mixture into manicotti shells. Spread 1 cup sauce into a greased 13x9-in. baking dish. Arrange manicotti over sauce. Pour remaining sauce over top.

3. Cover and bake at 350° for 35 minutes or until bubbly. Uncover; sprinkle with mozzarella cheese. Bake 10-15 minutes longer or until cheese is melted. If desired, garnish with avocado slices.

2 PIECES: 359 cal., 13g fat (5g sat. fat), 29mg chol., 625mg sod., 41g carb. (7g sugars, 5g fiber), 18g pro. **DIABETIC EXCHANGES:** 2 starch, 2 vegetable, 2 medium-fat meat, 1 fat.

**A LITTLE GOES
A LONG WAY**

*Using a small amount of a rich
ingredient, like heavy cream,
is a smart way keep a dish tasting
indulgent while keeping the
calories in check.*

CREAMY PASTA PRIMAVERA

This pasta dish is a wonderful blend of crisp, colorful vegetables and a creamy Parmesan cheese sauce.
—Darlene Brenden, Salem, OR

TAKES: 30 MIN. • **MAKES:** 6 SERVINGS

2 cups uncooked gemelli or spiral pasta
1 lb. fresh asparagus, trimmed and cut into 2-in. pieces
3 medium carrots, shredded
2 tsp. canola oil
2 cups cherry tomatoes, halved
1 garlic clove, minced
½ cup grated Parmesan cheese
½ cup heavy whipping cream
¼ tsp. pepper

1. Cook pasta according to the package directions. In a large skillet over medium-high heat, saute asparagus and carrots in oil until crisp-tender. Add tomatoes and garlic; cook 1 minute longer.

2. Stir in Parmesan cheese, cream and pepper. Drain pasta; toss with asparagus mixture.

1⅓ CUPS: 275 cal., 12g fat (6g sat. fat), 33mg chol., 141mg sod., 35g carb. (5g sugars, 3g fiber), 10g pro. **DIABETIC EXCHANGES:** 2 starch, 2 fat, 1 vegetable.

CHOPPED GREEK SALAD IN A JAR

Here's a lunchbox-friendly salad with lots of zesty flair. Prepare the jars on Sunday, and you'll have four grab-and-go lunches ready for the workweek.
—*Taste of Home* Test Kitchen

TAKES: 20 MIN. • **MAKES:** 4 SERVINGS

¼ cup pepperoncini juice
¼ cup extra virgin olive oil
¼ cup minced fresh basil
2 Tbsp. lemon juice
½ tsp. pepper
¼ tsp. salt
¼ cup finely chopped pepperoncini
1 can (15 oz.) garbanzo beans or chickpeas, rinsed and drained
2 celery ribs, sliced
½ cup Greek olives
1 medium tomato, chopped
½ cup crumbled feta cheese
8 cups chopped romaine

In a small bowl, whisk the first 6 ingredients. In each of four 1-qt. wide-mouth canning jars, divide and layer ingredients in the following order: olive oil mixture, pepperoncini, garbanzo beans, celery, Greek olives, tomato, feta and romaine. Cover and refrigerate until serving. Transfer salads into bowls; toss to combine.

1 SERVING: 332 cal., 23g fat (4g sat. fat), 8mg chol., 795mg sod., 25g carb. (5g sugars, 8g fiber), 9g pro.

THE BEST EGGPLANT PARMESAN

*I love eggplant and have many recipes that include it, but this one is
my favorites. The cheeses and seasonings make the dish unforgettable.*

—Dorothy Kilpatrick, Wilmington, NC

PREP: 1¼ HOURS • BAKE: 35 MIN. + STANDING • MAKES: 2 CASSEROLES (8 SERVINGS EACH)

- 3 garlic cloves, minced
- ⅓ cup olive oil
- 2 cans (28 oz. each) crushed tomatoes
- 1 cup pitted ripe olives, chopped
- ¼ cup thinly sliced fresh basil leaves or 1 Tbsp. dried basil
- 3 Tbsp. capers, drained
- 1 tsp. crushed red pepper flakes
- ¼ tsp. pepper

EGGPLANT
- 1 cup all-purpose flour
- 4 large eggs, beaten
- 3 cups dry bread crumbs
- 1 Tbsp. garlic powder
- 1 Tbsp. minced fresh oregano or 1 tsp. dried oregano
- 4 small eggplants (about 1 lb. each), peeled and cut lengthwise into ½-in. slices
- 1 cup olive oil

CHEESE
- 2 large eggs, beaten
- 2 cartons (15 oz. each) ricotta cheese
- 1¼ cups shredded Parmesan cheese, divided
- ½ cup thinly sliced fresh basil leaves or 2 Tbsp. dried basil
- ½ tsp. pepper
- 8 cups shredded part-skim mozzarella cheese
- Additional fresh basil, optional

1. In a Dutch oven over medium heat, cook garlic in oil 1 minute. Stir in tomatoes, olives, basil, capers, pepper flakes and pepper. Bring to a boil. Reduce heat; simmer, uncovered, 45-60 minutes or until thickened.

2. Meanwhile, for eggplant, place flour and beaten eggs in separate shallow bowls. In another bowl, combine bread crumbs, garlic powder and oregano. Dip eggplant in flour, eggs, then bread crumb mixture.

3. In a large skillet, cook eggplant in batches in oil until tender, 5 minutes on each side. Drain on paper towels. In a bowl, combine eggs, ricotta cheese, ½ cup Parmesan cheese, basil and pepper.

4. Preheat oven to 350°. In each of 2 greased 13x9-in. baking dishes, layer 1½ cups tomato sauce, 4 eggplant slices, 1 cup ricotta mixture and 2 cups mozzarella cheese. Repeat layers, sprinkling each with the remaining Parmesan cheese. Bake, uncovered, 35-40 minutes or until bubbly. Let stand for 10 minutes before cutting. If desired, sprinkle with additional fresh basil.

1 PIECE: 585 cal., 40g fat (14g sat. fat), 132mg chol., 935mg sod., 32g carb. (11g sugars, 7g fiber), 29g pro.

READER REVIEW

"We grew eggplant in our garden for the first time this year, and when I told my friends that I didn't know what to make with them, all said … eggplant Parmesan! I'm thrilled this is the recipe I tried. Although it was time-consuming, it was absolutely amazing! I used up our first-ever eggplants and shared the second casserole with friends. My husband liked it so much he asked if eggplants were sold at the grocery store and, if so, could we get them year round! I will definitely be making this again. Delicious!"

—WANDAHENDRIX, TASTEOFHOME.COM

GREEK OUZO
PORK KABOBS,
PAGE 211

BEEF, PORK & LAMB

Get ready to dig in. When it comes to serving up a satisfying meal that's full of flavor and heartiness, look no further than these meaty options.

PARMESAN PORK TENDERLOIN

I am of Danish descent and love all things pork, both old recipes and new. Here's a dish I came up with myself.
—John Hansen, Marstons Mills, MA

PREP: 25 MIN. • **COOK:** 25 MIN. • **MAKES:** 2 SERVINGS

1 pork tenderloin (¾ lb.)
6 Tbsp. grated Parmesan cheese
1 small sweet onion, sliced and separated into rings
1½ cups sliced fresh mushrooms
1 garlic clove, minced
2 tsp. butter, divided
2 tsp. olive oil, divided
¼ cup reduced-sodium beef broth
2 Tbsp. port wine or additional beef broth
⅛ tsp. salt, optional
⅛ tsp. each dried basil, thyme and rosemary, crushed
Dash pepper
½ tsp. cornstarch
3 Tbsp. water

1. Cut pork into ½-in. slices; flatten to ⅛-in. thickness. Coat with Parmesan cheese; set aside.

2. In a large skillet, saute onion, mushrooms and garlic in 1 tsp. butter and 1 tsp. oil until tender; remove and keep warm. In the same skillet, cook pork in remaining 1 tsp. butter and 1 tsp. oil in batches over medium heat until juices run clear, about 2 minutes on each side. Remove and keep warm.

3. Add broth to pan, scraping to loosen browned bits. Stir in wine or additional broth; add seasonings. Bring to a boil. Reduce heat; simmer, uncovered, for 5 minutes. Combine cornstarch and water until smooth; stir into pan. Bring to a boil; cook and stir until thickened, about 2 minutes. Serve with pork and onion mixture.

1 SERVING: 388 cal., 19g fat (8g sat. fat), 118mg chol., 472mg sod., 11g carb. (6g sugars, 2g fiber), 43g pro.

READER REVIEW

"The Parmesan cheese coating tasted wonderful! We added more mushrooms just because we like them so much. Don't worry if you don't have port wine on hand; additional beef broth works just as well. This is a nice dish for company or regular family dinners."
—NH-RESCUE, TASTEOFHOME.COM

FETA-STUFFED KIBBEH
WITH HARISSA

FETA-STUFFED KIBBEH WITH HARISSA

There are countless versions of this delicious dish throughout the Middle East.
This is our adaptation. You can substitute ground beef for the lamb.
—Chris Bugher, Fairview, NC

PREP: 30 MIN. • **BAKE:** 15 MIN. • **MAKES:** 6 SERVINGS

1 cup bulgur (fine grind)
¼ cup finely chopped red onion
3 garlic cloves, minced
2 tsp. ground allspice
1 tsp. ground cumin
½ tsp. salt
½ tsp. ground cinnamon
¼ tsp. pepper
1 lb. ground lamb
1 cup crumbled feta cheese
¼ cup pine nuts
2 Tbsp. harissa chili paste
  Refrigerated tzatziki sauce

1. Preheat oven to 375°. Soak bulgur according to package directions. Drain and transfer to a large bowl. Add onion, garlic and seasonings. Add lamb; mix lightly but thoroughly. Divide meat mixture into 18 portions. In another bowl, combine feta cheese, pine nuts and harissa. Shape each portion of meat mixture around 2 tsp. feta mixture to cover completely; form into a football shape.

2. Place on parchment-lined baking sheets. Bake until cooked through, 15-20 minutes. Serve with chilled tzatziki sauce.

3 KIBBEH: 324 cal., 17g fat (7g sat. fat), 60mg chol., 474mg sod., 21g carb. (1g sugars, 4g fiber), 20g pro.

◇◇

LAMB SHANKS DELUXE

I got this recipe from my mom. The lamb shanks are so tender and make an exquisitely flavored gravy.
—Sue Draheim, Waterford, WI

PREP: 30 MIN. + STANDING • **BAKE:** 2½ HOURS • **MAKES:** 4 SERVINGS

½ medium lemon
¼ tsp. garlic powder
4 lamb shanks (about 12 oz. each)
1 cup all-purpose flour, divided
2 tsp. salt
½ tsp. pepper
3 Tbsp. olive oil
2 cups beef consomme
1 cup water
½ cup dry vermouth
1 medium onion, chopped
4 medium carrots, cut into chunks
4 celery ribs, cut into chunks

1. Rub lemon and garlic over lamb shanks; let stand for 10 minutes. In a large airtight container, combine ¾ cup flour, salt and pepper. Add shanks, 1 at a time, and shake to coat.

2. In a large skillet, brown lamb in oil over medium-high heat. Transfer to a shallow roasting pan. Stir remaining flour into skillet; cook and stir until browned. Stir in consomme, water and vermouth until blended. Bring to a boil; cook and stir for 2-3 minutes or until thickened.

3. Stir in onion. Pour over lamb. Bake, uncovered, at 350° for 1½ hours. Turn shanks; add carrots and celery. Cover and bake 1 hour longer or until meat and vegetables are tender.

1 LAMB SHANK: 574 cal., 26g fat (8g sat. fat), 119mg chol., 2149mg sod., 36g carb. (6g sugars, 4g fiber), 40g pro.

PASTITSIO

Guests always seem to gobble up this authentic Greek beef and pasta casserole. The creamy white sauce is oh, so good.
—Amanda Briggs, Greenfield, WI

PREP: 35 MIN. • **BAKE:** 30 MIN. + STANDING • **MAKES:** 4 SERVINGS

- 1 pkg. (7 oz.) uncooked elbow macaroni
- 1 lb. ground beef or lamb
- 1 medium onion, chopped
- 1 garlic clove, minced
- 1 can (8 oz.) tomato sauce
- 1 tsp. salt, divided
- ¼ tsp. dried oregano
- ⅛ tsp. pepper
- ¼ tsp. ground cinnamon, optional
- ½ cup grated Parmesan cheese, divided
- 3 Tbsp. butter
- 3 Tbsp. all-purpose flour
- 1½ cups 2% milk
- 1 large egg, lightly beaten

1. Cook macaroni according to package directions. Meanwhile, in a large skillet, cook beef and onion over medium heat until meat is no longer pink. Add garlic; cook 1 minute longer. Drain. Stir in tomato sauce, ½ tsp. salt, oregano, pepper and, if desired, cinnamon; heat through.

2. Drain macaroni; place half of macaroni in a greased 9-in. square baking pan. Sprinkle with ¼ cup cheese. Layer with meat mixture and remaining macaroni. Set aside.

3. Preheat oven to 350°. In a small saucepan, melt butter; stir in flour and remaining salt until smooth. Gradually add milk. Bring to a boil; cook and stir 2 minutes or until thickened.

4. Remove from heat. Stir a small amount of the hot mixture into egg; return all to the pan, stirring constantly. Bring to a gentle boil; cook and stir 2 minutes. Remove from heat; stir in remaining cheese. Pour sauce over macaroni.

5. Bake, uncovered, 30-35 minutes or until golden brown. Let stand for 10 minutes before serving.

1 SERVING: 614 cal., 26g fat (13g sat. fat), 147mg chol., 1206mg sod., 57g carb. (10g sugars, 3g fiber), 38g pro.

READER REVIEW

"I've made this twice in the last few months. Once with beef and once with lamb. This is such a delicious, comforting meal! I've doubled it both times for my crew of teenage boys and husband. One tip I would add to reduce the number of pots/pans used is to make the bechamel sauce in the same pot that you've cooked the pasta in."
—THELOUWS, TASTEOFHOME.COM

GRILLED STEAKS WITH GREEK RELISH

My ribeye steak dinner showcases the flavors of Greece. These steaks go well with hummus and pita bread.
—Mary Lou Cook, Welches, OR

TAKES: 30 MIN. • **MAKES:** 2 SERVINGS

2 plum tomatoes, seeded and chopped
½ cup chopped red onion
⅓ cup pitted Greek olives
2 Tbsp. minced fresh cilantro
2 Tbsp. lemon juice, divided
1 Tbsp. olive oil
1 garlic clove, minced
1 beef ribeye steak (¾ lb.)
½ cup crumbled feta cheese

1. For relish, in a small bowl, combine tomatoes, onion, olives, cilantro, 1 Tbsp. lemon juice, oil and garlic.

2. Drizzle remaining lemon juice over steak. Grill steak, covered, over medium heat or broil 4 in. from heat 5-7 minutes on each side or until meat reaches the desired doneness (for medium-rare, a thermometer should read 135°; medium, 140°; medium-well, 145°). Let stand 5 minutes before cutting in half. Serve with relish and cheese.

4 OZ. COOKED STEAK WITH ⅔ CUP RELISH AND 2 TBSP. CHEESE: 562 cal., 42g fat (14g sat. fat), 108mg chol., 587mg sod., 10g carb. (4g sugars, 2g fiber), 34g pro.

🟡 PEPPERED PORK PITAS

Believe it: Cracked black pepper is all it takes to give my pork pitas some pop. With these sandwiches, any weeknight meal is a gourmet affair. I like to fill them up with caramelized onions and garlic mayo.
—Katherine White, Henderson, NV

TAKES: 20 MIN. • **MAKES:** 4 SERVINGS

1 lb. boneless pork loin chops, cut into thin strips
1 Tbsp. olive oil
2 tsp. coarsely ground pepper
2 garlic cloves, minced
1 jar (12 oz.) roasted sweet red peppers, drained and julienned
4 whole pita breads, warmed
Optional: Garlic mayonnaise and torn leaf lettuce

In a small bowl, combine pork, oil, pepper and garlic; toss to coat. Place a large skillet over medium-high heat. Add pork mixture; cook and stir until no longer pink. Stir in red peppers; heat through. Serve on pita breads. Top with mayonnaise and lettuce if desired.

1 SANDWICH: 380 cal., 11g fat (3g sat. fat), 55mg chol., 665mg sod., 37g carb. (4g sugars, 2g fiber), 27g pro. **DIABETIC EXCHANGES:** 3 lean meat, 2 starch, 1 fat.

DID YOU KNOW?

Usually associated with sweet recipes, nutmeg is the secret ingredient in flavorful bechamel or white sauces. Be careful not to overdo it, as a small amount of the spice goes a long way.

MOUSSAKA

Moussaka is traditionally made with lamb, but I often use ground beef instead. The recipe looks a bit daunting, but if you prepare one step while working on another, it will save time.
—Kim Powell, Knoxville, TN

PREP: 45 MIN. • **BAKE:** 30 MIN. + STANDING • **MAKES:** 8 SERVINGS

3 medium potatoes, peeled and cut lengthwise into ¼-in. slices
1 medium eggplant, cut lengthwise into ½-in. slices
1½ lbs. ground lamb or ground beef
1 small onion, chopped
2 garlic cloves, minced
2 plum tomatoes, chopped
1¼ cups hot water
1 can (6 oz.) tomato paste, divided
1¼ tsp. salt, divided
½ tsp. dried oregano
½ tsp. paprika
½ tsp. ground cinnamon
½ tsp. ground nutmeg, divided
3 Tbsp. butter
¼ cup all-purpose flour
4 cups 2% milk
2 cups shredded mozzarella cheese

1. Preheat oven to 450°. Arrange potato and eggplant slices in 2 greased 15x10x1-in. baking pans, overlapping as needed. Bake until cooked through, 20 minutes. Set aside; reduce oven setting to 400°.

2. In a large skillet, cook lamb, onion and garlic over medium heat until meat is no longer pink, 7-9 minutes, breaking into crumbles; drain. Stir in tomatoes, water, tomato paste, ¼ tsp. salt, oregano, paprika, cinnamon and ¼ tsp. nutmeg. Bring to a boil. Reduce heat; simmer, uncovered, 5 minutes.

3. In a large saucepan, melt butter over medium heat. Stir in flour until smooth; gradually whisk in milk. Bring to a boil, stirring constantly; cook and stir until thickened, 2-3 minutes. Stir in remaining 1 tsp. salt and ¼ tsp. nutmeg.

4. Arrange parcooked potatoes in a greased 13x9-in. baking dish, overlapping as needed. Top with lamb mixture. Arrange eggplant over top, overlapping as needed.

5. Top with bechamel sauce. Sprinkle with mozzarella cheese. Bake, uncovered, until bubbly and golden brown, about 30 minutes. Let stand 20 minutes before serving.

1 SERVING: 453 cal., 25g fat (13g sat. fat), 99mg chol., 700mg sod., 30g carb. (12g sugars, 4g fiber), 28g pro.

🍲 TENDER PORK CHOPS

Not only is it easy to use my slow cooker, but the results are fabulous. Meat cooked this way always comes out so tender and juicy. These pork chops are simmered in a thick tomato sauce.
—Bonnie Marlow, Ottoville, OH

PREP: 15 MIN. • **COOK:** 5 HOURS • **MAKES:** 6 SERVINGS

6   boneless pork loin chops
    (6 oz. each)
1   Tbsp. canola oil
1   medium green pepper, diced
1   can (6 oz.) tomato paste
1   jar (4½ oz.) sliced mushrooms,
    drained
½   cup water
1   envelope spaghetti sauce mix
½   to 1 tsp. hot pepper sauce

1. In a large skillet, brown pork chops in oil over medium heat 3-4 minutes on each side; drain. In a 5-qt. slow cooker, combine remaining ingredients. Top with pork chops.

2. Cover and cook on low 5-6 hours or until meat is tender.

FREEZE OPTION: Cool pork chop mixture. Freeze in freezer containers. To use, partially thaw in refrigerator overnight. Heat through slowly in a covered skillet, stirring occasionally, until a thermometer inserted in pork reads 165°.

1 PORK CHOP: 303 cal., 12g fat (4g sat. fat), 82mg chol., 763mg sod., 13g carb. (5g sugars, 3g fiber), 34g pro.

LAMB WITH APRICOTS

When I was a new bride, I decided to prepare a special Hanukkah meal for my husband, David, and me to share. The star was this lamb entree, which had been one of my favorites when I was growing up. Dried apricots add a touch of sweetness to the tender lamb, which is gently spiced.
—Rachel Delano, Tappahannock, VA

PREP: 15 MIN. • **BAKE:** 1½ HOURS • **MAKES:** 8 SERVINGS

1   large onion, chopped
2   Tbsp. olive oil
1   boneless lamb shoulder roast
     (2½ to 3 lbs.), cubed
1   tsp. each ground cumin, cinnamon
     and coriander
     Salt and pepper to taste
½   cup dried apricots, halved
¼   cup orange juice
1   Tbsp. ground almonds
½   tsp. grated orange zest
1¼   cups chicken broth
1   Tbsp. sesame seeds, toasted

1. In a large skillet, saute onion in oil until tender. Add lamb and seasonings. Cook and stir for 5 minutes or until meat is browned. Add apricots, orange juice, almonds and orange zest.

2. Transfer to a 2½-qt. baking dish. Stir in broth. Cover and bake at 350° for 1½ hours or until meat is tender. Sprinkle with sesame seeds.

1 CUP: 280 cal., 19g fat (7g sat. fat), 70mg chol., 198mg sod., 9g carb. (6g sugars, 2g fiber), 19g pro.

TENDER PORK CHOPS

GYRO SALAD TIPS

Is gyro salad healthy? *Gyro salad is a great way to get in more vegetables, and it's better for you than many gyros—but it's too high in saturated fat and sodium to meet our definition of a healthy recipe. To make the salad healthy, dial back the feta cheese and use ground beef that's at least 90% lean.*

What are some variations of gyro salad? *You can give this recipe a lighter twist by using lean ground chicken or turkey instead of lamb. To make it heartier, grill or toast some pita breads, cut into wedges and toss them into the mix. Or add fresh mint leaves for a refreshing, summer-perfect touch.*

How do you store gyro salad with tzatziki dressing? *Keep the tzatziki dressing separate whenever possible so it doesn't wilt your salad greens. Cover and refrigerate the leftovers for up to 3 days.*

GYRO SALAD WITH TZATZIKI DRESSING

If you're fond of gyros, you'll enjoy this garden-fresh salad showcasing ground lamb, crumbled feta cheese, Greek olives, tomatoes and a creamy cucumber dressing.
—*Taste of Home* Test Kitchen

TAKES: 30 MIN. • **MAKES:** 6 SERVINGS

DRESSING
- 1 cucumber, peeled and coarsely shredded
- ½ tsp. salt
- ½ cup sour cream
- ¾ cup plain yogurt
- 2 Tbsp. white vinegar
- 1 garlic clove, minced
- ½ tsp. dill weed
- ¼ tsp. cracked black pepper

SALAD
- ½ lb. ground lamb or ground beef
- 1 small onion, chopped
- 1 tsp. Greek seasoning or oregano leaves
- 8 cups mixed salad greens
- 2 tomatoes, chopped
- 1 pkg. (4 oz.) crumbled feta cheese
- ½ cup pitted Greek olives, drained
  Toasted pita bread wedges

1. In a large bowl, sprinkle cucumber with salt; mix well. Let stand for 5 minutes. Drain. Stir in remaining dressing ingredients. Cover and refrigerate.

2. In a large skillet over medium-high heat, cook lamb, onion and Greek seasoning until lamb is no longer pink, stirring to break the meat into crumbles; drain.

3. Arrange salad greens on a large serving platter; top with tomatoes, cheese, olives and lamb. Spoon dressing over salad. Serve immediately with toasted pita wedges.

1 SERVING: 236 cal., 16g fat (7g sat. fat), 43mg chol., 807mg sod., 10g carb. (4g sugars, 3g fiber), 14g pro.

PASTA WITH PROSCIUTTO, LETTUCE & PEAS

This elevated pasta dish will make your guests think you spent all day in the kitchen. It's the perfect holiday dish without a lot of work.
—Amy White, Manchester, CT

PREP: 20 MIN. • **COOK:** 15 MIN. • **MAKES:** 8 SERVINGS

1 lb. uncooked campanelle pasta
2 Tbsp. butter
3 Tbsp. olive oil, divided
12 green onions, sliced
1 shallot, finely chopped
½ cup white wine or reduced-sodium chicken broth
½ cup reduced-sodium chicken broth
¼ tsp. salt
⅛ tsp. pepper
1 head Boston lettuce, cut into ¾-in. slices
2 cups fresh or frozen peas
1 cup grated Parmesan cheese
4 oz. thinly sliced prosciutto or deli ham, cut into ½-in. strips
Additional Parmesan cheese, optional

1. Cook pasta according to package directions for al dente.

2. Meanwhile, in a large skillet, heat butter and 2 Tbsp. oil over medium-high heat. Add green onions and shallot; cook and stir until tender. Stir in wine. Bring to a boil; cook and stir 6-8 minutes or until liquid is almost evaporated.

3. Add broth, salt and pepper. Bring to a boil. Reduce heat; stir in lettuce and peas. Cook and stir until lettuce is wilted. Drain pasta; add to pan. Stir in Parmesan cheese and prosciutto; drizzle with remaining oil. If desired, top with additional Parmesan cheese.

1¼ CUPS: 220 cal., 13g fat (5g sat. fat), 29mg chol., 629mg sod., 14g carb. (5g sugars, 5g fiber), 13g pro.

LEBANESE STREET
SANDWICHES

LEBANESE STREET SANDWICHES

Arayes are grilled Lebanese-style pitas that are stuffed with a seasoned meat mixture. They're commonly found throughout the food stalls that line the streets of Beirut. If you'd rather not use a grill, they can be baked in the oven or made in a panini press too.
—Nikki Haddad, Germantown, MD

PREP: 30 MIN. • **GRILL:** 10 MIN. • **MAKES:** 6 SERVINGS

2   large onions, coarsely chopped
1½ cups packed fresh parsley sprigs
1½ lbs. ground beef
1   large egg, lightly beaten
1   tsp. salt
6   whole pita breads
2   Tbsp. olive oil
TAHINI SAUCE
⅓   cup tahini
2   garlic cloves, minced
¼   cup lemon juice
2   Tbsp. water
⅛   tsp. salt

1. Place onions in a food processor; pulse until finely chopped. Remove and pat dry; transfer to a large bowl. Add parsley to processor; pulse until minced. Stir into onions. Add beef, egg and salt; mix lightly but thoroughly.

2. Slice pitas horizontally in half. Spread bottoms with meat mixture to edge. Replace pita tops; press lightly to adhere. Brush outsides of sandwiches with oil. Grill sandwiches, uncovered, over medium heat 10-12 minutes or until a thermometer inserted into meat mixture reads 160°, turning every 2 minutes. Cool slightly before cutting into quarters.

3. Combine sauce ingredients; serve with sandwiches.

1 SERVING: 545 cal., 28g fat (7g sat. fat), 101mg chol., 852mg sod., 42g carb. (3g sugars, 4g fiber), 30g pro.

◇◇◇

CHARD & BACON LINGUINE

I use Swiss chard every way I can, and that includes stirring it into this breezy linguine. When you're short on time, this dish keeps life simple.
—Diane Nemitz, Ludington, MI

TAKES: 30 MIN. • **MAKES:** 4 SERVINGS

8   oz. uncooked whole wheat linguine
4   bacon strips, chopped
4   garlic cloves, minced
½   cup reduced-sodium chicken broth
½   cup dry white wine or additional chicken broth
¼   tsp. salt
6   cups chopped Swiss chard (about 6 oz.)
⅓   cup shredded Parmesan cheese

1. Cook linguine according to package directions; drain. Meanwhile, in a large skillet, cook bacon over medium heat until crisp, stirring occasionally. Add garlic; cook 1 minute longer.

2. Add broth, wine, salt and Swiss chard to skillet; bring to a boil. Cook and stir 4-5 minutes or until chard is tender.

3. Add linguine; heat through, tossing to combine. Sprinkle with cheese.

1 CUP: 353 cal., 14g fat (5g sat. fat), 23mg chol., 633mg sod., 47g carb. (2g sugars, 7g fiber), 14g pro. **DIABETIC EXCHANGES:** 3 starch, 1 vegetable, 1 medium-fat meat.

🍲 MOROCCAN POT ROAST

My husband loves meat and I love veggies, so we're both happy with this spicy twist on beefy pot roast. With garbanzo beans, eggplant, honey and mint, it's like something you'd eat at a Marrakesh bazaar.
—Catherine Dempsey, Clifton Park, NY

PREP: 25 MIN. • **COOK:** 7 HOURS • **MAKES:** 8 SERVINGS

- 2 Tbsp. olive oil
- 3 small onions, chopped
- 3 Tbsp. paprika
- 1 Tbsp. plus ½ tsp. garam masala, divided
- 1¼ tsp. salt, divided
- ¼ tsp. cayenne pepper
- 2 Tbsp. tomato paste
- 1 can (15 oz.) garbanzo beans or chickpeas, rinsed and drained
- 1 can (14½ oz.) beef broth
- ¼ tsp. pepper
- 1 boneless beef chuck roast (3 lbs.)
- 4 medium carrots, cut diagonally into ¾-in. pieces
- 1 small eggplant, cubed
- 2 Tbsp. honey
- 2 Tbsp. minced fresh mint
   Optional: Hot cooked couscous or flatbreads

1. In a large skillet, heat oil over medium heat; saute onions with paprika, 1 Tbsp. garam masala, ½ tsp. salt and cayenne until tender, 4-5 minutes. Stir in tomato paste; cook and stir 1 minute longer. Stir in garbanzo beans and broth; transfer to a 5- or 6-qt. slow cooker.

2. Mix pepper and remaining ½ tsp. garam masala and ¾ tsp. salt; rub over roast. Place in slow cooker. Add carrots and eggplant. Cook, covered, until meat and vegetables are tender, 7-9 hours.

3. Remove roast from slow cooker; break into pieces. Remove vegetables with a slotted spoon; skim fat from cooking juices. Stir in honey. Return beef and vegetables to slow cooker and heat through. Sprinkle with mint. If desired, serve with couscous or flatbreads.

FREEZE OPTION: Freeze cooled beef and vegetable mixture in freezer containers. To use, partially thaw in the refrigerator overnight. Microwave, covered, on high in a microwave-safe dish until heated through, stirring gently.

1 SERVING: 435 cal., 21g fat (7g sat. fat), 111mg chol., 766mg sod., 23g carb. (10g sugars, 6g fiber), 38g pro.

READER REVIEW

"Excellent! I like the shortcut of using the Indian spice blend—garam masala. I added a small zucchini and a handful of golden raisins to the roast. I didn't think it needed the honey."
—ACF7, TASTEOFHOME.COM

MAKE IT YOUR OWN

For a little more bite to your shells, opt for a spicy Italian sausage. Otherwise, try using ground beef or ground chicken in place of the sausage. You could also swap in the minced parsley for basil. Finally, add some finely chopped spinach to get more veggies into the meal.

SAUSAGE-STUFFED SHELLS

I wanted to make manicotti one day but was out of the noodles. So I came up with this recipe, using jumbo shells instead. They were much easier to work with.

—Lori Daniels, Beverly, WV

PREP: 25 MIN. • **BAKE:** 20 MIN. • **MAKES:** 2 SERVINGS

⅓ lb. bulk Italian sausage
1 can (8 oz.) tomato sauce
¼ cup tomato paste
2 Tbsp. water
1 tsp. brown sugar
½ tsp. Italian seasoning
⅓ cup 4% cottage cheese
¾ cup shredded part-skim
   mozzarella cheese, divided
2 Tbsp. beaten egg
½ tsp. minced fresh parsley
6 jumbo pasta shells, cooked
   and drained
   Grated Parmesan cheese, optional

1. Preheat oven to 350°. In a small saucepan, cook sausage over medium heat until no longer pink; drain. Reserve half the sausage for filling. Add tomato sauce, tomato paste, water, brown sugar and Italian seasoning to sausage in pan. Bring to a boil. Reduce heat; simmer, uncovered, 15 minutes, stirring occasionally.

2. In a small bowl, combine cottage cheese, ½ cup mozzarella cheese, egg, parsley and reserved sausage. Stuff into shells. Spread ¼ cup meat sauce in an ungreased 1-qt. shallow baking dish. Place stuffed shells in dish; drizzle with remaining meat sauce.

3. Sprinkle with remaining mozzarella cheese and, if desired, Parmesan cheese. Bake, uncovered, 20-25 minutes or until filling reaches 160°. Garnish with additional parsley.

3 STUFFED SHELLS: 437 cal., 14g fat (7g sat. fat), 67mg chol., 1371mg sod., 40g carb. (13g sugars, 4g fiber), 36g pro.

GROUND BEEF GYROS

If your family likes gyros as much as mine, they'll love this easy version that's made with ground beef instead of lamb. I found the recipe in a newspaper and adapted it to fit our tastes. They're very much like the ones served at a local restaurant. A cucumber yogurt sauce adds an authentic finishing touch.

—Ruth Stahl, Shepherd, MT

TAKES: 30 MIN. • **MAKES:** 4 SERVINGS

1   cup plain yogurt
⅓   cup chopped seeded cucumber
2   Tbsp. finely chopped onion
1   garlic clove, minced
1   tsp. sugar
GYROS
1½ tsp. dried oregano
1   tsp. garlic powder
1   tsp. onion powder
1   tsp. salt, optional
¾   tsp. pepper
1   lb. ground beef
4   pita pocket halves
3   cups shredded lettuce
1   large tomato, chopped
1   small onion, sliced

1. In a small bowl, combine first 5 ingredients; chill. In a large bowl, combine seasonings; crumble beef over mixture and mix lightly but thoroughly. Shape into 4 patties.

2. Grill patties, covered, over medium heat or broil 4 in. from heat for 6-7 minutes on each side or until a thermometer reads 160°. Cut patties into thin slices; stuff into pita halves. Add lettuce, tomato and onion. Serve with yogurt sauce.

1 GYRO: 357 cal., 16g fat (6g sat. fat), 78mg chol., 257mg sod., 27g carb. (7g sugars, 3g fiber), 26g pro.

READER REVIEW

"I was pleasantly surprised how flavorful this was considering so few ingredients go in to season the beef mixture. The gyros turned out amazing! I used sour cream instead of yogurt for the sauce, as that's all I had on hand. I will definitely make it again."

—SHANNONDOBOS, TASTEOFHOME.COM

🍲 TOMATO-TOPPED ITALIAN PORK CHOPS

Time to bring out the slow cooker! You're only seven ingredients away from a delicious meal.
—Krystle Chasse, Radium Hot Springs, BC

PREP: 25 MIN. • **COOK:** 8 HOURS • **MAKES:** 6 SERVINGS

6 bone-in pork loin chops (7 oz. each)
1 Tbsp. canola oil
1 small onion, chopped
½ cup chopped carrot
1 can (14½ oz.) diced tomatoes, drained
¼ cup reduced-fat balsamic vinaigrette
2 tsp. dried oregano

1. In a large skillet, brown chops in oil in batches. Transfer to a 4- or 5-qt. slow cooker coated with cooking spray. Saute onion and carrot in drippings until tender. Stir in tomatoes, vinaigrette and oregano; pour over chops.

2. Cover and cook on low for 8-10 hours or until meat is tender.

1 PORK CHOP: 267 cal., 12g fat (3g sat. fat), 86mg chol., 234mg sod., 7g carb. (4g sugars, 2g fiber), 31g pro. **DIABETIC EXCHANGES:** 4 lean meat, 1 vegetable, 1 fat.

🍲 ⑤ SLAMMIN' LAMB

This meat is easy, flavorful and best when marinated overnight.
You can even mix it up and freeze it until you want to throw it in the cooker!
Make sure you have lots of pita bread on hand to soak up the juices.
—Ruth Hartunian-Alumbaugh, Willimantic, CT

PREP: 20 MIN. + MARINATING • **COOK:** 4 HOURS • **MAKES:** 6 SERVINGS

2 small garlic bulbs
¾ cup plus 2 Tbsp. minced fresh mint, divided
½ cup balsamic vinegar
¼ cup olive oil
2 lbs. boneless lamb, cut into 1-in. cubes
   Hot cooked rice or pita bread, optional

1. Remove papery outer skin from garlic bulbs; cut off tops of bulbs, exposing individual cloves. Peel and halve cloves. In a large dish, combine garlic, ¾ cup mint, vinegar and oil. Add lamb; turn to coat. Cover and refrigerate up to 24 hours.

2. Transfer lamb and marinade to a 3-qt. slow cooker. Cook, covered, on low until meat is tender, 4-5 hours. Sprinkle with remaining mint. Serve with hot cooked rice or pita bread as desired.

1 SERVING: 323 cal., 17g fat (4g sat. fat), 98mg chol., 102mg sod., 10g carb. (6g sugars, 1g fiber), 31g pro.

MEDITERRANEAN KOFTA MEATBALLS

For a new take on meatballs, try this quick version of kofta—*flavorful Mediterranean meatballs full of spices and herbs. Shape meat mixture around soaked wooden skewers and grill them for a more authentic twist.*
—Rashanda Cobbins, Aurora, CO

TAKES: 25 MIN. • **MAKES:** 4 SERVINGS

1   **small onion, chopped**
½   **cup packed fresh parsley sprigs**
¼   **cup fresh mint leaves**
1   **Tbsp. minced fresh oregano**
2   **garlic cloves**
1   **tsp. lemon-pepper seasoning**
½   **tsp. salt**
½   **tsp. paprika**
¼   **tsp. ground cumin**
1   **lb. ground lamb**
1   **Tbsp. canola oil**
    Hot cooked couscous
1   **cup plain Greek yogurt**
2   **plum tomatoes, cut into wedges**
3   **Tbsp. minced red onion**
    Fresh mint leaves
2   **lemons, cut into wedges**

1. Place onion, parsley, mint, oregano and garlic in a food processor. Pulse until minced. In a large bowl, combine herb mixture, lemon pepper, salt, paprika and cumin. Add lamb; mix lightly but thoroughly. With wet hands, shape into 16 balls.

2. In a large skillet, heat oil over medium heat. Brown meatballs in batches; drain. Remove and keep warm. Serve meatballs over cooked couscous. Top with yogurt, tomato wedges and red onion. Garnish with mint leaves and lemon wedges.

4 MEATBALLS WITH ¼ CUP YOGURT AND ½ TOMATO: 339 cal., 24g fat (10g sat. fat), 90mg chol., 482mg sod., 8g carb. (4g sugars, 2g fiber), 22g pro.

READER REVIEW

"These were delicious! We love lamb and are always looking for new ways to make it. We skipped the couscous and served the meatballs with pita bread, tzatziki sauce, cucumber and tomatoes. I will definitely make this again."
—SHAWNBA, TASTEOFHOME.COM

LEHMEJUN (ARMENIAN PIZZA)

This pizza-style recipe came from my friend Ruby's mom, who is a crazy-good cook.
I added my own flair and tweaked it by using flour tortillas instead of making a dough.
—Tamar Yacoubian, Ketchum, ID

PREP: 20 MIN. • **COOK:** 15 MIN. • **MAKES:** 8 SERVINGS

1 lb. ground beef
1 lb. ground lamb
1 medium onion, halved and sliced
1 can (6 oz.) tomato paste
2 jalapeno peppers, seeded and diced
¼ cup minced fresh parsley
2 Tbsp. harissa chili paste
2 Tbsp. dry red wine
1 Tbsp. ground sumac
½ tsp. ground cinnamon
¼ tsp. salt
¼ tsp. pepper
8 flour tortillas (6 in.)
Cooking spray
1 medium lemon, cut in wedges

1. Preheat broiler. In a large skillet, cook and crumble beef and lamb with onion over medium-high heat until meat is no longer pink, 5-7 minutes; drain.

2. Mix together next 9 ingredients. Add to meat mixture; cook, stirring occasionally, until well blended and heated through. Remove from heat.

3. In batches, spritz both sides of tortillas with cooking spray and place on a baking sheet; broil 4-5 in. from heat until crisp and lightly browned, 45-60 seconds per side. Spread meat mixture over tortillas. Serve with lemon wedges.

NOTE: Wear disposable gloves when cutting hot peppers; the oils can burn skin. Avoid touching your face.

1 FILLED TORTILLA: 371 cal., 19g fat (7g sat. fat), 72mg chol., 464mg sod., 24g carb. (3g sugars, 3g fiber), 24g pro.

PORK WITH ARTICHOKES & CAPERS

After dating my husband for a month, I wanted to impress him with my cooking.
When I fixed this recipe, it convinced him I was "the one"!
—Lindy Bonnell, Loveland, CO

PREP: 20 MIN. • **COOK:** 20 MIN. • **MAKES:** 4 SERVINGS

2 pork tenderloins (¾ lb. each)
1 Tbsp. butter
1 green onion, finely chopped
1 can (14 oz.) water-packed artichoke hearts, rinsed, drained and chopped
¼ cup reduced-sodium chicken broth
1 Tbsp. capers, drained
1 tsp. Dijon mustard
1 Tbsp. minced fresh parsley
Lemon slices

1. Cut pork into 1-in. slices; flatten to ¼-in. thickness. In a large nonstick skillet over medium heat, cook pork in butter in batches until tender. Transfer to a serving platter and keep warm.

2. In same skillet, cook and stir onion until tender. Stir in artichokes, broth, capers and mustard; heat through. Serve over pork; sprinkle with parsley. Garnish with lemon.

1 SERVING: 263 cal., 9g fat (4g sat. fat), 102mg chol., 479mg sod., 7g carb. (0 sugars, 0 fiber), 37g pro. **DIABETIC EXCHANGES:** 5 lean meat, 1 vegetable.

LEHMEJUN
(ARMENIAN PIZZA)

PILE ON THE VEGGIES

If you want more toppings on this Armenian-style pizza, sprinkle them over the meat mixture, then fold the lehmejun in half to eat. It's great with tomatoes, peppers, onions and roasted eggplant.

GREEK OUZO PORK KABOBS

Do dinner like the Mediterraneans with these delightfully different kabobs. The ouzo,
an anise-flavored liqueur, and the tzatziki dipping sauce give you a real taste of the Greek islands.
—Francine Lizotte, Langley, BC

PREP: 25 MIN. + MARINATING • **GRILL:** 15 MIN. • **MAKES:** 6 SERVINGS

½ cup olive oil
¼ cup lemon juice
¼ cup honey
2 Tbsp. balsamic vinegar
1 Tbsp. minced garlic
1 Tbsp. minced fresh oregano or
   1 tsp. dried oregano
1 Tbsp. minced fresh thyme or
   1 tsp. dried thyme
1½ tsp. minced fresh rosemary or
   ¾ tsp. dried rosemary, crushed
½ tsp. salt
¼ tsp. pepper
¼ cup ouzo or anise liqueur
2 lbs. pork tenderloin, cut into
   1½-in. cubes
2 large sweet yellow or green
   peppers, cut into 1½-in. pieces
24 cherry tomatoes
1 large red or sweet onion, cut into
   1½-in. pieces
   Optional: Lettuce leaves,
   crumbled feta cheese and
   refrigerated tzatziki sauce

1. In a small bowl, whisk the first 10 ingredients until blended. Pour ½ cup marinade into a shallow dish; stir in ouzo. Add pork; turn to coat. Refrigerate 8 hours or overnight. Cover and refrigerate remaining marinade.

2. Drain pork, discarding marinade in dish. On 12 metal or soaked wooden skewers, alternately thread pork and vegetables. Grill kabobs, uncovered, over medium heat or broil 4 in. from heat until pork is tender and vegetables are crisp-tender, 12-15 minutes, turning occasionally and basting frequently with remaining marinade during the last 5 minutes. If desired, serve on lettuce leaves with crumbled feta and tzatziki sauce.

2 KABOBS: 336 cal., 15g fat (3g sat. fat), 85mg chol., 178mg sod., 17g carb. (13g sugars, 2g fiber), 32g pro. **DIABETIC EXCHANGES:** 4 lean meat, 2 fat, 1 vegetable, ½ starch.

RACK OF LAMB WITH FIGS

I've been making rack of lamb for years. My grandma gave me this recipe because she knew how much I love figs. And the toasted walnuts sprinkled on top give it just the right finishing touch.
—Sylvia Castanon, Long Beach, CA

PREP: 30 MIN. • **BAKE:** 45 MIN. • **MAKES:** 8 SERVINGS

2 racks of lamb (2 lbs. each)
1 tsp. salt, divided
1 cup water
1 small onion, finely chopped
1 Tbsp. canola oil
1 garlic clove, minced
2 Tbsp. cornstarch
1 cup port wine, or ½ cup grape juice plus ½ cup reduced-sodium beef broth
10 dried figs, halved
¼ tsp. pepper
½ cup coarsely chopped walnuts, toasted
   Chopped fresh parsley, optional

1. Rub lamb with ½ tsp. salt. Place meat side up on a rack in a greased roasting pan. Bake, uncovered, at 375° for 45-60 minutes or until meat reaches desired doneness (for medium-rare, a thermometer should read 135°; medium, 140°; medium-well, 145°).

2. Remove to a serving platter; cover loosely with foil. Add 1 cup water to roasting pan; stir to loosen browned bits from pan. Using a fine sieve, strain mixture; set drippings aside.

3. In a small saucepan, saute onion in oil until tender. Add garlic; cook 1 minute longer. Stir in cornstarch until blended; gradually add wine, drippings, figs, pepper and remaining salt. Bring to a boil. Reduce heat to medium-low; cook, uncovered, until figs are tender and sauce is thickened, about 10 minutes, stirring occasionally.

4. Sprinkle walnuts over lamb; serve with fig sauce. If desired, top with chopped parsley.

2 LAMB CHOPS: 363 cal., 16g fat (4g sat. fat), 66mg chol., 362mg sod., 23g carb. (14g sugars, 3g fiber), 23g pro.

HERBED PUMPKIN FLATBREAD,
PAGE 223

SIDE DISHES

*These standout dishes will turn a good entree
into a great meal. So go ahead and grab seconds ...
these bright sides are just too tasty to pass up.*

SPICED PEARL COUSCOUS WITH PINE NUTS

This side dish is great for entertaining, as you can prepare the topping ahead of time, and the couscous takes only minutes. Try adding a cup of drained and rinsed garbanzo beans to boost the protein!

—Cindy Beberman, Orland Park, IL

TAKES: 30 MIN. • **MAKES:** 4 SERVINGS

2 Tbsp. olive oil
1¾ cups finely chopped sweet onions
1½ cups uncooked pearl (Israeli) couscous
1¾ cups water
¾ tsp. salt
½ tsp. ground cinnamon
½ tsp. curry powder
¼ tsp. ground cumin
¼ tsp. ground coriander
⅓ cup dried currants
¼ cup minced fresh cilantro
2 Tbsp. finely chopped mint leaves
2 tsp. grated lemon zest
⅓ cup pine nuts, toasted
Lemon wedges, optional

1. In a large saucepan, heat oil over medium heat. Add onions; cook and stir until tender, 6-8 minutes. Add couscous; cook and stir until couscous is lightly browned, 2-3 minutes.

2. Add water, salt, cinnamon, curry powder, cumin and coriander; bring to a boil. Reduce heat; simmer covered until liquid is absorbed and couscous is tender, 7-10 minutes. Stir in currants, cilantro, mint and lemon zest; let stand 5 minutes. Fluff with a fork. Sprinkle with toasted pine nuts. If desired, serve with lemon wedges.

1 CUP: 414 cal., 15g fat (2g sat. fat), 0 chol., 449mg sod., 63g carb. (12g sugars, 3g fiber), 10g pro.

---

⑤ BRUSSELS SPROUTS WITH GOLDEN RAISINS

Take a break from ordinary steamed Brussels sprouts by combining them with raisins and a slightly tart dressing. Thinly slicing the sprouts makes them appeal to people who normally don't like the texture.

—Michaela Rosenthal, Indio, CA

TAKES: 30 MIN. • **MAKES:** 5 SERVINGS

1 lb. fresh Brussels sprouts, thinly sliced
1 Tbsp. olive oil
2 Tbsp. water
¼ tsp. celery salt
⅛ tsp. white pepper
⅓ cup golden raisins
1 tsp. white balsamic vinegar

In a large skillet, saute Brussels sprouts in oil until crisp-tender. Add water, celery salt and pepper. Reduce heat; cover and cook for 4-5 minutes or until tender. Stir in raisins and vinegar.

⅔ CUP: 93 cal., 3g fat (0 sat. fat), 0 chol., 98mg sod., 16g carb. (8g sugars, 4g fiber), 3g pro. **DIABETIC EXCHANGES:** 1 vegetable, ½ fruit, ½ fat.

SPICED PEARL COUSCOUS WITH PINE NUTS

ZUCCHINI FRIES

These aren't anything like potato fries—in a good way! They are air-fried to crispy perfection and oh, so flavorful. Enjoy them as an appetizer or a low-carb alternative to french fries. Don't have an air fryer? You can convection-bake the fries for the same time.

—Jen Pahl, West Allis, WI

PREP: 20 MIN. • **COOK:** 10 MIN./BATCH • **MAKES:** 4 SERVINGS

2 medium zucchini
1 cup panko bread crumbs
2 tsp. dried basil, divided
1½ tsp. seasoned salt
1 tsp. garlic powder
1 tsp. dried oregano
½ cup plus 2 Tbsp. grated
   Parmesan cheese, divided
2 large eggs, lightly beaten
   Cooking spray
   Marinara sauce, warmed

1. Preheat air fryer to 375°. Cut each zucchini in half lengthwise and then in half crosswise. Cut each piece lengthwise into ¼-in. slices.

2. In a shallow bowl, mix panko, 1 tsp. basil, salt, garlic powder, oregano and ½ cup Parmesan. Place eggs and remaining 1 tsp. basil in a separate shallow bowl. Dip zucchini slices in egg mixture and then in crumb mixture, patting to help coating adhere.

3. In batches, place zucchini in a single layer on greased tray in air-fryer basket; spritz with cooking spray. Cook until lightly browned, 6-8 minutes. Flip each piece; fry until golden brown, 3-5 minutes longer.

4. Sprinkle hot fries with remaining 2 Tbsp. Parmesan and serve with marinara sauce.

1 CUP: 91 cal., 4g fat (2g sat. fat), 52mg chol., 389mg sod., 9g carb. (2g sugars, 1g fiber), 6g pro. **DIABETIC EXCHANGES:** 1 vegetable, 1 fat.

CLEANING THE COIL

Oil or residue on the air fryer's heating coil can cause smoking and odors. To clean, unplug and cool the machine, then wipe the coil with a damp cloth— just like an electric stove's heating element.

🍲 SLOW-COOKED RATATOUILLE

I get my son to eat eggplant by cooking this classic French veggie dish low and slow. A side of rice and some garlic cheese bread also help.
—Diane Goedde, Red Lodge, MT

PREP: 25 MIN. + STANDING • **COOK:** 5 HOURS • **MAKES:** 10 SERVINGS

1 medium eggplant, peeled and cut into 1-in. cubes
1 Tbsp. plus 1 tsp. salt, divided
2 medium onions, halved and thinly sliced
4 medium tomatoes, chopped
3 medium zucchini, cut into ¾-in. slices
2 celery ribs, chopped
3 Tbsp. olive oil
2 tsp. dried basil or 2 Tbsp. minced fresh basil
4 garlic cloves, minced
½ tsp. pepper
1 can (6 oz.) tomato paste
1 can (2¼ oz.) sliced ripe olives, drained
⅓ cup coarsely chopped fresh basil

1. Place eggplant in a strainer over a plate; sprinkle with 1 Tbsp. salt and toss. Let stand 45 minutes. Rinse and drain well; blot dry with paper towels.

2. Place eggplant and remaining vegetables in a 5- or 6-qt. slow cooker. Add oil, basil, garlic, pepper and remaining 1 tsp. salt; toss to combine.

3. Cook, covered, on low 5-6 hours or until onions are tender. Stir in tomato paste, olives and fresh basil; heat through.

FREEZE OPTION: Freeze cooled ratatouille in freezer containers. To use, partially thaw in refrigerator overnight. Microwave, covered, on high in a microwave-safe dish until heated through, stirring gently.

¾ CUP: 102 cal., 5g fat (1g sat. fat), 0 chol., 380mg sod., 13g carb. (7g sugars, 4g fiber), 3g pro. **DIABETIC EXCHANGES:** 2 vegetable, 1 fat.

READER REVIEW
"Delicious! Best slow-cooked version I have found. I serve it with pasta as a side with fish."
—MARY4057, TASTEOFHOME.COM

GOLDEN GREEK LEMON POTATOES

This recipe was inspired by a tiny Greek restaurant we used to go to during grad school.
To make the potatoes extra delicious, use a high-quality olive oil and a nice kosher or sea salt.
—Karol Chandler-Ezell, Nacogdoches, TX

TAKES: 30 MIN. • MAKES: 4 SERVINGS

2 Tbsp. olive oil
1 Tbsp. butter
¼ cup chopped onion
1¼ lbs. baby Yukon Gold potatoes
¼ cup water
3 Tbsp. minced fresh chives or
 2 green onions, thinly sliced
1½ tsp. Greek seasoning
1 to 1½ tsp. grated lemon zest
1 garlic clove, minced
½ tsp. pepper
¼ tsp. kosher salt
1 to 2 Tbsp. lemon juice
1 Tbsp. minced fresh parsley

1. In a small skillet, heat oil and butter over medium heat. Add onion; cook and stir 1-2 minutes or until softened. Reduce heat to medium-low; cook until deep golden brown, 12-15 minutes, stirring occasionally.

2. Meanwhile, place potatoes and water in a large microwave-safe dish. Microwave, covered, on high until tender, 6-8 minutes.

3. Add chives, Greek seasoning, lemon zest, garlic, pepper and salt to onion mixture; cook and stir 1 minute longer. Drain potatoes; add onion mixture. Flatten potatoes with a fork, tossing them to coat with onion mixture. Add lemon juice and parsley; toss to combine.

1 SERVING: 219 cal., 10g fat (3g sat. fat), 8mg chol., 523mg sod., 30g carb. (3g sugars, 3g fiber), 4g pro.

ARUGULA PESTO

Arugula pesto is garden-fresh goodness. If your greens are too peppery,
substitute spinach for half of the arugula to balance it out beautifully.
—Courtney Stultz, Weir, KS

TAKES: 10 MIN. • MAKES: ¾ CUP

4 cups fresh arugula
1 cup fresh basil leaves
½ cup grated Parmesan cheese
¼ cup pine nuts
½ tsp. minced garlic
1 tsp. sea salt
½ cup olive oil

Pulse first 6 ingredients in a food processor until chopped. While processing, gradually add oil in a steady stream until mixture is smooth. Store tightly covered in refrigerator; use within 5 days.

2 TBSP.: 43 cal., 4g fat (0 sat. fat), 0 chol., 324mg sod., 1g carb. (0 sugars, 1g fiber), 1g pro.
DIABETIC EXCHANGES: 1 fat.

HERBED PUMPKIN FLATBREAD

HERBED PUMPKIN FLATBREAD

These flatbreads benefit from the flavor and texture of pumpkin, and herbs provide an autumnal twist. They are great served with soup or salad, and of course with curries. The chickpea flour adds a protein boost and unique flavor.
—Kayla Capper, Ojai, CA

PREP: 20 MIN. + STANDING • **COOK:** 5 MIN./BATCH • **MAKES:** 4 SERVINGS

1 cup all-purpose flour
½ cup chickpea flour
1 tsp. garlic salt
½ tsp. dried rosemary, crushed
¼ tsp. baking powder
¼ tsp. dried thyme
½ cup canned pumpkin
1 Tbsp. plus 2 tsp. canola oil, divided
1 tsp. water
Optional: Fresh thyme, fresh rosemary and tzatziki sauce

1. In a bowl, whisk first 6 ingredients. Add pumpkin, 1 Tbsp. oil and water; stir until mixture resembles coarse crumbs. Turn onto a floured surface; knead 8-10 times, forming a soft dough. Cover and let rest 15 minutes.

2. Divide dough into 4 pieces. On a lightly floured surface, roll each piece into a 6-in. circle. Brush flatbreads on both sides with remaining 2 tsp. oil. Heat a large skillet over medium-high heat. Working in batches, cook flatbreads 1-2 minutes on each side or until golden brown. Serve warm; if desired, top with fresh thyme and rosemary and serve with tzatziki sauce.

1 FLATBREAD: 231 cal., 7g fat (1g sat. fat), 0 chol., 525mg sod., 35g carb. (3g sugars, 4g fiber), 7g pro.

STUFFED GRILLED ZUCCHINI

Pair these zucchini boats with charred pork chops, smoked fish or other grilled greats.
—Nancy Zimmerman, Cape May Court House, NJ

PREP: 25 MIN. • **GRILL:** 10 MIN. • **MAKES:** 4 SERVINGS

4 medium zucchini
5 tsp. olive oil, divided
2 Tbsp. finely chopped red onion
¼ tsp. minced garlic
½ cup dry bread crumbs
½ cup shredded part-skim mozzarella cheese
1 Tbsp. minced fresh mint
½ tsp. salt
3 Tbsp. grated Parmesan cheese

1. Cut zucchini in half lengthwise; scoop out flesh, leaving ¼-in. shells. Brush with 2 tsp. oil; set aside. Chop zucchini flesh.

2. In a large skillet, saute flesh and onion in remaining oil. Add garlic; cook 1 minute longer. Add bread crumbs; cook and stir until golden brown, about 2 minutes.

3. Remove from heat. Stir in mozzarella cheese, mint and salt. Spoon into zucchini shells. Sprinkle with Parmesan cheese.

4. Grill, covered, over medium heat until zucchini is tender, 8-10 minutes.

2 STUFFED ZUCCHINI HALVES: 186 cal., 10g fat (3g sat. fat), 11mg chol., 553mg sod., 17g carb. (4g sugars, 3g fiber), 9g pro. **DIABETIC EXCHANGES:** 1 vegetable, 1 lean meat, 1 fat, ½ starch.

ROASTED BEETS WITH ORANGE GREMOLATA & GOAT CHEESE

My grandma always grew beets then pickled or canned them, but I prefer to prepare them differently.
—Courtney Archibeque, Greeley, CO

PREP: 25 MIN. • **BAKE:** 55 MIN. + COOLING • **MAKES:** 12 SERVINGS

3 medium fresh golden beets (about 1 lb.)
3 medium fresh beets (about 1 lb.)
2 Tbsp. lime juice
2 Tbsp. orange juice
½ tsp. fine sea salt
1 Tbsp. minced fresh parsley
1 Tbsp. minced fresh sage
1 garlic clove, minced
1 tsp. grated orange zest
3 Tbsp. crumbled goat cheese
2 Tbsp. sunflower kernels

1. Preheat oven to 400°. Scrub beets and trim tops by 1 in. Place beets on a double thickness of heavy-duty foil (about 24x12 in.). Fold foil around beets, sealing tightly. Place on a baking sheet. Roast until tender, 55-65 minutes. Open foil carefully to allow steam to escape.

2. When cool enough to handle, peel, halve and slice beets; place in a serving bowl. Add lime juice, orange juice and salt; toss to coat. Combine parsley, sage, garlic and orange zest; sprinkle over beets. Top with goat cheese and sunflower kernels. Serve warm or chilled.

¾ CUP: 49 cal., 1g fat (0 sat. fat), 2mg chol., 157mg sod., 9g carb. (6g sugars, 2g fiber), 2g pro. **DIABETIC EXCHANGES:** 1 vegetable.

---

⑤ CILANTRO POTATOES

Fresh cilantro gives an exotic Syrian-style flavor to these easy, delicious skillet potatoes. They're a creative complement to Mom's tangy kabobs.
—Weda Mosellie, Phillipsburg, NJ

PREP: 25 MIN. • **COOK:** 20 MIN. • **MAKES:** 8 SERVINGS

1 bunch fresh cilantro, chopped
1 garlic clove, minced
¼ cup olive oil
3 lbs. potatoes, peeled and cubed
½ tsp. salt

In a large cast-iron or other heavy skillet, cook cilantro and garlic in oil over medium heat for 1 minute. Add potatoes; cook and stir until tender and lightly browned, 20-25 minutes. Drain. Sprinkle with salt.

¾ CUP: 160 cal., 7g fat (1g sat. fat), 0 chol., 153mg sod., 23g carb. (2g sugars, 2g fiber), 2g pro. **DIABETIC EXCHANGES:** 1½ starch, 1½ fat.

HONEY
BAKED
LENTILS

HONEY BAKED LENTILS

This recipe originally had bacon in it, but I eliminated it in order to make a vegetarian dish. I added liquid smoke and additional vegetables. Serve the side with brown rice and additional soy sauce.

—Suzanne Rumsey, Fort Wayne, IN

PREP: 30 MIN. • **BAKE:** 1 HOUR • **MAKES:** 10 SERVINGS

- 1 pkg. (16 oz.) dried lentils, rinsed
- 6 cups water, divided
- 2 tsp. salt
- 1 bay leaf
- 2 cups chopped onions
- 4 medium carrots, finely chopped
- 1 Tbsp. reduced-sodium soy sauce
- 1 tsp. ground mustard
- 1 tsp. liquid smoke
- ¼ tsp. ground ginger
- ⅓ cup honey

1. Preheat oven to 350°. In a large saucepan, combine lentils, 5 cups water, salt and bay leaf. Bring to a boil. Reduce heat; cover and simmer until lentils are tender, 20-25 minutes. Discard bay leaf.

2. In a large bowl, combine onions, carrots, soy sauce, mustard, liquid smoke, ginger and remaining water. Gently stir in lentils. Transfer to a greased 13x9-in. baking dish. Drizzle with honey.

3. Bake, covered, 30 minutes. Uncover; bake until carrots are tender, 30-35 minutes longer.

¾ CUP: 219 cal., 1g fat (0 sat. fat), 0 chol., 551mg sod., 43g carb. (13g sugars, 6g fiber), 12g pro.

---

⑤ SPANAKOPITA MASHED POTATOES

I learned to cook by watching my mom in the kitchen. Most of the recipes I make use only five or six ingredients and have a healthier bent. I created this recipe after I tried a spinach-topped baked potato. Flecks of red and green from the potato skin and spinach make these potatoes look festive and special. By not peeling the potatoes, you not only keep some nutrients, but you also save on prep time.

—Ashley Laymon, Lititz, PA

PREP: 10 MIN. • **COOK:** 25 MIN. • **MAKES:** 6 SERVINGS

- 6 medium red potatoes, quartered
- 1 pkg. (6 oz.) fresh baby spinach
- ¼ cup 2% milk
- 1 Tbsp. butter
- ½ tsp. salt
- ½ tsp. pepper
- ¾ cup crumbled feta cheese

1. Place potatoes in a large saucepan and cover with water. Bring to a boil. Reduce heat; cover and cook for 15-20 minutes or until tender.

2. Meanwhile, in another large saucepan, bring ½ in. water to a boil. Add spinach; cover and boil for 3-5 minutes or until wilted. Drain and coarsely chop; keep warm.

3. Drain potatoes and return to the saucepan. Add milk, butter, salt and pepper; mash until smooth. Fold in cheese and spinach.

¾ CUP: 145 cal., 5g fat (3g sat. fat), 13mg chol., 379mg sod., 20g carb. (2g sugars, 3g fiber), 6g pro. **DIABETIC EXCHANGES:** 1 starch, 1 fat.

5i SYRIAN GREEN BEANS WITH FRESH HERBS

This how my mom always made green beans. She got the recipe from a neighbor when we lived in Turkey. Make a double batch, as they make an excellent healthy snack straight from the fridge. Add a thinly sliced onion and red bell pepper if you like. You can also make them ahead and add to a salad.

—Trisha Kruse, Eagle, ID

TAKES: 25 MIN. • **MAKES:** 6 SERVINGS

- **2 Tbsp. olive oil**
- **2 garlic cloves, minced**
- **1 lb. fresh green beans, cut into 2-in. pieces**
- **½ tsp. salt**
- **¼ tsp. pepper**
- **2 Tbsp. each minced fresh cilantro, parsley and mint**

In a large skillet, heat oil over medium heat. Add garlic; cook 1 minute. Add green beans, salt and pepper. Cook, covered, until crisp-tender, 8-10 minutes, stirring occasionally. Add herbs; cook and stir just until beans are tender, 1-2 minutes.

¾ CUP: 66 cal., 5g fat (1g sat. fat), 0 chol., 203mg sod., 6g carb. (2g sugars, 3g fiber), 2g pro. **DIABETIC EXCHANGES:** 1 vegetable, 1 fat.

5i CUMIN-ROASTED CARROTS

Carrots make a super side—they are big on flavor and a breeze to cook. Plus, I can actually get my husband to eat these spiced veggies.

—Taylor Kiser, Brandon, FL

PREP: 20 MIN. • **COOK:** 35 MIN. • **MAKES:** 12 SERVINGS

- **2 Tbsp. coriander seeds**
- **2 Tbsp. cumin seeds**
- **3 lbs. carrots, peeled and cut into 4x½-in. sticks**
- **3 Tbsp. coconut oil or butter, melted**
- **8 garlic cloves, minced**
- **1 tsp. salt**
- **½ tsp. pepper**
- **Minced fresh cilantro, optional**

1. Preheat oven to 400°. In a dry small skillet, toast coriander and cumin seeds over medium heat 45-60 seconds or until aromatic, stirring frequently. Cool slightly. Grind in a spice grinder, or with a mortar and pestle, until finely crushed.

2. Place carrots in a large bowl. Add coconut oil, garlic, salt, pepper and spices; toss to coat. Divide carrots between two 15x10x1-in. baking pans coated with cooking spray, spreading evenly.

3. Roast 35-40 minutes or until crisp-tender and lightly browned, stirring and rotating pans halfway through cooking. Sprinkle with cilantro if desired.

NOTE: You may substitute ground coriander and ground cumin (about 4 tsp. each) for the whole spices. Before using, toast ground spices in a dry skillet until aromatic, stirring frequently.

1 SERVING: 86 cal., 4g fat (3g sat. fat), 0 chol., 277mg sod., 13g carb. (5g sugars, 4g fiber), 1g pro. **DIABETIC EXCHANGES:** 1 vegetable, 1 fat.

SYRIAN GREEN BEANS
WITH FRESH HERBS

VEGETABLE TIAN

This colorful, hearty and delicious dish originated in Provence, France. A mandoline makes easy work of slicing all the vegetables but a knife will work just fine if you don't have one.

—Francine Lizotte, Langley, BC

PREP: 1 HOUR • **BAKE:** 1¼ HOURS + STANDING • **MAKES:** 8 SERVINGS

1 cup panko bread crumbs
2 cups finely chopped red onions
2 Tbsp. olive oil
3 garlic cloves, minced
½ tsp. crushed red pepper flakes
2 Tbsp. dry red wine
½ small butternut squash
   (about ¾ lb.), peeled
2 large russet potatoes
1 large zucchini
2 large tomatoes
2 Tbsp. fresh lemon juice
1½ tsp. herbes de Provence
1 tsp. sea salt or Himalayan pink salt
1 tsp. coarsely ground pepper

TOPPING
1 cup shredded Gruyere cheese
½ cup panko bread crumbs
2 Tbsp. clarified butter or ghee,
   melted

1. Preheat oven to 400°. Lightly grease a 10-in. cast-iron skillet; sprinkle with 1 cup panko bread crumbs. In another skillet, cook onions in oil over medium heat until tender, 4-5 minutes. Add garlic and red pepper flakes; cook 1 minute longer. Stir in red wine; cook until mixture is almost dry, 1-2 minutes. Spread onion mixture in the bottom of prepared cast-iron pan; set aside.

2. With a mandoline or sharp knife, cut squash, potatoes, zucchini and tomatoes into ¼-in.-thick slices. On a flat surface, layer vegetables into stacks, starting with a potato slice, tomato, squash and zucchini. Arrange stacks on their sides around outside edge of prepared skillet in a circular pattern. Make a second, alternating circle in the center. Drizzle lemon juice over vegetables and sprinkle with herbes de Provence, salt and pepper. Cover with foil; bake until vegetables are almost tender, about 1 hour. Meanwhile, in a small bowl, combine cheese, ½ cup panko and clarified butter.

3. Remove foil; sprinkle with topping. Bake until cheese is melted and starting to brown, about 15 minutes. Remove and let stand at least 10 minutes before serving.

1 PIECE: 287 cal., 12g fat (6g sat. fat), 26mg chol., 387mg sod., 36g carb. (6g sugars, 6g fiber), 9g pro.

AIR-FRYER GREEK BREADSTICKS

Get ready for rave reviews. These crisp breadsticks are twisted with Greek-inspired goodness and are best served warm with cool tzatziki sauce.

—Jane Whittaker, Pensacola, FL

PREP: 20 MIN. • **COOK:** 15 MIN./BATCH • **MAKES:** 32 BREADSTICKS

¼ cup marinated quartered artichoke hearts, drained
2 Tbsp. pitted Greek olives
1 pkg. (17.3 oz.) frozen puff pastry, thawed
1 carton (6½ oz.) spreadable spinach and artichoke cream cheese
2 Tbsp. grated Parmesan cheese
1 large egg
1 Tbsp. water
2 tsp. sesame seeds
  Refrigerated tzatziki sauce, optional

1. Preheat air fryer to 325°. Place artichokes and olives in a food processor; cover and pulse until finely chopped. Unfold 1 pastry sheet on a lightly floured surface; spread half the cream cheese over half the pastry. Top with half the artichoke mixture. Sprinkle with half the Parmesan cheese. Fold plain half over filling; press gently to seal.

2. Repeat with remaining pastry, cream cheese, artichoke mixture and Parmesan cheese. Whisk egg and water; brush over tops. Sprinkle with sesame seeds. Cut each rectangle into sixteen ¾-in.-wide strips. Twist each strip several times.

3. In batches, arrange breadsticks in a single layer on greased tray in air-fryer basket. Cook until golden brown, 12-15 minutes. Serve warm with tzatziki sauce if desired.

1 BREADSTICK: 99 cal., 6g fat (2g sat. fat), 11mg chol., 108mg sod., 9g carb. (0 sugars, 1g fiber), 2g pro.

BAKE 'EM INSTEAD

If you don't have an air fryer, you can bake these at 400° until golden brown, 12-14 minutes.

⑤ⓘ BULGUR WITH PINE NUTS

Bulgur wheat is not only good for you ... it's great for your budget!
Here our culinary experts use simple ingredients to flavor it wonderfully.
—*Taste of Home* Test Kitchen

TAKES: 20 MIN. • **MAKES:** 4 SERVINGS

1 cup uncooked bulgur
2 cups chicken broth
3 Tbsp. chopped green onions
¼ cup pine nuts, toasted

1. In a large saucepan, combine bulgur, broth and onions; bring to a boil over high heat. Reduce heat; cover and simmer for 15-18 minutes or until broth is absorbed. Add pine nuts; stir to combine.

½ CUP: 177 cal., 5g fat (1g sat. fat), 0 chol., 472mg sod., 29g carb. (1g sugars, 7g fiber), 7g pro.

KALE & FENNEL SKILLET

I love to mix different vegetables together and use a variety of herbs and spices to change things up. If you can't find apple sausage for this skillet, a good mild Italian sausage would work too.
—Patricia Levenson, Santa Ana, CA

PREP: 10 MIN. • **COOK:** 25 MIN. • **MAKES:** 6 SERVINGS

2 Tbsp. extra virgin olive oil
1 small onion, thinly sliced
1 small fennel bulb, thinly sliced
½ lb. fully cooked apple chicken sausage links or cooked Italian sausage links, halved lengthwise and sliced into half-moons
2 garlic cloves, minced
3 Tbsp. dry sherry or dry white wine
1 Tbsp. herbes de Provence
⅛ tsp. salt
⅛ tsp. pepper
1 bunch kale, trimmed and torn into bite-sized pieces

1. In a large cast-iron or other heavy skillet, heat olive oil over medium-high heat. Add onion and fennel; cook and stir 6-8 minutes or until onion begins to brown. Add sausage, garlic, sherry and seasonings; cook until sausage starts to caramelize, 4-6 minutes.

2. Add kale; cook, covered, stirring occasionally, until kale is tender, 15-17 minutes.

NOTE: Look for herbes de Provence in the spice aisle.

¾ CUP: 167 cal., 8g fat (2g sat. fat), 27mg chol., 398mg sod., 16g carb. (6g sugars, 3g fiber), 9g pro. **DIABETIC EXCHANGES:** 2 vegetable, 1 lean meat, 1 fat.

GREEK-STYLE STUFFED ACORN SQUASH

*With a truckload of acorn squash in my pantry, I wanted to make stuffed squash
in lots of different ways. A bottle of Greek seasoning got my creativity flowing.*
—Teri Rasey-Schloessmann, Tulsa, OK

PREP: 45 MIN. • **BAKE:** 30 MIN. • **MAKES:** 12 SERVINGS

3   medium acorn squash, halved
    and seeds removed
1   cup lentils
2   cups chicken broth
¾   cup uncooked orzo pasta
1   lb. bulk pork sausage
½   cup crumbled feta cheese
2   tsp. Greek seasoning
2   Tbsp. all-purpose flour
1   cup french-fried onions
    Additional crumbled feta cheese,
    optional

1. Preheat oven to 350°. Place squash halves, cut side up, on a large baking sheet; roast until they can just be pierced with a fork, about 40 minutes. Remove to a wire rack to cool.

2. Meanwhile, place lentils in a large saucepan; add water to cover. Bring to a boil. Reduce heat; cook, covered, until tender, 20-25 minutes. Drain. Remove and set aside. In the same saucepan, bring chicken broth to a boil. Add orzo; cook according to package directions for al dente. Drain, reserving broth.

3. In a large skillet, cook sausage, crumbling meat, until no longer pink, 6-8 minutes; drain. Add lentils and orzo to skillet; remove from heat. Add feta cheese and Greek seasoning; mix well.

4. Pour reserved chicken broth back into saucepan. Over medium heat, whisk in flour until thickened, then pour into sausage mixture.

5. When cool enough to handle, quarter squash and return to baking sheet. Top with sausage mixture. Bake until squash are tender, about 30 minutes. Before serving, sprinkle with french-fried onions and, if desired, additional crumbled feta.

1 SERVING: 335 cal., 14g fat (4g sat. fat), 29mg chol., 704mg sod., 41g carb. (5g sugars, 5g fiber), 13g pro.

READER REVIEW
"Delish! Didn't have acorn squash, so I used butternut, scooping out the squash in the neck and mixing it in with filling to make a bigger pocket for the stuffing."
—CAROL353, TASTEOFHOME.COM

⑤ SWEET POTATO LATKES

I have great memories of making this recipe for family holidays. Shredded russet potatoes can be used instead of sweet for a change of pace. Serve these with sour cream, applesauce or a sprinkling of chopped chives.
—Paula Freud, Minden, NV

PREP: 15 MIN. • **COOK:** 5 MIN./BATCH • **MAKES:** 8 SERVINGS

1   medium onion, finely chopped
¼   cup all-purpose flour
¾   tsp. salt
¼   tsp. pepper
2   large eggs, lightly beaten
2   lbs. medium sweet potatoes, peeled and shredded
½   cup peanut or canola oil
    Optional: Minced chives, sour cream and applesauce

1. In a large bowl, combine the first 4 ingredients. Stir in eggs until blended. Add potatoes; toss to coat.

2. Heat ¼ cup oil in a large nonstick skillet over medium heat. Drop batter by ¼ cupfuls into oil; press lightly to flatten. Fry in batches until golden brown on both sides, using remaining oil as needed. Drain on paper towels. If desired, top with minced chives and serve with sour cream and applesauce.

2 LATKES: 259 cal., 15g fat (3g sat. fat), 47mg chol., 250mg sod., 28g carb. (11g sugars, 3g fiber), 4g pro.

OVERNIGHT HERBED RATATOUILLE

When I lived in Florida, I went for dinner at a friend's home. His wife, who is Greek, served a beautiful side dish that she called an eggplant fan, and she shared the recipe with me. While I've made her version many times with success, I was inspired by the movie Ratatouille *and created this version.*
—Joe Sherwood, Tryon, NE

PREP: 30 MIN. + CHILLING • **BAKE:** 45 MIN. • **MAKES:** 13 SERVINGS

1   small eggplant
2   small zucchini
2   small yellow summer squash
4   plum tomatoes
1   large sweet onion
½   cup butter, melted
½   cup minced fresh parsley
3   garlic cloves, minced
½   tsp. salt
½   tsp. each dried thyme, oregano, tarragon and basil
½   tsp. dried rosemary, crushed
½   tsp. pepper
1   cup shredded part-skim mozzarella cheese

1. Cut vegetables into ¼-in.-thick slices.

2. In a greased 13x9-in. baking dish, layer eggplant, zucchini, squash, tomatoes and onion. In a small bowl, combine butter, parsley, garlic and seasonings; pour over vegetables. Cover and refrigerate overnight.

3. Remove from refrigerator 30 minutes before baking. Bake, uncovered, at 375° for 35 minutes. Sprinkle with cheese. Bake 10-15 minutes longer or until cheese is melted. Serve with a slotted spoon.

¾ CUP: 120 cal., 9g fat (5g sat. fat), 24mg chol., 190mg sod., 8g carb. (5g sugars, 3g fiber), 4g pro.

SWEET POTATO
LATKES

OLIVE OIL KNOW-HOW

Common olive oil works better for cooking at high heat than virgin or extra-virgin oil. These higher grades have ideal flavor for cold foods, but they smoke at lower temperatures.

GRILLED VEGETABLE PLATTER

This recipe is the best of summer in one dish! These pretty veggies are perfect for entertaining. Grilling brings out their natural sweetness, and the easy marinade really perks up the flavor.
—Heidi Hall, North St. Paul, MN

PREP: 20 MIN. + MARINATING • **GRILL:** 10 MIN. • **MAKES:** 6 SERVINGS

¼ cup olive oil
2 Tbsp. honey
4 tsp. balsamic vinegar
1 tsp. dried oregano
½ tsp. garlic powder
⅛ tsp. pepper
   Dash salt
1 lb. fresh asparagus, trimmed
3 small carrots, cut in half lengthwise
1 large sweet red pepper, cut into 1-in. strips
1 medium yellow summer squash, cut into ½-in. slices
1 medium red onion, cut into wedges

1. In a small bowl, whisk first 7 ingredients. Place 3 Tbsp. marinade in a large bowl. Add vegetables; turn to coat. Cover; marinate 1½ hours at room temperature.

2. Transfer vegetables to a grilling grid; place grid on grill rack. Grill vegetables, covered, over medium heat until crisp-tender, 8-12 minutes, turning occasionally.

3. Place vegetables on a large serving plate. Drizzle with remaining marinade.

NOTE: If you do not have a grilling grid, use a disposable foil pan. Poke holes in the bottom of pan with a meat fork to allow liquid to drain.

1 SERVING: 144 cal., 9g fat (1g sat. fat), 0 chol., 50mg sod., 15g carb. (11g sugars, 3g fiber), 2g pro. **DIABETIC EXCHANGES:** 2 vegetable, 2 fat.

AIR-FRYER HERB & LEMON CAULIFLOWER

A standout cauliflower side is easy to prepare with just a few ingredients. Crushed red pepper flakes add a touch of heat.
—Susan Hein, Burlington, WI

TAKES: 20 MIN. • **MAKES:** 4 SERVINGS

1   medium head cauliflower, cut into florets (about 6 cups)
4   Tbsp. olive oil, divided
¼   cup minced fresh parsley
1   Tbsp. minced fresh rosemary
1   Tbsp. minced fresh thyme
1   tsp. grated lemon zest
2   Tbsp. lemon juice
½   tsp. salt
¼   tsp. crushed red pepper flakes

Preheat air fryer to 350°. In a large bowl, combine cauliflower and 2 Tbsp. olive oil; toss to coat. In batches, arrange cauliflower in a single layer on tray in air-fryer basket. Cook until florets are tender and edges are browned, 8-10 minutes, stirring halfway through cooking. In a small bowl, combine remaining ingredients; stir in remaining 2 Tbsp. oil. Transfer cauliflower to a large bowl; drizzle with herb mixture and toss to combine.

¾ CUP: 161 cal., 14g fat (2g sat. fat), 0 chol., 342mg sod., 8g carb. (3g sugars, 3g fiber), 3g pro. **DIABETIC EXCHANGES:** 3 fat, 1 vegetable.

CARROT RAISIN COUSCOUS

Golden raisins add a slightly sweet flavor to this unique side dish featuring couscous and carrots. The recipe will brighten any dinner table.
—Jordan Sucher, Brooklyn, NY

PREP: 15 MIN. • **COOK:** 20 MIN. • **MAKES:** 10 SERVINGS

⅓   cup port wine or chicken broth
⅓   cup golden raisins
1   medium onion, chopped
3   Tbsp. olive oil, divided
1   pkg. (10 oz.) couscous
2   cups chicken broth
¼   tsp. salt, divided
¼   tsp. pepper, divided
4   medium carrots, julienned
1   Tbsp. sugar
1   tsp. molasses

1. In a small saucepan, heat wine until hot. In a small bowl, soak raisins in wine for 5 minutes. Drain raisins, reserving wine.

2. In a large saucepan, saute onion in 1 Tbsp. oil until tender. Stir in couscous. Cook and stir until lightly browned. Stir in broth, raisins and half each of salt and pepper. Bring to a boil. Cover and remove from heat. Let stand 5 minutes; fluff with a fork.

3. In a small skillet, saute carrots in remaining oil until crisp-tender. Combine sugar, molasses, reserved wine and the remaining salt and pepper. Stir into carrots; heat through.

4. In a large bowl, combine couscous mixture and carrots; toss to combine.

¾ CUP: 188 cal., 5g fat (1g sat. fat), 1mg chol., 277mg sod., 32g carb. (8g sugars, 2g fiber), 5g pro. **DIABETIC EXCHANGES:** 1½ starch, 1 vegetable, 1 fat.

AIR-FRYER
HERB & LEMON
CAULIFLOWER

ZESTY
MEDITERRANEAN
POTATO SALAD,
PAGE 252

SOUPS & SALADS

From warm, cozy soups to crisp, cool salads, look here for the perfect way to round out your menu. These flavors will transport you to the Mediterranean coast.

BEAN COUNTER CHOWDER

This hearty chowder is one of our favorite vegetarian dishes. Loaded with beans, noodles and bright herbs, it's so comforting on a chilly day.
—Vivian Haen, Menomonee Falls, WI

TAKES: 30 MIN. • **MAKES:** 8 SERVINGS (2 QT.)

½ cup chopped onion
1 Tbsp. canola oil
2 garlic cloves, minced
1 medium tomato, chopped
2 cans (14½ oz. each) chicken or vegetable broth
1¾ cups water
½ tsp. each dried basil, oregano and celery flakes
¼ tsp. pepper
3 cans (15½ oz. each) great northern beans, rinsed and drained
1 cup uncooked elbow macaroni
1 Tbsp. minced parsley

1. In a large saucepan, saute onion in oil until tender. Add garlic; cook 1 minute longer. Add tomato; simmer for 5 minutes. Add broth, water and seasonings. Bring to a boil; cook for 5 minutes. Add beans and macaroni; return to a boil.

2. Reduce heat; simmer, uncovered, until macaroni is tender, about 15 minutes. Sprinkle with parsley.

1 CUP: 196 cal., 3g fat (0 sat. fat), 2mg chol., 676mg sod., 33g carb. (2g sugars, 9g fiber), 10g pro. **DIABETIC EXCHANGES:** 2 starch, ½ fat.

---

⑤ MINT WATERMELON SALAD

I invented this refreshing fruit salad one sultry afternoon while my friends were gathered around my pool. It was quick to prepare and disappeared from their plates even quicker. The kids loved it too!
—Antoinette DuBeck, Huntingdon Valley, PA

TAKES: 20 MIN. • **MAKES:** 8 SERVINGS

6 cups cubed seedless watermelon
2 Tbsp. minced fresh mint
1 Tbsp. lemon juice
1 Tbsp. olive oil
2 tsp. sugar

Place watermelon and mint in a large bowl. In a small bowl, whisk lemon juice, oil and sugar until sugar is dissolved. Drizzle over salad; toss gently to combine.

¾ CUP: 56 cal., 2g fat (0 sat. fat), 0 chol., 2mg sod., 9g carb. (9g sugars, 1g fiber), 1g pro. **DIABETIC EXCHANGES:** ½ fruit.

ORANGE &
OLIVES SALAD

⑤ ORANGE & OLIVES SALAD

My grandmother made sure this salad was on our holiday table every year. We always celebrated the rustic Italian way and she made lots of delicious food. This is so light and simple to make, and it didn't fill you up before one of her great meals. It also looks pretty on the table.
—Angela David, Lakeland, FL

TAKES: 10 MIN. • **MAKES:** 16 SERVINGS

4   large navel oranges, peeled and sliced
2   cans (6 oz. each) pitted ripe olives, drained
1   Tbsp. canola oil
⅛   tsp. pepper

Arrange orange slices along the outer edge of a serving dish, leaving the center open. Place olives in the center of dish. Drizzle with oil; sprinkle with pepper.

1 SERVING: 54 cal., 3g fat (0 sat. fat), 0 chol., 185mg sod., 7g carb. (4g sugars, 2g fiber), 1g pro. **DIABETIC EXCHANGES:** ½ fruit, ½ fat.

🍲 TURKEY SAUSAGE SOUP WITH FRESH VEGETABLES

Our family is big on soup. This favorite is quick to make and very tasty, and it gives me plenty of time to have fun with my kids and grandkids while it slow-cooks.
—Nancy Heishman, Las Vegas, NV

PREP: 30 MIN. • **COOK:** 6 HOURS • **MAKES:** 10 SERVINGS (ABOUT 3¼ QT.)

1   pkg. (19½ oz.) Italian turkey sausage links, casings removed
3   large tomatoes, chopped
1   can (15 oz.) garbanzo beans or chickpeas, rinsed and drained
3   medium carrots, thinly sliced
1½   cups cut fresh green beans (1-in. pieces)
1   medium zucchini, quartered lengthwise and sliced
1   large sweet red or green pepper, chopped
8   green onions, chopped
4   cups chicken stock
1   can (12 oz.) tomato paste
½   tsp. seasoned salt
⅓   cup minced fresh basil

1. In a large skillet, cook sausage over medium heat 8-10 minutes or until no longer pink, breaking into crumbles; drain and transfer to a 6-qt. slow cooker.

2. Add tomatoes, garbanzo beans, carrots, green beans, zucchini, pepper and green onions. In a large bowl, whisk stock, tomato paste and seasoned salt; pour over vegetables.

3. Cook, covered, on low 6-8 hours or until vegetables are tender. Just before serving, stir in basil.

FREEZE OPTION: Freeze cooled soup in freezer containers. To use, partially thaw in refrigerator overnight. Heat through in a saucepan, stirring occasionally; add stock if necessary.

1⅓ CUPS: 167 cal., 5g fat (1g sat. fat), 20mg chol., 604mg sod., 21g carb. (8g sugars, 5g fiber), 13g pro. **DIABETIC EXCHANGES:** 2 vegetable, 2 lean meat, ½ starch.

SPANISH CHICKEN SOUP

A hearty soup made from scratch is the perfect antidote for chilly weather. Save leftovers for weekday lunches sent to work in a thermos or quickly reheated in the microwave.
—*Taste of Home* Test Kitchen

PREP: 15 MIN. **COOK:** 50 MIN. • **MAKES:** 12 SERVINGS

1   broiler/fryer chicken
    (3 to 4 lbs.), cut up
2   tsp. adobo seasoning
2   Tbsp. olive oil
2   celery ribs, chopped
1   medium onion, chopped
1   medium carrot, chopped
¼   cup sofrito tomato cooking base
2   qt. water
1   bay leaf
2   medium Yukon Gold potatoes,
    peeled and cubed
12 oz. fideo noodles or uncooked
    angel hair pasta, broken into
    1-in. pieces
1   tsp. salt
½   tsp. pepper
    Fresh cilantro leaves, optional

1. Sprinkle chicken with adobo seasoning. In a large stockpot, heat oil over medium heat. Brown chicken on both sides in batches. Remove chicken from pot. Add celery, onion, carrot and sofrito to same pot; cook and stir until onion is tender, 3-4 minutes.

2. Return chicken to pot. Add water and bay leaf; bring to a boil. Reduce heat; cover and simmer 30 minutes. Add potatoes. Simmer, uncovered, until potatoes are almost tender, 8-10 minutes.

3. Remove chicken and bay leaf; discard bay leaf. Let chicken stand until cool enough to handle. Skim fat from broth. Return broth to a simmer; add noodles. Simmer, uncovered, until noodles are tender, 5-7 minutes.

4. Meanwhile, remove chicken from bones; discard bones. Cut chicken into bite-sized pieces; add chicken to broth. Add salt and pepper. Cook and stir until heated through. If desired, garnish with cilantro.

1 CUP: 324 cal., 12g fat (3g sat. fat), 52mg chol., 530mg sod., 31g carb. (2g sugars, 2g fiber), 22g pro. **DIABETIC EXCHANGES:** 3 lean meat, 2 starch, ½ fat.

MAKE IT YOUR OWN

There aren't many limitations to what you can add to this soup. If you're looking to incorporate more vegetables, try adding some celery, peas or finely chopped fresh spinach. To boost the flavor, sprinkle in parsley or garlic powder. It really comes down to your personal preferences!

CREAMLESS CREAMY SQUASH SOUP

Here's my go-to recipe for get-togethers with family and friends. Everyone asks for seconds, and they can't believe they are eating something so healthy and vegetarian! It's also a hearty dish for those with food allergies.
—Sharon Verea, Thomasville, GA

PREP: 20 MIN. • **COOK:** 35 MIN. • **MAKES:** 8 SERVINGS (2 QT.)

2 Tbsp. olive oil
2 small onions, chopped
2 celery ribs, chopped
2 medium carrots, chopped
1 medium butternut squash (3 lbs.), peeled, seeded and cut into 1-in. cubes
1 medium sweet potato (about 8 oz.), peeled and cut into 1-in. cubes
1 yellow summer squash, halved lengthwise and sliced
4 garlic cloves, minced
4 cups vegetable broth
2 tsp. dried savory or herbes de Provence
¼ tsp. pepper
Grated Parmesan cheese, optional

1. In a Dutch oven, heat oil over medium heat. Add onions, celery and carrots; cook and stir until onion is tender, 6-8 minutes. Stir in butternut squash, sweet potato and summer squash. Cook and stir until squash and potato are lightly browned, 5-7 minutes. Add garlic; cook 1 minute longer.

2. Add broth, savory and pepper; bring to a boil. Reduce heat; simmer, uncovered, until vegetables are tender, 20-25 minutes.

3. Puree soup using an immersion blender, or cool slightly and, in batches, puree in a blender and return to pan; heat through. If desired, serve with cheese.

FREEZE OPTION: Freeze cooled soup in freezer containers. To use, partially thaw in refrigerator overnight. Heat through in a saucepan, stirring occasionally and adding a little broth if necessary.

1 CUP (CALCULATED WITHOUT CHEESE): 138 cal., 4g fat (1g sat. fat), 0 chol., 497mg sod., 27g carb. (8g sugars, 7g fiber), 2g pro. **DIABETIC EXCHANGES:** 1½ starch, 1 vegetable, ½ fat.

READER REVIEW

"This soup is creamy, smooth, colorful and flavorful. Experiment with cinnamon, chili and garlic powders, and paprika for a spicy variation. Garnish choices could include cilantro, Greek yogurt, bacon bits, green onions, garlic croutons and your favorite shredded cheese."
—JENNIFERH, TASTEOFHOME.COM

🅢 APRICOT SPINACH SALAD

*This easy-to-make salad is full of flavor. The vinaigrette
is a great complement to the spinach and apricots.*
—*Taste of Home* Test Kitchen

TAKES: 10 MIN. • **MAKES:** 8 SERVINGS

1   pkg. (10 oz.) fresh baby spinach
1   cup canned apricot halves, drained
    and sliced
½   cup golden raisins
½   cup raspberry vinaigrette
1   tsp. grated lemon zest

In a large salad bowl, combine spinach, apricots and raisins. Drizzle with vinaigrette and sprinkle with lemon zest; toss to coat.

1 CUP: 132 cal., 8g fat (1g sat. fat), 0 chol., 155mg sod., 16g carb. (12g sugars, 2g fiber), 1g pro.

WATERMELON GAZPACHO

*My refreshing gazpacho is a delightfully simple, elegant dish.
Serve as a side or with pita and hummus for a meal.*
—Nicole Deelah, Nashville, TN

TAKES: 25 MIN. • **MAKES:** 4 SERVINGS (1 QT.)

4   cups cubed watermelon,
    seeded, divided
2   Tbsp. lime juice
1   Tbsp. grated lime zest
1   tsp. minced fresh gingerroot
1   tsp. salt
1   cup chopped tomato
½   cup chopped cucumber
½   cup chopped green pepper
¼   cup minced fresh cilantro
2   Tbsp. chopped green onion
1   Tbsp. finely chopped seeded
    jalapeno pepper
    Watermelon wedges, optional

1. Puree 3 cups watermelon in a blender. Cut remaining watermelon into ½-in. pieces; set aside.

2. In a large bowl, combine pureed watermelon, lime juice and zest, ginger and salt. Stir in tomato, cucumber, green pepper, cilantro, green onion, jalapeno and cubed watermelon. Refrigerate until serving. If desired, serve with wedge of watermelon.

NOTE: Wear disposable gloves when cutting hot peppers; the oils can burn skin. Avoid touching your face.

1 CUP: 58 cal., 0 fat (0 sat. fat), 0 chol., 599mg sod., 18g carb. (15g sugars, 2g fiber), 1g pro. **DIABETIC EXCHANGES:** 1 fruit.

ZESTY MEDITERRANEAN POTATO SALAD

*I love this recipe that incorporates many of the vegetables I plant in my summer garden.
The dressing is light and fresh—perfect for a picnic or barbecue.*
—Terri Crandall, Gardnerville, NV

PREP: 25 MIN. • **COOK:** 15 MIN. + CHILLING • **MAKES:** 8 SERVINGS

4   large Yukon Gold potatoes,
    peeled and cubed
1½ tsp. salt, divided
½   cup olive oil
¼   cup lemon juice
½   tsp. pepper
⅛   tsp. crushed red pepper flakes
1   medium sweet red pepper,
    finely chopped
½   small red onion, finely chopped
⅓   cup Greek olives, pitted and
    chopped
4   bacon strips, cooked and crumbled
½   cup crumbled feta cheese
¼   cup loosely packed basil leaves,
    torn

1. Place potatoes in a large saucepan; add water to cover. Add 1 tsp. salt. Bring to a boil. Reduce heat; cook, uncovered, until tender, 8-10 minutes. Drain and place in a large bowl.

2. In a small bowl, whisk olive oil, lemon juice, remaining ½ tsp. salt, pepper and red pepper flakes until blended. Spoon over potato mixture; toss to coat. Refrigerate, covered, about 1 hour.

3. Just before serving, add sweet red pepper, onion, olives and bacon to potatoes. Sprinkle with feta and basil.

¾ CUP: 341 cal., 18g fat (3g sat. fat), 8mg chol., 685mg sod., 40g carb. (4g sugars, 3g fiber), 6g pro.

KITCHEN TIP

This soup thickens slightly as it stands. If you have leftovers, keep extra broth on hand in case you need it when the soup is reheated.

🍲 GREEK-STYLE LENTIL SOUP

This healthy, warming soup is a satisfying vegetarian recipe,
but you can use chicken broth or add cooked meat if you like.
—Mary E. Smith, Columbia, MO

PREP: 20 MIN. • **COOK:** 5 HOURS • **MAKES:** 12 SERVINGS (3 QT.)

4 cups water
4 cups vegetable broth
2 cups dried lentils, rinsed
2 medium carrots, chopped
1 small onion, chopped
1 celery rib, chopped
1 tsp. dried oregano, divided
1 cup chopped fresh spinach
½ cup tomato sauce
1 can (2¼ oz.) sliced ripe olives, drained
3 Tbsp. red wine vinegar
2 garlic cloves, minced
½ tsp. salt
¼ tsp. pepper
Optional: Chopped red onion, chopped parsley and lemon wedges

1. Place water, broth, lentils, carrots, onion, celery and ½ tsp. oregano in a 5- or 6-qt. slow cooker. Cook, covered, on low for 4-5 hours or until lentils are tender.

2. Stir in spinach, tomato sauce, olives, vinegar, garlic, salt, pepper and remaining ½ tsp. oregano. Cook, covered, on low until spinach is wilted, about 1 hour longer. If desired, serve with red onion, parsley and lemon wedges.

1 CUP: 134 cal., 1g fat (0 sat. fat), 0 chol., 420mg sod., 24g carb. (2g sugars, 4g fiber), 9g pro. **DIABETIC EXCHANGES:** 1½ starch, 1 lean meat.

SUMMER SALAD

*In this dish, I combine traditional Caprese salad flavors with summer peaches and blueberries.
I also add prosciutto for saltiness, creating a balanced, flavor-packed side dish.*
—Emily Falke, Santa Barbara, CA

TAKES: 25 MIN. • **MAKES:** 12 SERVINGS

⅔ cup extra virgin olive oil
½ cup julienned fresh basil
⅓ cup white balsamic vinegar
¼ cup julienned fresh mint leaves
2 garlic cloves, minced
2 tsp. Dijon mustard
1 tsp. sea salt
1 tsp. sugar
1 tsp. pepper
2 cups cherry tomatoes
8 cups fresh arugula
1 carton (8 oz.) fresh mozzarella
cheese pearls, drained
2 medium peaches, sliced
2 cups fresh blueberries
6 oz. thinly sliced prosciutto,
julienned
Additional mint leaves

1. In a small bowl, whisk the first 9 ingredients. Add tomatoes; let stand while preparing salad.

2. In a large bowl, combine arugula, mozzarella, peaches, blueberries and prosciutto. Pour tomato mixture over top; toss to coat. Garnish with additional mint leaves. Serve immediately.

1 CUP: 233 cal., 18g fat (5g sat. fat), 27mg chol., 486mg sod., 10g carb. (8g sugars, 2g fiber), 8g pro.

READER REVIEW
"My favorite part was the little mozzarella balls together with the ripe peaches and tomatoes. It's a delicious salad."
—CURLYLIS85, TASTEOFHOME.COM

CALAMARI SALAD

CALAMARI SALAD

This is one of the seven fish dishes we serve at Christmas time. It is easy to make and quite delicious!
I enjoy it served both warm and cold. Either way, it has become one of our traditional dishes each year.
The recipe has been passed down to me through my grandparents, who were excellent cooks.
—Paul Rinaldi, Easton, PA

TAKES: 25 MIN. • **MAKES:** 8 SERVINGS

- 2½ lbs. cleaned fresh or frozen calamari (squid), thawed
- ½ cup olive oil
- 3 anchovy fillets, minced, optional
- 2 tsp. minced fresh Italian parsley
- 1 garlic clove, minced
- ½ cup dry white wine or dry vermouth
- 1 can (8 oz.) mushroom stems and pieces, drained, optional
- ¼ tsp. salt
- ¼ tsp. pepper
- ½ cup chopped celery
- ½ cup pitted Italian olives, sliced
- 3 Tbsp. lemon juice

1. Chop calamari tentacles; cut body into ½-in. rings.

2. In a large saucepan, heat oil over medium heat. Add anchovies if desired; stir in parsley and garlic. Cook for 1 minute. Add wine; stir in mushrooms if desired, and seasonings. Add calamari; bring to a boil. Reduce heat; simmer, covered, until calamari is tender, 2-3 minutes. Remove pan from heat; cool slightly.

3. In a serving bowl, toss celery, olives, lemon juice and calamari mixture. Serve warm, or refrigerate and serve cold.

½ CUP: 273 cal., 16g fat (2g sat. fat), 330mg chol., 204mg sod., 6g carb. (0 sugars, 0 fiber), 22g pro.

TZATZIKI POTATO SALAD

My son has an egg allergy, so this potato salad is perfect for him.
For extra color, add radish, apple and garlic dill pickles.
—Cindy Romberg, Mississauga, ON

PREP: 25 MIN. + CHILLING • **MAKES:** 12 SERVINGS

- 3 lbs. small red potatoes, halved
- 1 carton (12 oz.) refrigerated tzatziki sauce
- 2 celery ribs, thinly sliced
- ½ cup plain Greek yogurt
- 2 green onions, chopped
- 2 Tbsp. snipped fresh dill
- 2 Tbsp. minced fresh parsley
- ½ tsp. salt
- ¼ tsp. celery salt
- ¼ tsp. pepper
- 1 Tbsp. minced fresh mint, optional

1. Place potatoes in a Dutch oven; add water to cover. Bring to a boil. Reduce heat; cook, uncovered, until tender, 10-15 minutes. Drain; cool completely.

2. In a small bowl, mix tzatziki sauce, celery, yogurt, green onions, dill, parsley, salt, celery salt, pepper and, if desired, mint. Spoon over potatoes; toss to coat. Refrigerate, covered, until cold.

¾ CUP: 128 cal., 3g fat (2g sat. fat), 7mg chol., 190mg sod., 21g carb. (3g sugars, 2g fiber), 4g pro. **DIABETIC EXCHANGES:** 1½ starch, ½ fat.

GRILLED MEDITERRANEAN ZUCCHINI SALAD

This zucchini salad with Mediterranean dressing is the best side dish. I also like to add summer squash for a variation, or crumbled goat cheese when I want some extra creaminess.
—Rashanda Cobbins, Aurora, CO

TAKES: 20 MIN. • **MAKES:** 4 SERVINGS

3   medium zucchini, thinly sliced
¼   cup olive oil, divided
¼   tsp. salt
¼   tsp. pepper
¼   cup chopped red onion
3   Tbsp. minced fresh mint
2   Tbsp. minced fresh parsley
1   medium lemon, juiced and zested
⅓   cup crumbled feta cheese
3   Tbsp. pine nuts, toasted

1. In a large bowl, combine zucchini and 2 Tbsp. olive oil. Add salt and pepper; toss to coat. Transfer to a grill wok or open grill basket; place on grill rack. Grill, covered, over medium-high heat until zucchini is crisp-tender, 5-10 minutes, turning occasionally.

2. Transfer zucchini to a serving bowl; sprinkle with remaining 2 Tbsp. olive oil and red onion. When it cools slightly, sprinkle with mint, parsley, lemon juice and zest, and feta cheese. Stir gently. Sprinkle with pine nuts before serving.

1 CUP: 220 cal., 20g fat (3g sat. fat), 5mg chol., 252mg sod., 8g carb. (4g sugars, 3g fiber), 5g pro.

🍲 PROVENCAL HAM & BEAN SOUP

There is nothing quite like the wonderful aroma of this delicious soup bubbling away!
—Lyndsay Wells, Ladysmith, BC

PREP: 15 MIN. + SOAKING • **COOK:** 7 HOURS • **MAKES:** 10 SERVINGS (3½ QT.)

2   cups assorted dried beans for soup
1   can (28 oz.) whole plum tomatoes, undrained
2   cups cubed fully cooked ham
1   large Yukon Gold potato, peeled and chopped
1   medium onion, chopped
1   cup chopped carrot
1   celery rib, chopped
2   garlic cloves, minced
2   tsp. herbes de Provence
1½   tsp. salt
1   tsp. pepper
1   carton (32 oz.) unsalted chicken stock
     French bread

1. Rinse and sort beans; soak according to package directions. Drain and rinse beans, discarding liquid.

2. Transfer beans to a 6-qt. slow cooker. Add tomatoes; crush with a wooden spoon until chunky. Stir in ham, vegetables, garlic, seasonings and stock. Cook, covered, on low 7-9 hours or until beans are tender. Serve with bread.

1⅓ CUPS: 212 cal., 2g fat (0 sat. fat), 17mg chol., 887mg sod., 33g carb. (5g sugars, 9g fiber), 17g pro.

GRILLED
MEDITERRANEAN
ZUCCHINI SALAD

HUMMUS PASTA SALAD

Adding the dressing while the pasta is still warm allows the pasta to absorb some of the dressing. It's a hearty side dish but could be a nice meatless main dish as well.
—Michelle Morrow, Newmarket, NH

PREP: 25 MIN. • **BAKE:** 20 MIN. + CHILLING • **MAKES:** 18 SERVINGS

2   cans (16 oz. each) garbanzo beans or chickpeas, rinsed and drained
2   Tbsp. olive oil
¾   tsp. salt, divided
½   tsp. pepper, divided
1   pkg. (16 oz.) uncooked whole wheat spiral pasta
4   cups chopped fresh kale
2   medium lemons
½   cup water
6   Tbsp. tahini
4   garlic cloves, minced
2   Tbsp. Greek olive juice
1   pint cherry tomatoes, quartered
1   cup Greek olives, chopped

1. Preheat oven to 350°. Place garbanzo beans on a parchment-lined rimmed baking sheet. Drizzle with oil and sprinkle with ½ tsp. salt and ¼ tsp. pepper; toss to coat. Bake until golden brown, about 20 minutes.

2. Meanwhile, cook pasta according to package directions for al dente. Drain pasta; rinse with cold water and drain well. Place kale in a large mixing bowl; massage until tender, 3-5 minutes. Add pasta.

3. Finely grate zest from 1 lemon. Cut lemons crosswise in half; squeeze juice from lemons. In a small bowl, whisk water, tahini, garlic, olive juice, lemon juice and zest, and remaining ¼ tsp. salt and ¼ tsp. pepper. Pour over pasta mixture; toss to coat. Stir in garbanzo beans, tomatoes and olives. Refrigerate, covered, at least 3 hours before serving.

¾ CUP: 219 cal., 8g fat (1g sat. fat), 0 chol., 316mg sod., 30g carb. (2g sugars, 6g fiber), 7g pro. **DIABETIC EXCHANGES:** 2 starch, 1½ fat.

⑤ SUMMER STRAWBERRY SOUP

Laden with strawberries, this chilled soup is certain to become a new hot-weather favorite.
—Verna Bollin, Powell, TN

PREP: 15 MIN. + CHILLING • **MAKES:** 6 SERVINGS

2   cups vanilla yogurt
½   cup orange juice
2   lbs. fresh strawberries, halved (8 cups)
½   cup sugar
   Optional: Additional vanilla yogurt and fresh mint leaves

In a blender, combine yogurt, orange juice, strawberries and sugar in batches; cover and process until blended. Refrigerate for at least 2 hours. Garnish with additional yogurt and mint leaves if desired.

1 CUP: 192 cal., 1g fat (1g sat. fat), 4mg chol., 55mg sod., 42g carb. (37g sugars, 3g fiber), 5g pro.

YELLOW SQUASH & WATERMELON SALAD

I always like to bring this healthy option to parties and potlucks, and people seem to really appreciate that. No oil is necessary for this salad; the lemon juice combines with the feta to lightly coat the bright, fresh ingredients.
—Camille Parker, Chicago, IL

TAKES: 20 MIN. • **MAKES:** 12 SERVINGS

6 cups cubed seedless watermelon
2 medium yellow summer squash, chopped
2 medium zucchini, chopped
½ cup lemon juice
12 fresh mint leaves, torn
1 tsp. salt
8 cups fresh arugula or baby spinach
1 cup (4 oz.) crumbled feta cheese

In a large bowl, combine the first 6 ingredients. Just before serving, add arugula and feta cheese; toss gently to combine.

1 CUP: 61 cal., 2g fat (1g sat. fat), 5mg chol., 299mg sod., 10g carb. (8g sugars, 2g fiber), 3g pro. **DIABETIC EXCHANGES:** 1 vegetable, ½ fruit.

🍲 FRENCH LENTIL & CARROT SOUP

It's crazy how just a few ingredients can make such a difference. Using finely chopped rotisserie chicken in this recipe makes it perfect for a busy weeknight meal, but you can leave the chicken out if you prefer.
—Colleen Delawder, Herndon, VA

PREP: 15 MIN. • **COOK:** 6¼ HOURS • **MAKES:** 6 SERVINGS (2¼ QT.)

5 large carrots, peeled and sliced
1½ cups dried green lentils, rinsed
1 shallot, finely chopped
2 tsp. herbes de Provence
½ tsp. pepper
¼ tsp. kosher salt
6 cups reduced-sodium chicken broth
2 cups cubed rotisserie chicken
¼ cup heavy whipping cream

1. Combine the first 7 ingredients in a 5- or 6-qt. slow cooker; cover. Cook on low for 6-8 hours or until lentils are tender.

2. Stir in chicken and cream. Cover and continue cooking until heated through, about 15 minutes longer.

1½ CUPS: 338 cal., 8g fat (3g sat. fat), 53mg chol., 738mg sod., 39g carb. (5g sugars, 7g fiber), 29g pro. **DIABETIC EXCHANGES:** 3 lean meat, 2 starch, 1 vegetable.

BEST LASAGNA SOUP

All the traditional flavors of lasagna come together in this heartwarming bowl of comfort.
—Sheryl Olenick, Demarest, NJ

TAKES: 30 MIN. • **MAKES:** 8 SERVINGS (ABOUT 2¾ QT.)

1 lb. lean ground beef (90% lean)
1 large green pepper, chopped
1 medium onion, chopped
2 garlic cloves, minced
2 cans (14½ oz. each) diced tomatoes, undrained
2 cans (14½ oz. each) reduced-sodium beef broth
1 can (8 oz.) tomato sauce
1 cup frozen corn
¼ cup tomato paste
2 tsp. Italian seasoning
¼ tsp. pepper
2½ cups uncooked spiral pasta
½ cup shredded Parmesan cheese

1. In a large saucepan, cook beef, green pepper and onion over medium heat 6-8 minutes or until meat is no longer pink, breaking up beef into crumbles. Add garlic; cook 1 minute longer. Drain.

2. Stir in tomatoes, broth, tomato sauce, corn, tomato paste, Italian seasoning and pepper. Bring to a boil. Stir in pasta. Return to a boil. Reduce the heat; simmer, covered, 10-12 minutes or until pasta is tender. Sprinkle with cheese.

1⅓ CUPS: 280 cal., 7g fat (3g sat. fat), 41mg chol., 572mg sod., 35g carb. (8g sugars, 4g fiber), 20g pro. **DIABETIC EXCHANGES:** 2 vegetable, 2 lean meat, 1½ starch.

READER REVIEW

"My very, very picky spouse loved this! We all had second helpings, and I beat everyone to lunch leftovers! This is my new favorite recipe. I'll try adding more and different veggies."
—FREDERICKBUCKLEY, TASTEOFHOME.COM

🟢 TAHINI DRESSING

I like to serve this dressing over a salad of romaine lettuce, baby red potatoes, asparagus and snap peas. It's a healthy and tasty way to start a meal.
—Amy Lyons, Mounds View, MN

TAKES: 5 MIN. • **MAKES:** 1¼ CUPS

½ cup water
½ cup tahini
3 Tbsp. lemon juice
4 garlic cloves
1 tsp. ground cumin
¼ tsp. salt
¼ tsp. cayenne pepper
⅛ tsp. pepper

Place all ingredients in a blender; cover and process until blended.

2 TBSP.: 88 cal., 8g fat (1g sat. fat), 0 chol., 62mg sod., 3g carb. (0 sugars, 1g fiber), 3g pro. **DIABETIC EXCHANGES:** 1½ fat.

SHRIMP GAZPACHO

Here's a refreshing take on the classic chilled tomato soup. Our twist features shrimp, lime and plenty of avocado.
—*Taste of Home* Test Kitchen

PREP: 15 MIN. + CHILLING • **MAKES:** 12 SERVINGS (3 QT.)

6 cups spicy hot V8 juice
2 cups cold water
½ cup lime juice
½ cup minced fresh cilantro
½ tsp. salt
¼ to ½ tsp. hot pepper sauce
1 lb. peeled and deveined cooked shrimp (31-40 per lb.), tails removed
1 medium cucumber, seeded and diced
2 medium tomatoes, seeded and chopped
2 medium ripe avocados, peeled and chopped

In a large nonreactive bowl, mix first 6 ingredients. Gently stir in remaining ingredients. Refrigerate, covered, 1 hour before serving.

1 CUP: 112 cal., 4g fat (1g sat. fat), 57mg chol., 399mg sod., 9g carb. (5g sugars, 3g fiber), 10g pro. **DIABETIC EXCHANGES:** 2 vegetable, 1 lean meat, 1 fat.

TABBOULEH

Tabbouleh (also known as tabouleh) is a classic Middle Eastern salad.
The fresh veggies and mint leaves make it light and refreshing on a hot day.
—Michael & Mathil Chebat, Lake Ridge, VA

TAKES: 30 MIN. + COOLING • **MAKES:** 8 SERVINGS

- ¼ cup bulgur
- 3 bunches fresh parsley, minced (about 2 cups)
- 3 large tomatoes, finely chopped
- 1 small onion, finely chopped
- ¼ cup lemon juice
- ¼ cup olive oil
- 5 fresh mint leaves, minced
- ½ tsp. salt
- ½ tsp. pepper
- ¼ tsp. cayenne pepper

Prepare bulgur according to package directions; cool. Transfer to a large bowl. Stir in remaining ingredients. If desired, chill before serving.

NOTE: Bulgur is a type of whole grain wheat. It has more fiber than quinoa, oats and corn. Since it's precooked then dried, it needs to boil for only about 10 minutes to be ready to eat.

⅔ CUP: 100 cal., 7g fat (1g sat. fat), 0 chol., 164mg sod., 9g carb. (3g sugars, 2g fiber), 2g pro. **DIABETIC EXCHANGES:** 1½ fat, ½ starch.

FRESH MOZZARELLA & TOMATO SALAD

A splash of lemon and hint of refreshing mint brighten up the medley of red tomatoes,
creamy mozzarella and ripe avocados in this sensational salad.
—Lynn Scully, Rancho Santa Fe, CA

PREP: 25 MIN. + CHILLING • **MAKES:** 8 SERVINGS

- 6 plum tomatoes, chopped
- 2 cartons (8 oz. each) fresh mozzarella cheese pearls, drained
- ⅓ cup minced fresh basil
- 1 Tbsp. minced fresh parsley
- 2 tsp. minced fresh mint
- ¼ cup lemon juice
- ¼ cup olive oil
- ¾ tsp. salt
- ¼ tsp. pepper
- 2 medium ripe avocados, peeled and chopped

1. In a large bowl, combine tomatoes, cheese, basil, parsley and mint; set aside.

2. In a small bowl, whisk lemon juice, oil, salt and pepper. Pour over tomato mixture; toss to coat. Cover and refrigerate for at least 1 hour before serving.

3. Just before serving, stir in avocados. Serve with a slotted spoon.

¾ CUP: 305 cal., 26g fat (10g sat. fat), 45mg chol., 309mg sod., 8g carb. (3g sugars, 4g fiber), 11g pro.

TABBOULEH

FATTOUSH

*This type of bread salad is very popular in the Middle East. It uses sumac,
which is a distinctive spice that adds an acidic flavor to dishes, as does lemon juice.*
—Stephanie Khio, Bloomingdale, IL

TAKES: 25 MIN. • **MAKES:** 6 SERVINGS

2 whole pita breads
1 Tbsp. extra virgin olive oil
¼ tsp. salt
2 bunches romaine, chopped
2 medium tomatoes, chopped
2 medium cucumbers, halved
  and sliced
1 medium green pepper, cut into
  1-in. pieces
5 radishes, sliced
½ cup chopped fresh parsley
¼ cup chopped fresh mint

DRESSING
¼ cup extra virgin olive oil
1 medium lemon, juiced (2-3 Tbsp.)
½ tsp. salt
½ tsp. ground sumac
¼ tsp. pepper

1. Preheat oven to 375°. Arrange pita breads in a single layer on an ungreased baking sheet; brush with oil and sprinkle with salt. Bake until crisp, 8-10 minutes, turning once. Cool.

2. Meanwhile, in a large bowl, toss lettuce, tomatoes, cucumbers, green pepper, radishes, parsley and mint. Break toasted pitas into small pieces over salad.

3. In a small bowl, whisk olive oil, lemon juice, salt, sumac and pepper. Drizzle over salad; toss to coat.

1½ CUPS: 200 cal., 12g fat (2g sat. fat), 0 chol., 436mg sod., 20g carb. (4g sugars, 5g fiber), 6g pro. **DIABETIC EXCHANGES:** 2½ fat, 2 vegetable, ½ starch.

GREEK TORTELLINI SALAD

A bold homemade dressing gives this pasta salad a burst of flavor.
Watch it disappear from your buffet table!
—Sue Braunschweig, Delafield, WI

PREP: 20 MIN. + CHILLING • **MAKES:** 10 SERVINGS

16 to 18 oz. refrigerated or frozen
    cheese tortellini
1 medium sweet red pepper,
    julienned
1 medium green pepper, julienned
¾ cup sliced red onion
¼ cup sliced ripe olives
½ cup olive oil
½ cup white wine vinegar
3 Tbsp. minced fresh mint or
    1 Tbsp. dried mint flakes
3 Tbsp. lemon juice
1½ tsp. seasoned salt
1 tsp. garlic powder
½ tsp. pepper
⅛ to ¼ tsp. crushed red pepper flakes
½ cup crumbled feta cheese

1. Cook tortellini according to package directions; drain and rinse in cold water. In a large bowl, combine tortellini, peppers, onion and olives.

2. In a jar with a tight-fitting lid, combine oil, vinegar, mint, lemon juice, seasoned salt, garlic powder, pepper and red pepper flakes; shake well. Pour over salad and toss to coat. Refrigerate, covered, for at least 4 hours.

3. Just before serving, sprinkle with feta cheese.

¾ CUP: 267 cal., 16g fat (4g sat. fat), 23mg chol., 477mg sod., 24g carb. (3g sugars, 2g fiber), 8g pro.

GREEK TORTELLINI SALAD TIPS

What else can you put in your Greek tortellini salad? *Like most potluck salads, this recipe is perfect for mixing and matching your favorite ingredients. Stir in classics such as Kalamata olives, grape tomatoes or sliced artichokes.*

How long will this last in the refrigerator? *For the best flavor and texture, serve this salad within 1-2 days (though you could keep it for up to 3-4 days).*

How can you tell if the tortellini is done cooking? *Tortellini doesn't take long to cook. You can tell it's done when it starts to float.*

Can this be made into a main dish? *You can turn this salad into a main dish by stirring in shredded rotisserie chicken or shrimp sauteed in garlic and butter.*

🍲 BEEF BARLEY LENTIL SOUP

I serve this soup often to family and friends on cold nights, along with homemade rolls and a green salad. For variety, you can substitute jicama for the potatoes.
—Judy Metzentine, The Dalles, OR

PREP: 20 MIN. • **COOK:** 8 HOURS • **MAKES:** 10 SERVINGS (ABOUT 3¾ QT.)

1 lb. lean ground beef (90% lean)
1 medium onion, chopped
2 cups cubed red potatoes
   (¼-in. pieces)
1 cup chopped celery
1 cup chopped carrots
1 cup dried lentils, rinsed
½ cup medium pearl barley
8 cups water
2 tsp. beef bouillon granules
½ tsp. lemon-pepper seasoning
2 cans (14½ oz. each) stewed
   tomatoes, coarsely chopped
1 tsp. salt

1. In a nonstick skillet, cook beef and onion over medium heat until meat is no longer pink, 6-8 minutes, breaking up beef into crumbles; drain.

2. Transfer to a 5-qt. slow cooker. Layer with potatoes, celery, carrots, lentils and barley. Combine water, bouillon and lemon pepper; pour over vegetables. Cook, covered, on low for 6 hours or until vegetables and barley are tender.

3. Add tomatoes and salt; cook 2 hours longer.

1½ CUPS: 232 cal., 4g fat (2g sat. fat), 28mg chol., 603mg sod., 33g carb. (6g sugars, 6g fiber), 16g pro. **DIABETIC EXCHANGES:** 2 lean meat, 1½ starch, 1 vegetable.

CHERRY TOMATO SALAD

This recipe evolved from a need to use the bumper crops of cherry tomatoes that we regularly grow. It's become a summer favorite, especially at cookouts.
—Sally Sibley, St. Augustine, FL

PREP: 15 MIN. + MARINATING • **MAKES:** 6 SERVINGS

1 qt. cherry tomatoes, halved
¼ cup canola oil
3 Tbsp. white vinegar
½ tsp. salt
½ tsp. sugar
¼ cup minced fresh parsley
1 to 2 tsp. minced fresh basil
1 to 2 tsp. minced fresh oregano

Place tomatoes in a shallow bowl. In a small bowl, whisk oil, vinegar, salt and sugar until blended; stir in herbs. Pour over tomatoes; gently toss to coat. Refrigerate, covered, overnight.

¾ CUP: 103 cal., 10g fat (1g sat. fat), 0 chol., 203mg sod., 4g carb. (3g sugars, 1g fiber), 1g pro. **DIABETIC EXCHANGES:** 2 fat, 1 vegetable.

NECTARINE FRUIT SALAD WITH LIME SPICE DRESSING

*The lime spice dressing gives this fruit salad a little something extra. It's a crowd-pleaser
as a side dish or as a light and healthy way to end an outdoor meal with friends.
Mix and match fruit with what's in season.*

—Paula Hudson, Cary, NC

PREP: 20 MIN. + CHILLING • **MAKES:** 8 SERVINGS

1½ tsp. grated lime zest
2 Tbsp. lime juice
2 Tbsp. honey
½ tsp. ground ginger
¼ tsp. cayenne pepper
6 medium nectarines, cut into
   1-in. pieces (about 4 cups)
2 cups seedless red grapes
¼ cup chopped fresh mint
½ cup mascarpone cheese
2 Tbsp. confectioners' sugar
2 Tbsp. 2% milk
¼ tsp. vanilla extract
⅓ cup chopped pistachios
   Fresh mint leaves

1. In a small bowl, whisk the first 5 ingredients. Place nectarines, grapes and mint in a large bowl. Drizzle with honey mixture; stir gently. Refrigerate, covered, 1-2 hours.

2. For topping, mix mascarpone, confectioners' sugar, milk and vanilla. Serve fruit salad with topping, pistachios and fresh mint leaves.

1 SERVING: 254 cal., 16g fat (7g sat. fat), 35mg chol., 44mg sod., 27g carb. (22g sugars, 3g fiber), 4g pro.

HEARTY SOUP

If you like a thicker minestrone, add 2-4 Tbsp. tomato paste. Adding more beans, cheese or other veggies will also make the soup more hearty.

CONTEST-WINNING EASY MINESTRONE

This recipe is special to me because it's one of the few dinners my entire family loves.
And I can feel good about serving it because it's full of nutrition and low in fat.
—Lauren Brennan, Hood River, OR

PREP: 25 MIN. • **COOK:** 40 MIN. • **MAKES:** 11 SERVINGS (2¾ QT.)

2   large carrots, diced
2   celery ribs, chopped
1   medium onion, chopped
1   Tbsp. olive oil
1   Tbsp. butter
2   garlic cloves, minced
2   cans (14½ oz. each) reduced-sodium chicken broth
2   cans (8 oz. each) no-salt-added tomato sauce
1   can (16 oz.) kidney beans, rinsed and drained
1   can (15 oz.) chickpeas, rinsed and drained
1   can (14½ oz.) diced tomatoes, undrained
1½ cups shredded cabbage
1   Tbsp. dried basil
1½ tsp. dried parsley flakes
1   tsp. dried oregano
½   tsp. pepper
1   cup uncooked whole wheat elbow macaroni
11 tsp. grated Parmesan cheese

1. In a large saucepan, saute carrots, celery and onion in oil and butter until tender. Add garlic; cook 1 minute longer.

2. Stir in broth, tomato sauce, kidney beans, chickpeas, tomatoes, cabbage, basil, parsley, oregano and pepper. Bring to a boil. Reduce heat; cover and simmer for 15 minutes.

3. Add macaroni; cook, uncovered, 6-8 minutes or until macaroni and vegetables are tender. Ladle soup into bowls. Sprinkle with cheese.

FREEZE OPTION: Before adding cheese, freeze cooled soup in freezer containers. To use, partially thaw in refrigerator overnight. Heat through in a saucepan, stirring occasionally and adding a little broth or water if necessary.

1 CUP: 180 cal., 4g fat (1g sat. fat), 4mg chol., 443mg sod., 29g carb. (7g sugars, 7g fiber), 8g pro. **DIABETIC EXCHANGES:** 2 starch, 1 lean meat.

FLOURLESS OLIVE OIL
CHOCOLATE CAKE,
PAGE 317

YIAYIA'S SWEETS

Time for everyone's favorite course—dessert!
And nobody makes it quite like Grandma.
Best of all, you can feel good about serving these
wholesome, nutty and fruit-forward treats.

HALVA & NUTELLA BABKA BUNS

This recipe is the result of many years of tweaking and perfecting.
It is a favorite request when visitors come to my farm.
—Dawn Lamoureux-Crocker, Machiasport, ME

PREP: 1 HOUR + RISING • **BAKE:** 15 MIN. • **MAKES:** 8 BUNS

3¾ to 4¼ cups all-purpose flour
⅓ cup sugar
¼ tsp. salt
1 Tbsp. active dry yeast
6 Tbsp. butter, softened
¾ cup warm 2% milk (110° to 115°)
½ tsp. vanilla extract
2 tsp. grated lemon zest
2 large eggs, room temperature
1 jar (13 oz.) Nutella
6 oz. halva with pistachio, crumbled (about 1 cup)
½ cup semisweet chocolate chips
½ cup sugar, optional
½ cup water, optional
2 Tbsp. butter, optional

1. In a large bowl, combine 1½ cups flour, sugar, salt and yeast. Cut in butter until crumbly. Add warm milk, vanilla and lemon zest to dry ingredients; beat just until moistened. Add eggs; beat on medium for 2 minutes. Stir in enough remaining flour to form a firm dough. Turn onto a floured surface; knead until smooth and elastic, 5-7 minutes. Place in a greased bowl, turning once to grease top. Cover and let rise in a warm place until doubled, about 1 hour.

2. Turn out dough onto a lightly floured surface; divide into 8 pieces. Roll each piece into a 10x5-in. rectangle about ⅛ in. thick. For each, spread Nutella to within ½ in. of edges, sprinkle with 2 Tbsp. halva and 1 Tbsp. chocolate chips, and roll up jelly-roll style, starting with a long side; pinch seam and ends to seal.

3. Using a sharp knife, cut each roll lengthwise in half; carefully turn each half cut side up. Loosely twist strips around each other, keeping cut surfaces facing up; pinch ends together to seal. Repeat for remaining buns. Place cut side up on parchment-lined baking sheets. Cover with kitchen towels; let rise in a warm place until almost doubled, about 30 minutes. Preheat oven to 375°.

4. Bake until golden brown, 15-20 minutes. If desired, in a small saucepan, bring sugar and water to a boil; reduce heat and simmer until sugar is dissolved, 1-2 minutes. Remove from heat; add butter, stirring until melted. Brush over buns. Serve buns warm.

1 BUN: 748 cal., 34g fat (11g sat. fat), 72mg chol., 196mg sod., 102g carb. (52g sugars, 5g fiber), 14g pro.

STORING BABKA BUNS

Store these buns in a sealed container for 2-3 days. They also freeze well! Freeze in a single layer in airtight containers for up to 3 months.

AUDREY'S LEMON MERINGUE BARS

In our backyard resides a prolific lemon tree. We are forever trying to find new ways to incorporate these lovely yellow fruits into our culinary endeavors so that none go to waste. My 13-year-old daughter, Audrey, knows my love of all things sweet. She decided to test her baking skill by combining two of my lemony favorites: lemon bars and lemon meringue pie. After several intense hours in the kitchen (warding off her horde of brothers), these delicious bars were born.
—Monica Fearnside, Rancho Palos Verdes, CA

PREP: 35 MIN. + COOLING • **BAKE:** 40 MIN. + CHILLING • **MAKES:** 2 DOZEN

- 2 **cups all-purpose flour**
- ½ **cup sugar**
- ¼ **tsp. salt**
- 1 **cup cold butter**

FILLING
- 1⅓ **cups sugar**
- ½ **cup lemon juice**
- 4 **large eggs, room temperature**
- ¼ **cup all-purpose flour**
- 2 **Tbsp. grated lemon zest**

MERINGUE
- 3 **large egg whites, room temperature**
- 1 **tsp. grated lemon zest**
- ¼ **tsp. cream of tartar**
- 7 **Tbsp. sugar**

1. Preheat oven to 350°. Line a 13x9-in. baking pan with parchment, letting ends extend up sides.

2. In a large bowl, combine flour, sugar and salt; cut in butter until mixture resembles coarse crumbs. Press into bottom of prepared pan. Bake until light golden brown, 20-25 minutes. Cool completely on a wire rack.

3. For filling, in another large bowl, mix sugar, lemon juice, eggs, flour and lemon zest until combined. Pour over crust. Bake until set and top is dry, 22-27 minutes.

4. Meanwhile, for meringue, in a bowl, beat egg whites with lemon zest and cream of tartar on medium speed until foamy. Gradually add sugar, 1 Tbsp. at a time, beating on high after each addition until sugar is dissolved. Continue beating until stiff glossy peaks form. Spread or pipe over hot filling.

5. Bake until meringue is golden brown, 15-18 minutes. Cool 1 hour on a wire rack. Refrigerate at least 4 hours before serving. Lifting with parchment, remove from pan. Cut into bars.

1 BAR: 200 cal., 9g fat (5g sat. fat), 51mg chol., 105mg sod., 29g carb. (19g sugars, 0 fiber), 3g pro.

READER REVIEW
"Yum! This recipe is delicious and a much easier way to make lemon meringue pie—in sheet form! Great job, Audrey!"
—MARTHAMYDEAR6, TASTEOFHOME.COM

WHITE CHOCOLATE FRUIT TART

*It takes a little time to make, but this tart is absolutely marvelous,
especially in summer when fresh fruit is in abundance.*
—Claire Dailey, New Castle, DE

PREP: 30 MIN. • **BAKE:** 25 MIN. + CHILLING • **MAKES:** 16 SERVINGS

¾ cup butter, softened
½ cup confectioners' sugar
1½ cups all-purpose flour
FILLING
1 pkg. (10 to 12 oz.) white baking
  chips, melted and cooled
¼ cup heavy whipping cream
1 pkg. (8 oz.) cream cheese, softened
1 can (11 oz.) mandarin oranges
1 can (8 oz.) pineapple chunks
1 pint fresh strawberries, sliced
2 kiwifruit, peeled and sliced
GLAZE
3 Tbsp. sugar
2 tsp. cornstarch
½ tsp. lemon juice
  Optional: Minced fresh basil
  or fresh mint

1. In a small bowl, cream butter and confectioners' sugar until light and fluffy, 3-4 minutes. Gradually add flour and mix well.

2. Press into an ungreased 11-in. fluted tart pan with removable bottom or 12-in. pizza pan with side. Bake at 300° for 25-30 minutes or until lightly browned. Cool on a wire rack.

3. For filling, in a small bowl, beat melted chips and cream. Add cream cheese; beat until smooth. Spread over crust. Refrigerate for 30 minutes.

4. Drain oranges and pineapple, reserving ½ cup fruit juices. Arrange oranges, pineapple, strawberries and kiwi over filling.

5. For glaze, in a small saucepan, combine sugar and cornstarch. Stir in lemon juice and reserved fruit juices until smooth. Bring to a boil over medium heat; cook and stir for 2 minutes or until thickened. Cool.

6. Brush glaze over fruit. Refrigerate for 1 hour before serving. If desired, sprinkle with fresh basil or mint. Refrigerate leftovers.

1 PIECE: 335 cal., 21g fat (13g sat. fat), 45mg chol., 133mg sod., 35g carb. (24g sugars, 1g fiber), 4g pro.

ITALIAN HONEY CLUSTERS

My mother made these treats, known as struffoli *in Italian, for neighbors, teachers and anyone who stopped by. This dish is an Easter, Christmas and special-occasion classic, and many call them cookies even though these are honey-coated bits of deep-fried dough.*
—Sarah Knoblock, Hyde Park, IN

PREP: 45 MIN. + STANDING • **COOK:** 5 MIN./BATCH • **MAKES:** ABOUT 2 DOZEN

3   cups all-purpose flour
½   tsp. ground cinnamon
½   tsp. aniseed, crushed
⅛   tsp. salt
4   large eggs, lightly beaten
⅓   cup 2% milk
    Oil for deep-fat frying
1   cup honey
¼   cup sugar
½   cup pine nuts, toasted
    Nonpareils, optional

1. Line 24 muffin cups with paper or foil liners. In a large bowl, whisk flour, cinnamon, aniseed and salt. Stir in eggs and milk. Turn dough onto a floured surface; knead until smooth and elastic, 6-8 minutes. Shape into a disk; wrap and let stand 1 hour.

2. Divide dough into 6 portions. Roll each portion into ½-in.-thick ropes; cut crosswise into ½-in. pieces. In an electric skillet or deep-fat fryer, heat oil to 350°. Fry pieces, a few at a time, for 2-3 minutes on each side or until golden brown. Drain on paper towels. Place dough pieces in a large heatproof bowl and keep warm in a 200° oven.

3. In a large heavy saucepan, combine honey and sugar. Bring to a boil over medium heat; boil 1 minute. Immediately remove from heat and drizzle over dough pieces. Stir to coat. Immediately spoon into prepared cups. Sprinkle with pine nuts and, if desired, nonpareils.

1 SERVING: 161 cal., 5g fat (1g sat. fat), 31mg chol., 27mg sod., 26g carb. (14g sugars, 1g fiber), 3g pro.

DID YOU KNOW?

Also known as pignolia or pinon, the pine nut is a small seed from one of several pine tree varieties. They are small, elongated ivory-colored nuts, measuring about ⅜ in. long and having a soft texture and buttery flavor. Frequently used in Italian dishes and a signature ingredient in pesto, pine nuts are often toasted to enhance their flavor.

ORANGE RICOTTA CAKE ROLL

I come from a big Italian family. When I was growing up, my mom cooked and baked many delicious meals and desserts from scratch. Now I do the same for my family. This cake is my finale to our special-occasion dinners.
—Cathy Banks, Encinitas, CA

PREP: 45 MIN. • **BAKE:** 10 MIN. + CHILLING • **MAKES:** 12 SERVINGS

- 4   large eggs, separated, room temperature
- ¼   cup baking cocoa
- 2   Tbsp. all-purpose flour
- ⅛   tsp. salt
- ⅔   cup confectioners' sugar, sifted, divided
- 1   tsp. vanilla extract
- ½   tsp. cream of tartar

FILLING
- 1   container (15 oz.) ricotta cheese
- 3   Tbsp. mascarpone cheese
- ⅓   cup sugar
- 1   Tbsp. Kahlua (coffee liqueur)
- 1   Tbsp. grated orange zest
- ½   tsp. vanilla extract
    Additional confectioners' sugar

1. Place egg whites in a bowl. Preheat oven to 325°. Line bottom of a greased 15x10x1-in. baking pan with parchment; grease paper. Sift cocoa, flour and salt together twice.

2. In a large bowl, beat egg yolks until slightly thickened. Gradually add ⅓ cup confectioners' sugar, beating on high speed until thick and lemon-colored. Beat in vanilla. Fold in cocoa mixture (batter will be very thick).

3. Add cream of tartar to egg whites; with clean beaters, beat on medium until soft peaks form. Gradually add remaining confectioners' sugar, 1 Tbsp. at a time, beating on high after each addition until sugar is dissolved. Continue beating until soft glossy peaks form. Fold a fourth of the whites into batter, then fold in remaining whites. Transfer to prepared pan, spreading evenly.

4. Bake until top springs back when lightly touched, 9-11 minutes. Cover cake with waxed paper; cool completely on a wire rack.

5. Remove waxed paper; invert cake onto an 18-in.-long sheet of waxed paper dusted with confectioners' sugar. Gently peel off parchment.

6. In a small bowl, beat cheeses and sugar until blended. Stir in Kahlua, orange zest and vanilla. Spread over cake to within ½ in. of edges. Roll up jelly-roll style, starting with a short side. Trim ends; place on a platter, seam side down.

7. Refrigerate, covered, at least 1 hour before serving. To serve, dust with confectioners' sugar.

1 PIECE: 169 cal., 9g fat (5g sat. fat), 94mg chol., 95mg sod., 17g carb. (14g sugars, 0 fiber), 7g pro. **DIABETIC EXCHANGES:** 2 fat, 1 starch.

⑤ⅰ GLUTEN-FREE ALMOND COOKIES

My friend loved these gluten-free almond cookies so much, she had to ask for the recipe! Quick and easy, they taste as good as the decadent treats I make using puff pastry and almond paste. Everyone loves them!
—Sherri Cox, Lucasville, OH

PREP: 15 MIN. • BAKE: 15 MIN./BATCH • MAKES: 2 DOZEN

1   can (8 oz.) almond paste
½   cup sugar
2   large egg whites,
     room temperature
⅛   tsp. salt

1. Preheat oven to 350°. In a large bowl, beat almond paste and sugar until crumbly. Beat in egg whites and salt until smooth. Drop by scant tablespoonfuls 1 in. apart onto parchment-lined baking sheets.

2. Bake until lightly browned, 15-18 minutes. Cool for 1 minute before removing from pans to wire racks. Store in an airtight container.

NOTE: Read all ingredient labels for possible gluten content prior to use. Ingredient formulas can change, and production facilities vary among brands. If you're concerned that your brand may contain gluten, contact the company.

1 COOKIE: 61 cal., 3g fat (0 sat. fat), 0 chol., 18mg sod., 9g carb. (8g sugars, 0 fiber), 1g pro. **DIABETIC EXCHANGES:** ½ starch, ½ fat.

---

⑤ⅰ LEMON-APRICOT FRUIT POPS

With just 31 calories, 4 teaspoons of sugar total and lots of vitamin C, this is one light and refreshing summer dessert everyone can find room for!
—Aysha Schurman, Ammon, ID

PREP: 15 MIN. + FREEZING • MAKES: 6 POPS

¼   cup orange juice
1   tsp. grated lemon zest
¼   cup lemon juice
4   tsp. sugar
1   cup sliced fresh apricots
     (4-5 medium)
½   cup ice cubes
1   tsp. minced fresh mint, optional
6   freezer pop pouches, molds or
     6 paper cups (3-oz. size) and
     wooden pop sticks

1. Place the first 6 ingredients in a blender; cover and process until blended. If desired, stir in mint.

2. Pour into pouches, molds or paper cups. Top molds with holders. If using cups, top with foil and insert sticks through foil. Freeze until firm.

1 POP: 31 cal., 0 fat (0 sat. fat), 0 chol., 0 sod., 8g carb. (6g sugars, 1g fiber), 0 pro. **DIABETIC EXCHANGES:** ½ fruit.

MINI BAKLAVA

MINI BAKLAVA

Baklava provides amazing memories for me: My best friend made it for my bridal and baby showers. And then she taught me how to make it! These delicious little miniatures give you the taste of baklava in a bite-sized package.
—Margaret Guillory, Eunice, LA

PREP: 20 MIN. • **BAKE:** 10 MIN. + COOLING • **MAKES:** ABOUT 2½ DOZEN

½ cup butter
¼ cup sugar
1 tsp. ground cinnamon
1 cup finely chopped pecans
1 cup finely chopped walnuts
2 pkg. (1.9 oz. each) frozen miniature phyllo tart shells
Honey

1. Preheat oven to 350°. In a small saucepan over medium heat, melt butter. Stir in sugar and cinnamon. Bring to a boil. Reduce heat; add pecans and walnuts, tossing to coat. Simmer, uncovered, until nuts are lightly toasted, 5-10 minutes.

2. Place phyllo shells on a parchment-lined baking sheet. Spoon nut and butter sauce mixture evenly into shells. Bake until golden brown, 9-11 minutes. Cool completely on pan on a wire rack. Drizzle a drop of honey into each shell; let stand, covered, until serving. Serve with additional honey if desired.

1 FILLED PHYLLO CUP: 105 cal., 9g fat (2g sat. fat), 8mg chol., 33mg sod., 5g carb. (2g sugars, 1g fiber), 1g pro.

LEMON & LIME STRAWBERRY ICE

My icy fruit dessert is perfect for summer. It's so refreshing after dinner.
—Marie Rizzio, Interlochen, MI

PREP: 30 MIN. + FREEZING • **MAKES:** 6 SERVINGS

1 cup sugar
¾ cup water
1 Tbsp. shredded orange zest
2 tsp. shredded lemon zest
1½ tsp. shredded lime zest
⅓ cup orange juice
3 Tbsp. lemon juice
2 Tbsp. lime juice
4 cups sliced fresh strawberries

1. In a small saucepan, combine the first 5 ingredients. Bring to a boil. Reduce heat; simmer, uncovered, 5-6 minutes or until slightly thickened. Strain; discard zest. Add juices to the syrup; cool slightly.

2. Place half of the juice mixture and 2 cups strawberries in a blender; cover and pulse until nearly smooth. Pour into a 2-qt. freezer container. Repeat with remaining juice mixture and berries.

3. Cover and freeze 12 hours or overnight, stirring several times. Ice may be frozen for up to 3 months. Just before serving, break apart with a large spoon.

⅔ CUP: 173 cal., 0 fat (0 sat. fat), 0 chol., 2mg sod., 44g carb. (39g sugars, 3g fiber), 1g pro.

LEMON-LIME BERRY ICE: Reduce strawberries to 2 cups and add 2 cups fresh raspberries.

ISRAELI MALABI WITH POMEGRANATE SYRUP

This is a very famous, easy-to-make sweet milk pudding from Israel. For this recipe, I learned from a friend, you can use rose syrup instead of pomegranate syrup.
—Kanwaljeet Chhabra, Eden Prairie, MN

PREP: 20 MIN. + CHILLING • **COOK:** 10 MIN. • **MAKES:** 4 SERVINGS

2 cups whole milk
⅓ cup sugar
4 Tbsp. cornstarch
½ cup cold water
¼ cup heavy whipping cream
1 tsp. rose water
POMEGRANATE SYRUP
½ cup sugar
½ cup pomegranate juice
¼ cup pomegranate seeds
2 Tbsp. chopped pistachios

In a small heavy saucepan, whisk milk and sugar. Cook and stir over medium heat until bubbly. In a small bowl, mix cornstarch and water until smooth; stir into pan. Bring to a boil; cook and stir until thickened, 1-2 minutes. Remove from heat. Stir in cream and rose water. Cool 15 minutes, stirring occasionally. Transfer to dessert dishes. Press plastic wrap onto the surface of pudding. Refrigerate until cold. For syrup, in a small saucepan, combine sugar and pomegranate juice. Cook and stir over medium heat until sugar is dissolved, 3-4 minutes. Remove from heat; cool completely. Spoon syrup over pudding; sprinkle with pomegranate seeds and pistachios.

1 SERVING: 346 cal., 11g fat (6g sat. fat), 29mg chol., 74mg sod., 58g carb. (50g sugars, 1g fiber), 5g pro.

🟤 ITALIAN PIGNOLI COOKIES

Cookies are the crown jewels of Italian confections. I can't let a holiday go by without baking these traditional almond cookies rolled in mild pine nuts.
—Maria Regakis, Saugus, MA

PREP: 30 MIN. • **BAKE:** 15 MIN./BATCH • **MAKES:** 2½ DOZEN

1¼ cups (12 oz.) almond paste
½ cup sugar
4 large egg whites,
   room temperature, divided
1 cup confectioners' sugar
1½ cups pine nuts

1. In a small bowl, beat almond paste and sugar until crumbly. Beat in 2 egg whites. Gradually add confectioners' sugar; mix well.

2. Whisk remaining egg whites in a shallow bowl. Place pine nuts in another shallow bowl. Shape dough into 1-in. balls. Roll in egg whites and coat with pine nuts. Place 2 in. apart on parchment-lined baking sheets. Flatten slightly.

3. Bake at 325° until lightly browned, 15-18 minutes. Cool for 1 minute before removing from pans to wire racks. Store in an airtight container.

1 COOKIE: 112 cal., 6g fat (1g sat. fat), 0 chol., 7mg sod., 13g carb. (11g sugars, 1g fiber), 3g pro.

ISRAELI MALABI WITH
POMEGRANATE SYRUP

MELOMAKARONA

Growing up in Cyprus, we would see this cookie everywhere during the holidays. Every year my mother, Thelma, would make plate after plate of these all Christmas long. It's just not the holidays without them.
—Paris Paraskeva, San Francisco, CA

PREP: 15 MIN. • **BAKE:** 20 MIN./BATCH • **MAKES:** 4½ DOZEN

1 cup sugar
1 cup water
¾ cup honey
COOKIES
1 cup confectioners' sugar
2 cups olive oil
½ cup Cognac
½ cup orange juice
1 Tbsp. honey
7½ cups all-purpose flour
4 tsp. grated orange zest
3 tsp. baking powder
1 tsp. ground cinnamon
½ cup ground toasted walnuts

1. Preheat oven to 350°. In a saucepan, combine sugar, water and honey; bring to a boil. Reduce heat; simmer, uncovered, 10 minutes. Cool completely.

2. Meanwhile, for cookies, in a large bowl, beat confectioners' sugar and oil until blended. Beat in Cognac, orange juice and honey. In another bowl, whisk flour, orange zest, baking powder and cinnamon; gradually beat into sugar mixture.

3. Shape tablespoons of dough into 1-in.-thick ovals. Place 1 in. apart on parchment-lined baking sheets. Bake until lightly browned, 20-25 minutes. Cool on pans 5 minutes. Remove to wire racks.

4. Float and turn warm cookies in syrup about 10 seconds; allow excess to drip off. Place on waxed paper; sprinkle with walnuts. Let stand until set. Store between pieces of waxed paper in airtight containers.

1 COOKIE: 172 cal., 9g fat (1g sat. fat), 0 chol., 27mg sod., 20g carb. (7g sugars, 1g fiber), 2g pro.

READER REVIEW
"These are now one of my all-time favorite cookies."
—EJSHELLABARGER, TASTEOFHOME.COM

OLIVE OIL CAKE

*A good olive oil cake isn't overly sweet, so it can just as easily be
a breakfast treat or an afternoon snack as a dessert.*
—Lisa Kaminski, Wauwatosa, WI

PREP: 15 MIN. • **BAKE:** 45 MIN. + COOLING • **MAKES:** 16 SERVINGS

- 3 large eggs, room temperature
- 1½ cups sugar
- ¾ cup extra virgin olive oil
- ¾ cup ground almonds
- ½ cup 2% milk
- 4 tsp. grated orange zest
- 1 tsp. vanilla extract
- 1¾ cups all-purpose flour
- 2 tsp. baking powder
- ½ tsp. salt
- ¾ cup confectioners' sugar
- 2 to 3 Tbsp. orange juice
  Sliced almonds, toasted, optional

1. Preheat oven to 350°. Grease and flour a 10-in. fluted tube pan. In a large bowl, beat eggs on high speed 3 minutes. Gradually add sugar, beating until thick and lemon-colored. Gradually beat in oil. Beat in ground almonds, milk, orange zest and vanilla.

2. In another bowl, whisk flour, baking powder and salt; fold into egg mixture. Transfer batter to prepared pan, spreading evenly. Bake until a toothpick inserted in center comes out clean, 45-50 minutes. Cool in pan 15 minutes before removing to a wire rack to cool completely.

3. For icing, in a small bowl, whisk confectioners' sugar and enough orange juice to reach a drizzling consistency. Drizzle over cake. If desired, sprinkle with almonds.

1 PIECE: 279 cal., 14g fat (2g sat. fat), 35mg chol., 152mg sod., 37g carb. (25g sugars, 1g fiber), 4g pro.

LEMON SORBETTO

🗑 LEMON SORBETTO

Whether you serve it in chilled bowls or scoop it into cut lemon halves, this creamy four-ingredient sorbet is both sweet and tart. It makes a delightfully refreshing finish to any meal.
—Goldene Petersen, Brigham City, UT

PREP: 15 MIN. + COOLING • **PROCESS:** 20 MIN. + FREEZING • **MAKES:** ABOUT 2 CUPS

1 cup sugar
1 cup water
3 Tbsp. grated lemon zest
¾ cup lemon juice
Optional: Cookie cups, lemon wedges and additional lemon zest

1. Place sugar and water in a small saucepan; bring to a boil over medium heat, stirring constantly. Reduce heat; simmer, uncovered, 2 minutes. Cool completely.

2. Stir in lemon zest and juice. Fill cylinder of ice cream maker no more than two-thirds full; freeze according to manufacturer's directions.

3. Transfer sorbet to a freezer container, allowing headspace for expansion. Freeze until firm, about 4 hours. If desired, serve in cookie cups with lemon wedges and top with additional lemon zest.

⅓ CUP: 138 cal., 0 fat (0 sat. fat), 0 chol., 1mg sod., 36g carb. (34g sugars, 0 fiber), 0 pro.

APRICOT DESSERT BRUSCHETTA

Years ago, my mother took a trip to Italy, and this recipe reminds her of the sun-kissed fruits from the orchards there. It's a lovely apricot dessert that's not overly sweet or heavy.
—Deborah Biggs, Omaha, NE

TAKES: 30 MIN • **MAKES:** 10 SERVINGS

10 slices French bread baguette (¼ in. thick)
½ cup chopped dried apricots
½ cup apricot nectar
1 tsp. grated lemon zest
¼ cup reduced-fat ricotta cheese
¼ cup apricot preserves
2 Tbsp. sliced almonds, toasted

1. Place bread on an ungreased baking sheet. Bake at 350° until toasted, 4-6 minutes. Cool.

2. Meanwhile, in a small saucepan, combine apricots, nectar and lemon zest. Bring to a boil. Reduce heat; simmer, uncovered, for 2 minutes. Remove from heat; cool to room temperature. Strain mixture, discarding liquid.

3. Combine cheese and preserves; spread over toasted bread. Top with apricot mixture. Sprinkle with almonds.

1 PIECE: 77 cal., 1g fat (0 sat. fat), 2mg chol., 49mg sod., 15g carb. (7g sugars, 1g fiber), 2g pro. **DIABETIC EXCHANGES:** 1 starch.

BAKLAVA

Baklava is a traditional Middle Eastern pastry made with flaky phyllo dough, chopped nuts and sweet honey. This dessert is very rich, so one pan goes a long way.
—Judy Losecco, Buffalo, NY

PREP: 30 MIN. • **BAKE:** 40 MIN. • **MAKES:** 4 DOZEN

1½ lbs. finely chopped walnuts
½ cup sugar
½ tsp. ground cinnamon
⅛ tsp. ground cloves
1 lb. butter, melted, divided
2 pkg. (16 oz. each, 14x9-in. sheet size) frozen phyllo dough, thawed

SYRUP
2 cups sugar
2 cups water
1 cup honey
1 Tbsp. grated lemon or orange zest

1. In a small bowl, combine walnuts, sugar, cinnamon and cloves; set aside. Brush a 15x10x1-in. baking pan with some butter. Unroll 1 pkg. phyllo dough; cut stack into a 10½x9-in. rectangle. Repeat with remaining phyllo. Discard scraps.

2. Line bottom of prepared pan with 2 sheets of phyllo dough (sheets will overlap slightly). Brush with butter. Repeat layers 14 times. (Keep dough covered with a damp towel until ready to use to prevent sheets from drying out.)

3. Spread with 2 cups walnut mixture. Top with 5 layers of phyllo dough, brushing with butter between each sheet. Spread with remaining walnut mixture. Top with 1 layer of phyllo dough; brush with butter. Repeat 14 times. Cut into 2½-in. squares; cut each square in half diagonally. Brush remaining butter over top. Bake at 350° until golden brown, 40-45 minutes.

4. In a large saucepan, bring syrup ingredients to a boil. Reduce heat; simmer for 10 minutes. Strain syrup, discarding zest; cool to lukewarm. Pour syrup over warm baklava.

1 BAKLAVA TRIANGLE: 271 cal., 16g fat (5g sat. fat), 21mg chol., 162mg sod., 30g carb. (17g sugars, 1g fiber), 5g pro.

CHOCOLATE BAKLAVA: For nut mixture, combine 1 lb. finely chopped walnuts, 1 pkg. (12 oz.) miniature semisweet chocolate chips, ¾ cup sugar, 1½ tsp. ground cinnamon and 1 tsp. grated lemon peel. Layer and bake as directed. For syrup, use 1 cup plus 2 Tbsp. orange juice, ¾ cup each sugar, water and honey and 3 Tbsp. lemon juice. Bring to a boil. Reduce heat; simmer, uncovered, 20 minutes. Pour over warm baklava. Cool completely on a wire rack.

DATE BAR TIPS

What kind of dates should you use to make these bars? Dates are very healthy, and there are two main kinds that are readily available, medjool or deglet noor dates. While it's really a personal preference, we like medjool dates for these bars. Medjool dates are naturally sweeter than deglet noor dates.

How can you make date bars your own? A simple and easy way to elevate these bars is to play around with some warm spices that would enhance these already delicious bars. Something as easy as adding a sprinkle of cardamom or cinnamon can really take these date bars to the next level.

BEST DATE BARS

BEST DATE BARS

These wholesome bar cookies freeze well. Simply cool them in the pan,
cut into squares and store them in airtight freezer containers.
—Dorothy DeLeske, Scottsdale, AZ

PREP: 25 MIN. • **BAKE:** 35 MIN. • **MAKES:** 40 BARS

2½ cups pitted dates, cut up
¼ cup sugar
1½ cups water
⅓ cup coarsely chopped walnuts,
    optional
1¼ cups all-purpose flour
½ tsp. salt
½ tsp. baking soda
1½ cups quick-cooking oats
1 cup packed brown sugar
½ cup butter, softened
1 Tbsp. water

1. In a saucepan, combine dates, sugar and water. Cook, stirring frequently, until very thick. Stir in walnuts if desired; cool.

2. Sift flour, salt and baking soda together in a large bowl; add oats and brown sugar. Cut in butter until mixture is crumbly. Sprinkle water over mixture; stir lightly. Pat half into a greased 13x9-in. baking pan. Spread with date mixture; cover with remaining oat mixture and pat lightly.

3. Bake at 350° until lightly browned, 35-40 minutes. Cool on a wire rack. Cut into bars.

1 BAR: 97 cal., 3g fat (2g sat. fat), 6mg chol., 65mg sod., 19g carb. (12g sugars, 1g fiber), 1g pro.

🔟 PEACH ICE

If the fresh peach you use is delicious, this recipe will be delicious! It's a very
light dessert for those counting calories, and it's truly a cinch to prepare.
—Carma Blosser, Livermore, CO

PREP: 15 MIN. + FREEZING • **MAKES:** 2 SERVINGS

⅓ cup warm water (120° to 130°)
2 Tbsp. sugar
1 small peach, peeled
2 tsp. lemon juice

1. In a small bowl, stir water and sugar until sugar is dissolved. Place peach, lemon juice and sugar mixture in a blender. Cover and process 1 minute or until blended. Transfer to a freezer container; cover and freeze 3 hours or until almost firm.

2. Transfer to blender. Cover and process 30-40 seconds or until slushy. Return to freezer container; cover and freeze overnight.

3. Remove from freezer just before serving. Using a fork, scrape into two dessert dishes.

1 SERVING: 65 cal., 0 fat (0 sat. fat), 0 chol., 0 sod., 17g carb. (16g sugars, 1g fiber), 0 pro. **DIABETIC EXCHANGES:** 1 starch.

CITRUS CORNMEAL CAKE

Cornmeal adds a rustic quality to this delicate dessert flavored with citrus and almond.
It makes a great holiday party hostess gift and is sure to be a staple in your recipe collection.
—Roxanne Chan, Albany, CA

PREP: 25 MIN. • **BAKE:** 25 MIN. + COOLING • **MAKES:** 8 SERVINGS

½ cup lemon yogurt
⅓ cup honey
¼ cup olive oil
1 large egg, room temperature
2 large egg whites,
   room temperature
¼ tsp. almond extract
¾ cup all-purpose flour
½ cup cornmeal
1 tsp. baking powder
½ tsp. grated orange zest
1 can (15 oz.) mandarin oranges,
   drained
3 Tbsp. sliced almonds

1. Coat a 9-in. fluted tart pan with removable bottom with cooking spray. In a large bowl, beat yogurt, honey, oil, egg, egg whites and extract until well blended. Combine flour, cornmeal and baking powder; gradually beat into yogurt mixture until blended. Stir in orange zest.

2. Pour into prepared pan. Arrange oranges over batter; sprinkle with almonds. Bake at 350° until a toothpick inserted in the center comes out clean, 25-30 minutes. Cool on a wire rack for 10 minutes before cutting. Serve warm or at room temperature.

1 PIECE: 240 cal., 9g fat (1g sat. fat), 27mg chol., 85mg sod., 36g carb. (20g sugars, 2g fiber), 5g pro.

5i WINTER FRUIT WITH PROSECCO SABAYON

This recipe is special to me because it allows me to treat my dinner guests to a special, unusual dessert.
The bright, vivid colors are perfect for the holidays. Omit the Prosecco when serving to children.
—Jerry Gulley, Pleasant Prairie, WI

TAKES: 25 MIN. • **MAKES:** 6 SERVINGS (¾ CUP SAUCE)

6 medium blood oranges, peeled
   and cut into ¼-in. slices
1 vanilla bean, split
¼ cup sugar plus 3 Tbsp. sugar,
   divided
½ cup Prosecco or other
   sparkling wine, divided
   Dash salt
3 large egg yolks

1. Arrange orange slices on a serving platter or individual plates. Scrape vanilla bean seeds into a small bowl. Add ¼ cup sugar, ¼ cup Prosecco and salt; combine and drizzle over oranges. Refrigerate until serving.

2. In a double boiler or metal bowl over simmering water, constantly whisk egg yolks and remaining sugar and Prosecco until mixture reaches 160° and coats the back of a spoon. Drizzle over oranges. Serve immediately.

1 SLICED ORANGE WITH 2 TBSP. SAUCE: 151 cal., 3g fat (1g sat. fat), 92mg chol., 249mg sod., 26g carb. (24g sugars, 2g fiber), 2g pro. **DIABETIC EXCHANGES:** 1 starch, 1 fruit, ½ fat.

CITRUS
CORNMEAL
CAKE

⑤ RHUBARB STRAWBERRY GRANITA

Fresh rhubarb and strawberries make this sweet and icy dessert such a treat. You'll love how quickly it comes together and that it's prepared without any special equipment.
—Christen Roye, Weatherford, TX

PREP: 15 MIN+ FREEZING • **MAKES:** 8 SERVINGS

3 cups water
1 cup plus 2 Tbsp. sugar
1 cup diced fresh or frozen rhubarb, thawed
½ cup halved fresh strawberries
2 Tbsp. orange liqueur or orange juice
Fresh mint leaves, optional

1. In a large saucepan, bring water, sugar, rhubarb and strawberries to a boil. Cook and stir until sugar is dissolved. Strain; discard pulp and seeds.

2. Transfer syrup to an 8-in. square dish. Stir in orange liqueur; cool to room temperature. Freeze for 1 hour; stir with a fork. Freeze 2-3 hours longer or until completely frozen, stirring every 30 minutes. Stir granita with a fork just before serving; spoon into dessert dishes. Garnish with mint if desired.

1 SERVING: 128 cal., 0 fat (0 sat. fat), 0 chol., 1mg sod., 31g carb. (30g sugars, 0 fiber), 0 pro.

SUGARED DATE BALLS

When I was a youngster, Mom always baked these tender old-fashioned cookies dotted with chewy dates and crunchy walnuts. Much to the delight of my family, I've continued her delicious tradition.
—Sandra Vautrain, Sugar Land, TX

PREP: 15 MIN. • **BAKE:** 25 MIN./BATCH • **MAKES:** 2½ DOZEN

½ cup butter, softened
⅓ cup confectioners' sugar
1 Tbsp. 2% milk
1 tsp. vanilla extract
1¼ cups all-purpose flour
¼ tsp. salt
⅔ cup chopped dates
½ cup chopped nuts
Additional confectioners' sugar

1. Preheat oven to 325°. In a bowl, cream butter and sugar. Beat in milk and vanilla. Combine flour and salt; gradually add to creamed mixture. Stir in dates and nuts.

2. Roll into 1-in. balls. Place 2 in. apart on ungreased baking sheets. Bake until bottoms are lightly browned, 22-25 minutes. Roll warm cookies in confectioners' sugar; cool on wire racks.

1 DATE BALL: 74 cal., 4g fat (2g sat. fat), 8mg chol., 44mg sod., 8g carb. (3g sugars, 1g fiber), 1g pro.

SENSATIONAL TIRAMISU

This light version of the popular Italian dessert is moist and creamy, and cuts so well into pretty layered squares. You'll love the blend of coffee, Kahlua and cream cheese flavors.
—Mary J. Walters, Westerville, OH

PREP: 25 MIN. • **COOK:** 10 MIN. + CHILLING • **MAKES:** 12 SERVINGS

1   pkg. (8 oz.) reduced-fat cream cheese
⅔   cup confectioners' sugar, divided
1½   cups reduced-fat whipped topping, divided
½   cup plus 1 Tbsp. sugar
3   large egg whites, room temperature
¼   cup water
2   pkg. (3 oz. each) ladyfingers, split
½   cup boiling water
2   Tbsp. coffee liqueur
1   Tbsp. instant coffee granules
½   tsp. baking cocoa

1. In a small bowl, beat cream cheese and confectioners' sugar until smooth. Fold in 1 cup whipped topping; set aside.

2. Combine ½ cup sugar, egg whites and water in a small heavy saucepan over low heat. With a hand mixer, beat on low speed for 1 minute. Continue beating on low over low heat 8-10 minutes or until mixture reaches 160°. Pour into a large bowl. Beat on high until stiff peaks form, about 7 minutes. Fold into cream cheese mixture.

3. Arrange half of ladyfingers in an ungreased 11x7-in. dish. Combine boiling water, coffee liqueur, coffee granules and remaining sugar; brush half of mixture over ladyfingers. Top with half of cream cheese mixture. Repeat layers. Spread remaining whipped topping over top; sprinkle with cocoa. Refrigerate for 2 hours before serving.

1 PIECE: 223 cal., 7g fat (4g sat. fat), 62mg chol., 127mg sod., 34g carb. (18g sugars, 0 fiber), 5g pro. **DIABETIC EXCHANGES:** 2 starch, 1 fat.

READER REVIEW
"This recipe truly is sensational! My whole family thought it was the best tiramisu recipe I've made. I'm making a double batch for an Italian-themed party we're having at work. I'm sure it will be a hit at the party."
—BAKE MASTER, TASTEOFHOME.COM

⑤ VANILLA MERINGUE COOKIES

These sweet little swirls are light as can be. They're all you need after a big, special dinner.
—Jenni Sharp, Milwaukee, WI

PREP: 20 MIN. • **BAKE:** 40 MIN. + COOLING • **MAKES:** ABOUT 5 DOZEN

3 **large egg whites**
1½ **tsp. clear or regular vanilla extract**
¼ **tsp. cream of tartar**
  Dash salt
⅔ **cup sugar**

TRY OTHER FLAVORS

This recipe calls for classic vanilla, but feel free to use other flavors of extract instead, such as almond, lemon, orange, peppermint, coconut, cherry or raspberry. If desired, add a little food coloring to help hint at the flavor (such as yellow or orange for citrus cookies).

1. Place egg whites in a small bowl; let stand at room temperature for 20 minutes.

2. Meanwhile, preheat oven to 250°. Add vanilla, cream of tartar and salt to egg whites; beat on medium speed until foamy. Gradually add sugar, 1 Tbsp. at a time, beating on high after each addition, until sugar is dissolved. Continue beating until stiff glossy peaks form, about 7 minutes.

3. Attach a #32 star tip to a pastry bag. Transfer meringue to bag. Pipe 1¼-in.-diameter cookies 2 in. apart onto parchment-lined baking sheets.

4. Bake until firm to touch, 40-45 minutes. Turn off oven; leave meringues in oven 1 hour (leave oven door closed). Remove from oven; cool completely on baking sheets. Remove meringues from paper; store in airtight containers at room temperature.

1 COOKIE: 10 cal., 0 fat (0 sat. fat), 0 chol., 5mg sod., 2g carb. (2g sugars, 0 fiber), 0 pro. **DIABETIC EXCHANGES:** 1 free food.

GREEK HOLIDAY
COOKIES

GREEK HOLIDAY COOKIES

Koulourakia are a traditional treat in Greece, where they are usually made for Easter and other celebrations. I enjoy making these buttery, golden cookies to keep me in touch with my heritage.
—Nicole Moskou, New York, NY

PREP: 30 MIN. + CHILLING • **BAKE:** 10 MIN./BATCH • **MAKES:** 6½ DOZEN

1½ cups butter, softened
1¼ cups sugar
4 large eggs, room temperature
2 Tbsp. orange juice
3 tsp. vanilla extract
5¼ cups all-purpose flour
1½ tsp. baking powder
¾ tsp. baking soda

1. In a large bowl, cream butter and sugar until light and fluffy, 5-7 minutes. Add 2 eggs; beat well. Beat in orange juice and vanilla. Combine flour, baking powder and baking soda; gradually add to creamed mixture. Cover and refrigerate for 1 hour or until easy to handle.

2. Roll dough into 1¼-in. balls. Shape each into a 6-in. rope; fold in half and twist twice. Place 2 in. apart on ungreased baking sheets.

3. In a small bowl, beat remaining 2 eggs; brush over dough. Bake at 350° for 7-12 minutes or until edges are golden brown. Remove to wire racks.

1 COOKIE: 79 cal., 4g fat (2g sat. fat), 19mg chol., 53mg sod., 10g carb. (3g sugars, 0 fiber), 1g pro.

🄕 STRAWBERRY & WINE SORBET

Bright and refreshing, this grown-up dessert tastes like you're biting into a just-picked strawberry. White wine and lemon juice enhance its not-too-sweet flavor.
—Donna Lamano, Olathe, KS

PREP: 20 MIN. + FREEZING • **MAKES:** 1 QT.

¾ cup sugar
½ cup water
1½ lbs. fresh strawberries, hulled
1 cup white wine
½ cup honey
¼ cup lemon juice

1. In a small saucepan, bring sugar and water to a boil. Cook and stir until sugar is dissolved; set aside to cool.

2. Place remaining ingredients in a food processor; add sugar syrup. Cover and process for 2-3 minutes or until smooth. Strain and discard seeds and pulp. Transfer puree to a 13x9-in. dish. Freeze for 1 hour or until edges begin to firm. Stir and return to freezer. Freeze 2 hours longer or until firm.

3. Just before serving, transfer to a food processor; cover and process for 2-3 minutes or until smooth.

⅔ CUP: 254 cal., 0 fat (0 sat. fat), 0 chol., 4mg sod., 59g carb. (54g sugars, 2g fiber), 1g pro.

5i QUICK MANGO SORBET

Last summer, I decided to try my hand at making a passion fruit and mango sorbet. But fresh fruits require more prep and are difficult to find ripened at the same time. So I experimented using frozen fruit and juice, and voila! Both are readily available and inexpensive too.
—Carol A Klein, Franklin Square, NY

TAKES: 5 MIN. • **MAKES:** 2½ CUPS

1 pkg. (16 oz.) frozen mango chunks, slightly thawed
½ cup passion fruit juice
2 Tbsp. sugar

Place all ingredients in a blender; cover and process until smooth. Serve immediately. If desired, for a firmer texture, cover and freeze at least 3 hours.

½ CUP: 91 cal., 0 fat (0 sat. fat), 0 chol., 2mg sod., 24g carb. (21g sugars, 2g fiber), 1g pro.

5i ROSE WATER RICE PUDDING

This rice pudding is a popular Middle Eastern treat. Pomegranate seeds and chopped pistachios add a simple yet elegant touch to this floral Lebanese specialty.
—Michael & Mathil Chebat, Lake Ridge, VA

PREP: 10 MIN. • **COOK:** 45 MIN. + CHILLING • **MAKES:** 14 SERVINGS

4 cups water
2 cups uncooked long grain rice
4 cups half-and-half cream
1½ cups sugar
1 to 2 tsp. rose water
Optional: Pomegranate seeds and chopped pistachios

In a heavy saucepan, combine water and rice; bring to a boil over medium heat. Reduce heat; cover and simmer 15 minutes or until water is absorbed. Add cream and sugar; bring to a boil. Reduce heat; simmer, uncovered, 30-40 minutes or until slightly thickened. Stir in rose water. Refrigerate at least 2 hours. Stir in additional cream to reach desired consistency. If desired, top with pomegranate seeds and pistachios.

½ CUP: 281 cal., 7g fat (5g sat. fat), 34mg chol., 35mg sod., 47g carb. (24g sugars, 0 fiber), 4g pro.

FLOURLESS OLIVE OIL CHOCOLATE CAKE

This flourless cake is baked with olive oil to create a rich and savory flavor. Top with ice cream, confectioners' sugar or anything sweet to balance out the deep chocolaty flavor.
—Jenna Barnard, Gilbert, AZ

PREP: 25 MIN. • **BAKE:** 25 MIN. + COOLING • **MAKES:** 8 SERVINGS

6 large eggs, separated
8 oz. bittersweet chocolate, chopped
½ cup extra virgin olive oil
1 Tbsp. vanilla extract
1½ tsp. instant espresso powder
1 cup sugar, divided
   Confectioners' sugar
   Optional: Mixed fresh berries
   and whipped cream

MAKE-AHEAD MAGIC

Because flourless chocolate cake is very moist, it's the perfect choice for a make-ahead sweet. Prepare it a day in advance and cool completely. Store the cake in the refrigerator in a covered container. Remove from the fridge four hours before serving to let it come to room temperature.

1. Preheat oven to 350°. Coat bottom of a 9-in. springform pan with cooking spray. Top with a sheet of parchment; secure springform ring on top and lock in place. Place egg whites in a clean bowl; let stand while melting chocolate.

2. In top of a double boiler or a metal bowl over simmering water, stir chocolate and oil until smooth. Remove from heat; stir in vanilla and espresso powder. Set aside.

3. Beat egg whites on high speed until soft peaks form. Slowly add ½ cup sugar while beating; beat until stiff peaks form. Beat remaining ½ cup sugar into chocolate mixture. Add yolks, 1 at a time, until combined. Add a fourth of egg whites to chocolate; mix until fully combined. Add remaining egg whites; gently fold to combine. Transfer batter to prepared pan. Bake until puffed and set, 25-30 minutes. Let cool 10 minutes before serving. Dust with confectioners' sugar; serve with toppings as desired.

1 PIECE: 438 cal., 27g fat (9g sat. fat), 140mg chol., 54mg sod., 30g carb. (28g sugars, 1g fiber), 7g pro.

RECIPE INDEX